Three Hundred

Years

in

Thirty

# THREE HUNDRED YEARS IN THIRTY

Memoir of Transition with the
Cree Indians of Lake Mistassini

Nicholas N. Smith

Polar Bear & Company
Solon Center for Research and Publishing
Solon, Maine

Polar Bear & Company
PO Box 311, Solon, ME 04979, U.S.A.
207.643.2795, www.polarbearandco.org

First edition 2011
First printing 2011; on demand from 2015

Polar Bear & Company ™ is an imprint of
the Solon Center for Research and Publishing

Library of Congress Control Number: 2011925681
ISBN 978-1-882190-02-7

Cover art & design by Ramona du Houx
Photo credits: Portrait of Nicholas N. Smith by Jeffrey S. Morris, the Pierce Studio, Brunswick, ME; All other photos courtesy of author.

Frontispiece: The beaver skins are still considered the best in the world and obtain top prices at the fur auction.

In memory of the Reverend
Kenneth R. J. Blaber, 1931–2008,
who introduced me to the
Mistassini people.

# Contents

# Foreword

In his memoir, Nicholas Smith has done something rarely experienced by others in recent times. Because of his deep interest in the original citizens of North America, particularly the northern Cree of Quebec, he has gone and lived among them, entering with intense interest and total commitment to their ancient way of life.

The results of this unique experience he shares with us in this insightful and fascinating account. Dr. Smith takes the reader right into the heart of the Canadian wilderness to dwell with the Mistassini and Waswanipi Cree as they go about their life as entrepreneurs of the Hudson's Bay Company.

In the course of this intriguing book we are introduced to a way of life that molded and shaped the Mistassini and Waswanipi Cree into a proud, wise, and resolute First Nations people with a most colourful history and attachment to the exciting days of the fur trade. Many individuals play a significant role in the story, among them, Hudson's Company officers, missionary clergy, and notable Cree leaders.

This is an engrossing book to be enjoyed by all who travel its pages. It is also an important historical document to be treasured by the northern Cree as a vivid portrayal and recollection of their old way of life and history.

The story is well told by a good man who greatly admired and esteemed them.

James Scanlon
Sometime "inlander"
Formerly Archdeacon of James Bay

FOREWORD

# Introduction

Over nearly six decades, Nicholas Smith has amassed an astounding compendium of historical and ethnographical information about the Algonquian-speaking peoples of northeastern North America. His quiet, unassuming manner, competency and unbridled enthusiasm, coupled with an historian's approach to understanding the past, have garnered respect from both First Nations and his peers. Innumerable publications, political advocacy, museum displays, an unpublished (but readily available) catalogue of Wabanaki (Abenaki, Maliseet, Passamaquoddy, Penobscot) textual resources, and an honourary doctorate attest to his many accomplishments and willingness to share information with indigenous peoples and non-Natives alike. Strongly committed to Native affairs, the author continues to contribute in various ways.

Following in the footsteps of Frank Goldsmith Speck, Fannie Eckstorm, and Edwin Tappan Adney, Smith focused first on the history of the Natives of the state of Maine. Not content to confine his interest to dusty tomes and archival papers, Smith gained firsthand knowledge by listening and learning from the Natives themselves. His eagerness to document the rapidly disappearing Wabanaki traditions, ceremonies and crafts led to an enduring friendship with Maliseet Peter Paul and his wife, Minnie. Peter Paul, having been raised by his grandparents, proved to be a marvelous bridge between the present and the past. With his remarkable memory and invaluable assistance songs, stories, and genealogies were tape-recorded, and canoe trips were undertaken to rediscover the routes, portages, and campsites used by Paul's Maliseet ancestors. In turn, this Maliseet work served as excellent preparation, first for research undertaken to help the Penobscot Nation to regain and reinstate certain rights, and second for his later visits to the Mistassini Cree in the province of Québec.

As the Maliseet and Penobscot way of life was rapidly becoming affected by encroaching external pressures, Smith believed that if he drove to the "end of the road," he would find indigenous peoples living as the Maliseet had done back in the 1850s. Consequently, nearly forty years ago, Nicholas Smith drove north to Mistassini in Québec where he found some of the Mistassini Cree camped close to lumber operations.

Similar encampments of neighbouring Waswanipi Cree were located near the mining towns of Chapais and Chibougamau and along the recently constructed road. This trip was the first of many carried out during all four seasons over fifteen years. For three of those years, grants from the Canadian Museum of Civilization in Ottawa allowed Smith to amass a significant collection of material and information for the museum. A grant from another source provided money for a portable generator and a 16 mm projector. Transported from camp to camp by the Crees, Smith showed films borrowed from the National Film Board. This marvelous opportunity to meet the Crees in their natural surroundings led to further invitations to join them in a winter hunting camp and for their culturally significant spring goose hunt. These invitations included the opportunity to photograph the Crees in a way of life that had existed for centuries but was soon to change.

These visits to Mistassini took place during a period of incipient change. Children no longer went into the bush with their families, but were sent to residential school in the Québec town of La Tuque, where their education was intended to obliterate their culture and language. The new road brought with it vast changes in technology and additional outside influences. The James Bay Power Corporation mapped the area in preparation for the massive system of dams for power generation. Concomitantly, anthropologists from McGill University were conducting research on the Mistassini and Waswanipi Crees. As well, both Edward S. Rogers of the Royal Ontario Museum and Adrian Tanner of McGill participated in Cree life for prolonged periods, documenting the physical and symbolic aspects of their hunting traditions. While all these studies resulted in important publications, they include only minimal photographic documentation. Therefore, this photographic edition is a most welcome addition to Cree publications, providing a highly significant visual documentation of everyday activities of the Mistassini Crees in their natural setting just prior to this period of immense change.

Cath Oberholtzer, PhD
Department of Anthropology
Trent University, Ontario

# Preface

Lake Mistassini had not been a place in my imagination as a destination for future plans. In 1969 it was by chance that I went there, really knowing only that I wanted to compare northern Quebec Indian camps with those of northern Maine and the Maritimes in 1850. I thought it would be a one-time visit.

In 1950, two weeks before graduation, Dr. David Trafford, my counselor in the History Department of the University of Maine, Orono, asked me what I was going to do with history, my major, after graduation. I replied, "Maritime History." Dr. Trafford responded that maritime history was such a popular field that it would be difficult to enter. He suggested Maine Indian history instead, since no one was working in that field. I had a passion for history, and opportunity offered me an opening on the ground floor. At that time there were no courses offered anywhere in Maine on Maine Indian history, anthropology, archaeology, or museum studies. Museums seemed to be the area to search for a job.

For me history is not just facts and dates, but it is the actions, passions, and frustrations of real people. Jobs in Maine Indian history were just as elusive as the courses were. My military service obligations had been fulfilled with duty in the Army Air Force in Europe, and I had earned my undergraduate college degree. The Korean War opened the job market. I found an opening in the second shift of a drop-forge plant in Rockport, Massachusetts. The shift from 3 to 11 p.m. made it possible for me to volunteer mornings at the Peabody Museum in Salem, where I was assigned to organize some ninety boxes of recently obtained Edwin Tappan Adney papers. Adney was recognized as the expert on the Canadian Maliseet Indians of New Brunswick's St. John River Valley watershed. He became fascinated with their simple but efficient way of life. I became captivated by Adney's papers filled with Maliseet history, folk tales, hunting and trapping methods, songs, language, archaeology, and marvelous sketches creating indelible images of their lifestyle. The names of his Maliseet teachers were included. I could not have had a better introduction to Wabanaki Indian lifestyle.

A summer position became available at the Abbe Museum in Bar Harbor in 1951. It was offered to me, and I accepted it. During the

summer I learned much from my work at the Abbe and from visits
to the Penobscot[1] at Indian Island, Old Town. In the fall I accepted
a position teaching English and history near Houlton. An easy drive
from the Houlton area brought me to the Woodstock Maliseet village,
where the late Peter Paul, one of Adney's esteemed collaborators, lived.
I, too, found Peter Paul and his wife Minnie marvelous and enthusiastic
teachers of Wabanaki culture. For a number of years we worked on a
comprehensive study of the Maliseet and their neighbors, often took
trips to museums, and studied the geographic land features as we wove
together the folk stories, material culture, ethnobotany, language, place-
names, and heritage into a meaningful lifestyle and history.

One of our most impressive accomplishments to the Maliseet was
canoeing lakes and rivers and hiking the portages of the Old Maliseet
Trail linking the St. John River to Indian Island at Old Town, Maine, a
trip that no living Maliseet had made. This was a challenging segment
of history in the raw that required both research, field work, and
determination, leading to a meaningful conclusion. The trail connected
to the Passamaquoddy and Penobscot, as well as other bands in western
Maine and New Hampshire. The earliest missionaries used the trail.
When the French offered the highest fur prices, the Penobscot brought
their furs north over the trail to them. When the British prices were best,
the Maliseet took their furs south over the trail. The early British settlers
used the route to their new homes in northeastern Maine. We learned not
only the hardships but also the magnificence of this almost forgotten
wilderness trail.[2]

After working with Peter Paul and other elders for several years, I felt
that I had a good knowledge of Maine maritime Indian life back to about
1850. Indian life changed little up to then. It would be interesting to see
life as it was in 1850. I surmised that if one went north as far as he could
drive, perhaps Indians were still living similar to the way Wabanaki lived
a hundred years ago. In the summer of 1969 my wife, Edyth, daughter
Wanda, and I drove to the St. Francis village of Odanak. From there we
traveled to Lake St. John and then continued to Chibougamau Park and
finally to Chibougamau, where the road ended. Indians were camped
near the park in small shelters that fit descriptions that Peter Paul recalled
Maliseet using when he was a boy. It was a short stay, but I saw enough
of Indian camps to intrigue me to make another, longer visit.

The following winter I contacted the Rev. Ken Blaber at the Anglican
Mission at Mistassini and arranged to stay there for several days during
the summer. A new road was in the planning to be constructed into the

village of Mistassini in the spring. In 1970 we drove to Mistassini and met Ken and Joyce Blaber and their three children, Paul, Andrew, and Sharon. Father Blaber let us use a small cabin that was set up as the village library. After observing how we adapted to frontier living, Ken broke the ice, so to speak, by explaining to me the role and duties expected of an Indian small mission village church in the twentieth century. The captivating words instilled in me a must to know more about the people Ken served. He presented an agenda that included visiting several nearby camps close to the road and an overnight visit to a camp about one hundred miles from the village by bush plane. This gave a quick but good introduction to Indian life in the wilderness conditions similar to that of the Wabanaki before 1850. It was a living history experience for me. I thought that the Mistassini Cree would be quite similar to the Wabanaki, and that these people were so similar that they could be the Indians Adney had studied in 1890.

Upon returning to Lake Mistassini, I expressed my gratitude to Ken Blaber, missionary, for permitting me to accompany him on the overnight visit in the bush. He proposed that if we wished to return, we could do a summer Bible school for the children, and I could have more trips to see bush camps. I later learned that Father Blaber was an expert at obtaining new programs and material for his isolated mission from those who came to him to learn about "his" Indians. And so my Mistassini adventures started. Ken was reassigned. Those who followed, some for short terms, others for longer terms, all welcomed me from 1970 to 1985. My visits provided new opportunities to observe Mistassini, a major supplier of furs to the world market, at a time when their world was in a state of great change.

This is a record of the Mistassini Cree Indians, from what we know of their history, and of my encounter with them in the height of the fur trade era prior to their entrance into the high-tech world. The biggest event influencing change in the area was the James Bay Hydro Project, that swallowed a large part of Mistassini Territory. Year by year, I marveled at the many changes that brought Mistassini from a small, summer fur-trading society to a modern Canadian community.

Brunswick, Maine                                                          NNS
June 2009

# Acknowledgments

This book would not have been possible without the help of the late Reverend Kenneth Blaber and his wife, Joyce, the first Anglican missionary family who were assigned full-time to St. John the Evangelist Mission at Lake Mistassini, Quebec, in 1966.

I am grateful to Canon James Scanlon and his wife, Doris, who gave us much good advice and encouragement. Thanks also to Kathy Bertrim and Simone Glendenning of Kingston, Ontario, and Chris Frink Madrid from Watertown, NY, who joined our summer Bible school group, giving us a talented, friendly crew. I wish to thank Charles Martijn, an archaeologist of the region, who has a very broad knowledge of the Quebec Indians and their land. He was always most helpful, providing information, sources, and encouragement, and had a reputation for bringing together those involved in similar research interests. My thanks go also to Suzanne McLaren of the Carnegie Museum of Natural History in Pittsburgh, PA, for updating information about the white freshwater seals of northern Quebec. I am grateful to Trinity Church Watertown, NY, who provided a grant for a 16 mm movie projector and a portable generator for the mission.

With much appreciation and gratitude to Richard Been and James Scanlon for reading and making suggestions regarding my manuscript. Many thanks to Jeff Morris, who prepared my photographs, slides and negatives for publication. I am indebted to Edward Caswell for designing pertinent maps of the Mistassini Territory and James Bay area for the period of great change to the region. My appreciation goes out to Patrick Paul, editor of *Wabanaki News*, for permission to publish the poem "Here's Why" by D. C. Butterfield.

Much appreciation to the Reverend Richard Janke and Herman Kummerle who at different times loaned us a travel trailer as accommodations for us and our volunteers during the time we lived among the Cree. Many thanks to all the Cree people who made us feel welcome and gave us insights into their history and culture, especially Philip Voyageur and his family, and the late John Gull.

I am grateful to my wife, Edyth, and my daughter, Wanda Morris, for their patience in reading, rereading and helping me edit each draft of the manuscript. Finally, I don't know how to thank my wife for her patience, support and understanding, while I was dedicating so much of my time to completing this book.

My thanks and appreciation go to the families of Philip Voyageur and Rupert Voyageur who provided me with a most unforgettable vacation in their winter hunting territory. Thanks go to all the Mistassini people who have successfully weathered the great changes in the last half of the twentieth century. Let the sun shine on them and the wind blow at their back as they continue in the twenty-first century.

Northwestern Québec Fur Trade Map 1800-1970

Drawn by Ed Caswell.

# I

# A Dream Comes True

I stood in the cold watching the bush plane, the umbilical cord to civilization, revving up on the snow-covered lake. I wondered if I had made a crazy decision to accept an Indian's invitation to give me a "wonderful vacation" in midwinter in the Northern Quebec bush. The day had dawned very cold, too cold for pilots to risk flying bush planes whose engines' fragile oil seals tend to break when temperatures drop below $-35°$F. Pilots waited until midday temperatures rose before deciding that it was safe to fly. After dropping me off in the northern bush, they were eager to return to Mistassini before temperatures began descending again. My tummy had a strange feeling as I watched the plane ski down the winter runway marked by several small black spruce trees planted in the snow by an Indian family at their winter hunting camp on a lake south of the Eastmain River. A hundred snow-covered miles of virgin bush lay between me and the nearest road or store. Many of my friends headed south this time of year to enjoy a break from northern New York or New England winters and returned with tans, to the envy of their friends. I anticipated that the sun reflecting off the snow, plus the ever-present wind, would color my cheeks to the envy of the Florida sun bathers. I hoped that the telltale white spots of frostbite would not blemish my face.

For a number of years, on cold winter days I often sat in the old Penobscot Indian houses built from the river-drive logs grounded on the shores, harvested by the Indians and sawed into lumber. Most of the boards had shrunk, permitting snow to drift in and dance to the floor. The atmosphere was ripe for elders to reminisce about winter hunting and trapping in the shadow of Mt. Katahdin. Those days were only memories, but both the tales and the cold winter nights were gripping.

PHILIP'S CAMP, ALSO MY HOME FOR SEVERAL WEEKS

Yarns were told with such fervor that one could almost feel the sharp wind and deep cold settling in for the night in Maine's most notable mountain area. I wondered what it would be like to experience such a life. When I was a boy, there was still much fascinating literature available in youth magazines, books, and films relating both factual and fictional stories about the rugged Indians and fur traders and their solitary life in Maine or beyond. Now I was much farther north of Maine's North Woods, south of the Eastmain River that flows into James Bay. It was 1979. The cold was real. I was about to experience typical Indian hunting and trapping in one of the few remaining fur-trading economies on Quebec's northern frontier. Although the cold would be more severe than that which my Penobscot, Passamaquoddy, and Maliseet friends had described, the isolation and life style would be very similar.

In the 1880s Frederick Remington went west to record the last days of the western frontier, published as *Men With the Bark On* by Harper & Brothers in 1900.[1] One hundred years later, I watched the bush plane that had brought me to Philip Voyageur's isolated winter camp begin its return trip over the vast hundred-mile expanse of virgin wilderness to the Mistassini Indian village. I was about to experience life with the Indian inhabitants of Quebec's northern frontier. I turned to see the Indians and their winter camp and expected that they, too, could well fit Remington's image of "men with the bark on."

It was too late to reconsider my plans. The plane was now a tiny speck over the wilderness. Many of my friends called my plan a crazy pipedream. There was no turning back now. I had to take what would come, smile and enjoy whatever was to be. I turned around and faced Philip Voyageur and other family members and followed them to their tent, which would also be my home for several weeks. The plane had delivered supplies for Philip and also for his brother Reuben, who camped ten miles away. While others us-

My room

ing sleds transported the supplies to the tent, Philip cordially led me to "my room," one corner of the tent. Early on the morning of October 1, 1978, Philip had telephoned inviting me for "a wonderful winter vacation" in his winter bush hunting camp in Northern Quebec wilderness. I had met Philip several years earlier and had made short visits to his winter camp. This presented a marvelous opportunity to observe the Mistassini Lake Indians' culture, a culture based on centuries of experience in the subarctic. Philip knew that his life of being dependent on the beaver economy with Hudson's Bay Company's traders would soon be over. Therefore, he wanted pictures of this life to provide his grandchildren with a better understanding of their heritage. I spluttered over the phone, not quite believing my ears. Philip insisted that I give him a date. They were leaving for their winter camp later in the day and needed to make plane reservations for me right away. I quickly thought through my winter schedule and said the middle of February. In less than five minutes, Philip's generous vacation offer became a firm date. It was just as important for me to relive a nineteenth-century version of Maine maritime Indian life as it was for a maritime historian to experience firsthand a voyage on a sailing vessel.

The Mistassini were a remote group wanting little to do with those who immigrated to Canada. They were one of the tribes who traded with the French in the sixteenth century on the St. Lawrence River and then retreated to their northern territory. They never made a treaty with Canada or engaged in war with England, France, the United States, or Canada. They were slow to permit fur traders, missionaries, or others from the outside world to enter their territory. They were primarily a self-sufficient, independent, loosely organized people with limited community and social services. Canada did not make a survey of Mistassini until A. P. Low conducted his Mistassini Expedition for the Survey of Canada in 1885. The Ungava Peninsula north of the Eastmain River was added to the province of Quebec by the Quebec Boundaries Extension Act of 1912. The Dominion Indian agent made an annual visit to the chief. The agent was primarily interested in information concerning the health, welfare, and changes in population. This required only a short visit. The Mistassini happily controlled their territory until the Quebec Government showed an interest in the area in 1960. In 1964 Laval and McGill Universities provided grants for preliminary research for the Cree Developmental Change Project, a program to develop socioeconomic opportunities never before available to the Cree. This was probably the first time that a group of specialists had an opportunity to present an orientation program to such an unsophisticated tribe to help them meld successfully into the twentieth century. Anthropology students were offered the challenge to do specific projects or studies in an actual hunting and trapping culture situation that had been little affected by life beyond their borders. Academia assumed that the Mistassini people wanted the changes and would look forward to them. In actuality the Mistassini would be a low-paid, low-level, muscular labor market for corporations looking for new resources.

The Mistassini lands were divided into units of individual hunting territories. Each was large enough to include all types of terrain and geographic conditions, creating a variety of environments to attract all species of wildlife and plants necessary for sustaining their type of life. The hunting territory, a segment of a vast virgin forest, was their "supermarket" providing everything from food to wigwam frames. There was no need to trespass on another's hunting territory. The chief had a record of all the territories, which families were using them, and the exact location of each family, in case one needed to be visited in an emergency.

These territories were not gifts or grants of land in the European fashion. Indian families were privileged to have the use of the land and its resources but not outright ownership. The Indians believed that they were the caretakers of land that belonged to a creator. On the demise of the headman, the territory usually was passed on to his eldest son, son-in-law, or to a designated family leader whom the surviving family recommended. As long as a family retained a hunter-leader, meaning a provider for the entire welfare of the family, the tract of land remained for that family to use. Hunters regularly left their territory or a portion of it vacant for a year or two, so the wildlife would replenish their numbers, just as many farmers leave fields to lie fallow for a season. When the fur traders came, establishing trading posts and instituting a beaver economy, they too learned and kept records of the families' territories and promoted this system, since they would benefit from it.

In the middle of the twentieth century, the Hudson's Bay Company (HBC) was the central unit around which the Mistassini Band evolved. The ice does not go out of Lake Mistassini until early or mid June. July and August were the months when most Indian trappers returned to the trading post from their bush winter quarters. By late August and September, most families had returned to the bush to set up their camps before the snow settled in for the winter. They were a happy, cooperative unit, working together to survive the long winter months. Now I was going to observe how this stalwart race had persevered for unknown centuries.

# II

# THE MISTASSINI TERRITORY

Mistassini had almost a mystical atmosphere about it. It seemed that time had stopped several centuries ago. Few people dared attempt to enter it until the eighteenth century. Its exact size and boundaries were unknown. No two people who described the climate could agree, other than that it was cold. But how cold was it?

June 21, 2007, was a magnificent morning in Maine. Summer would officially arrive shortly after 2:00 p.m. I checked the weather for Mistassini, Quebec. The early morning temperature was 36°F, influenced by the lake temperatures. It must have been a magnificent morning there also with bright sunshine; the ice would be out of the lake, except for some stubborn ice cakes blown into shaded coves by the ever-present winds. The British from the southern half of the kingdom would find it much more difficult to face the harsh climate than the adventurers from the northern islands of Scotland.

Even in the twentieth century, writers and researchers often were not certain of the exact limits of Mistassini. Some included the entire Ungava Peninsula and Labrador; others only estimated the areas of the Indian hunting territories surrounding Lake Mistassini, and there are other definitions.

The difference between the elevation at water level at the coast and the height of land just east of Lake Mistassini creates noticeable variances in the weather. Easterly winds bring fair weather; James Bay to the west is the weather maker.

Lake Mistassini was the target of the James Bay lake-effect condition. James Bay freezes well into the bay, but the center seldom, if ever, freezes. The sun draws moisture from the open water. As the moisture drifts eastward over the mainland, it quickly transforms into snow dumped on Mistassini. Sudden squalls that create whiteouts are common. Most of the snow is a light powder. About once in a normal lifetime, the east side of Hudson Bay will freeze over much farther into the bay, creating a walkable land bridge to the Belcher Islands.

Since weather on coasts is normally milder than that of the interior, winters in Ungava and the Labrador coasts and even Greenland's inhabited coastal areas are warmer than winters in Mistassini. Temperatures fluctuate a great deal in this vast territory. It does make a difference where the reporting person is situated. It is more the norm for temperatures to be as much as ten degrees colder out on the ice of Lake Mistassini than in the tiny, sheltered Indian community that finds some protection from the winds. Temperatures have always been important to the fur traders, who have maintained some of the longest weather records in Canada. Kenneth Hare of the Canadian Weather Service described Ungava weather.

> The most significant of these features is the heaviness of the snowfall all across the central and southern districts of the Plateau of Labrador-Ungava. More than half the entire peninsula has falls of over 100 inches. This, moreover, is the belt of the most frequent snowfall, the axis of highest frequency (over 100 days with 0.1 inches of Snow per annum) running from Lake Abitibi to the Meanly Mountains via Lakes Mistassini, Nitchequon and Ashupipi.[1]

Water flowing from the west side of Lake Mistassini forms into a large river system that flows west into James Bay at Rupert House, a village with a trading post at the mouth of the Rupert River. From the east side of the lake, the waters flow southeast to Lake St. John and enter the St. Lawrence River at Tadoussac. The Rupert River was the first route Hudson's Bay traders took to the interior to reach Lake Mistassini. Indians found that starting from the Rupert River and crossing over to the Broadback River was a much easier and shorter trip, reducing the number of portages. Most of the rivers have many falls and rapids. It is said that the Rupert River has 150 portages between Mistassini and James Bay. Therefore the Indian inhabitants found easier ways to make the trip, though they were still no joyride. These "Inlanders," as they were sometimes called, met the winter season with a smile on their face, a noble challenge. The ability to defy successfully the forces of nature was considered a part of being Indian.

Establishing a specific time when people came into the region is difficult. Archaeologists consider the whole area from the east coast of James Bay to Ungava and Labrador a unit. It was the last large northeastern area to come under the archaeologist's scrutiny. Unfortunately the James Bay Hydro Project has not allowed an extensive and proper investigation project in the western section. The hydro project has drowned and changed the area, preventing further study of early man in the region, especially many rich sites that were habitable by Archaic people along the shores of rivers and lakes. An attempt was made to enlist a team of archaeologists in an emergency program to discover and study many known sites and retrieve as many artifacts as possible. All too often, the construction contractors were one step ahead of the archaeologists. The archaeologists' priority became the collection of artifacts to be stored away in labs for later study, a plan which is still in progress. Unfortunately the hydro project makes further on-site study impossible, just as the Churchill Falls Hydro Project in Labrador stopped archaeological work there. At this time the bulk of the material discovered is still being studied in labs and has not been documented in published reports. Our knowledge regarding early man in the subarctic will increase and may change when these studies are completed.

Fifty years ago archaeologists theorized that the earliest time when man could have come to Maine was 4,000 years ago. Since then, archaeologists have revised the figure several times, and much new information has increased our knowledge about these early inhabitants. Now scientists believe that man arrived in Maine 13,000 years ago. A recent discovery in Europe has revised man's arrival date to the continent to more than a million years ago. It should be no surprise if the information from the stored Mistassini artifacts in labs will provide important new results and may even change present theories about early man in the Ungava Peninsula.

The locations chosen for work under the emergency archeological plan were almost exclusively limited to those previously known and those suspected of producing a large number of artifacts. The gradual retreat of the ice is thought to have begun about 8000 BP (before the present time), probably the beginning of a warming period. Ice and snow cleared from the coast first, including the coast of Ungava and Labrador north of Mistassini. Larch could have been growing on the northern Labrador coast as early as 6300 BP. Gradually, with melting, the ice receded. It is believed that by 5500 BP the snow and ice had cleared from the Mistassini Territory, and human life could be sustained by 4400 BP. The typical flora that now covers the forest floor was creating the forest as we know it today.[2] I watched the return of growth after the Bar Harbor, Maine, fire of 1947. In places the rich forest duff burned off completely, leaving the rock subsurface entirely exposed. The Acadia National Park personnel made a very conservative estimate for the return of growth. The full sun in the open spaces and the ash were factors in the reforestation. Everyone, including the park personnel, was astounded at how fast the regrowth took place. However, The regrowth of an area after a forest fire or from rich volcanic lavas probably cannot be compared to the first growth arising from completely barren ground.

I have seen the ice go out in rivers and lakes overnight at Mistassini, on the Moose River at Moose Factory, and on the St. Lawrence River, and in the morning I marveled at the waterfowl enjoying the open water. It took only a few hours for waterfowl to discover the open water and occupy it. Various kinds of life were moving into the center of the subarctic barrens from all sides of its warmer surroundings. I expect that all forms of life were ready to move into the barren ground just as soon as conditions made it possible. Who knows what seeds could be embedded in the heavy winter feathers or fur and then scattered by wildlife penetrating the shores of the newly established lakes and rivers?

As one who has experienced the winter life of the Mistassini people, I feel that the earliest people who entered the subarctic would not let snow, ice, wind, and cold delay the exploration or hunting excursions into the virgin areas after the wildlife became established there. The earliest excursions into the area were probably of short duration but became longer as reforestation became more intense and travel routes better known and established. Many important subarctic archaeological sites of northern Quebec and Labrador were found along important rivers that are still the principal travel routes in use in twenty-first century Mistassini and Naskapi. The early archaeological reports concerning this area suggest that there were both a lower level Archaic Period and an upper level Late Archaic Period. At least one archaeologist suggests that the Later Archaic people may have been those who were living in the Mistassini area when the first Europeans arrived. One site turned up tools very similar to those known on the Maritime and Maine coast. No one can truthfully say who these early inhabitants were or from where they came. Early Maine man, who was so well adapted to a cold, harsh climate, may have been an early migrant after the ice and snow left Maine and the Maritimes. At some time, Late Archaic people may have migrated from as far west as upper Lake Michigan and today's province of Ontario.

Apparently some wanderers discovered sites that produced the finest stone material for knives, arrows, and spears that were known at that time. These best sought materials were the Ramah chert from northern Labrador, Labrador Trough cherts from the north-south chain of rivers and lakes in western Labrador, and Mistassini quartzite. Artifacts of one or more of these very high-grade materials are found in many sites that archaeologists have discovered. Somehow people found these widespread sites and were willing to travel long distances in harsh conditions to obtain superior materials for their needs. Some important sites included many artifacts and even bulk pieces of the prized materials for future manufacturing of artifacts cached there. It appears that people went to the same sites for some important annual events, such as hunting caribou and waterfowl. They cached material and artifacts at these sites expecting to return for their future hunts. Stealing was unknown, but a hungry person in need of food who happened along and found a needed weapon was welcome to take what he needed for his survival. Starvation must have been a problem in the early days, just as it was in the first half of the twentieth century; I was told in 1970 that everyone had at least one relative who had starved to death.

Early people established sites along major chains of lakes and rivers. These inhabitants must have acquired excellent skills for building a proper craft for navigating the fast-flowing rivers and mastered the control of their craft in the many rapids and portages needed to cover long distances to their destinations. Their routes can be followed, and most are the same still in use today by the Mistassini people. A raft or log would not meet the requirements necessary for these northern water travel conditions. The birchbark canoe meets the criteria for summer travel in the Northeast on rivers with many rapids and portages.

Winter travel would be impossible without snowshoes, since a twenty-minute struggle without them in the hip-deep, fine snow is extremely tiring. The more one attempts to extricate oneself, the farther one sinks—exhausted, one would quickly freeze to death. The earliest people had to have both canoes and snowshoes when they first came to the region.

The presence of Mistassini quartzite dispersed at sites on the St. Maurice River at Chicoutimi and Lake St. John is evidence that there were well-established trade routes long before Europeans arrived. Those early people followed the waterways that only a craft with the qualities of the birch canoe could navigate. The deep, dry, fine snow of winter made snowshoes a requirement for travel. Both the bark canoe and the snowshoe are of very ancient vintage.

Many people, even archaeologists and anthropologists, assumed that those first inhabitants who made the Mistassini area their homeland lacked intelligence; some scientists feel that the present-day Indians are lacking in intelligence. Unfortunately there are no IQ tests designed to give accurate measurements for the Indians' intelligence. If the critics had the opportunity to observe these people in their winter surroundings, they would have to admit that the Mistassini people have adapted extremely well to the harsh winter environment. Most who survived to adulthood had to be of high intelligence in order to meet the everyday challenges presented to them. That intelligence has been passed down to the present day. The Mistassini culture requires special aspects that have to be learned on the site, just as our city survival skills do. Mistassini hunters cannot be burdened with unnecessary material goods. A hunter is not ready to rush to acquire the latest gimmick or paraphernalia. He will consider how the article can improve his life before making the change. He is not interested in a new device that could possibly become a burden to him.

A beaver is a very difficult animal to skin. I was surprised to see people using bone scrapers fashioned from a caribou or moose leg. The same style fleshers for skinning beaver have been found in coastal Maine archaeological sites. The Cree told me that they had not found a steel tool that did the job as well as the ancient bone scrapers. In Mistassini I actually saw these traditional tools in use.

# III

# TADOUSSAC

Tadoussac has a fascinating history that unfortunately is omitted from the chronicles of our American history books. Much history stops at borders as if there were an impenetrable wall between the two countries, despite how much both countries may have in common. In 1534 Jacques Cartier sailed on his first of four voyages to Quebec and the Maritimes. One objective of the trip was to found the Colony of Quebec under the governorship of Jean-François de la Roque de Roberval. In addition they planned to establish a settlement on the Isle of Orleans in the St. Lawrence River east of Quebec City and organize commercial relations with the Indians.

Cartier did not just go off on a whim. The two assignments were not what one would expect for a first exploratory expedition. The Basques, who inhabited a small independent state between France and Spain, were considered the top seamen and had developed unequaled ships in the sixteenth century. They were fishing and whaling in northern Newfoundland waters by 1520, and some think even earlier.[1] The French and other European fishermen soon followed, finding the rich fishing banks near Newfoundland, and returned with full cargoes of fish for Catholic Europe. Frequently the fishermen topped off their loads with furs. It is thought that a Portuguese settlement was established on Cape Breton Island by 1521. Cartier found Indians who were ready to trade at Tadoussac. Although the average fisherman of that time could not read or write, he enjoyed meeting at certain pubs or taverns, exchanging tales. Fleets of the small fishing boats left together under the direction of an experienced navigator. Unfortunately, finding records of these voyages is difficult. Very few, if any, of the documents have survived the destructive fires that were all too common in the crowded French seaports at that time. Few navigators left written records.[2]

Tadoussac, where the Saguenay River meets the St. Lawrence River, was the first place where the Mistassini Cree met Europeans. This summer meeting place for many tribes on both sides of the St. Lawrence River was known as the Kingdom of Saguenay. Jacques Cartier, who made his first trip up the St. Lawrence River in 1534, apparently knew that Tadoussac was the most important trading site along the St. Lawrence River and coast of Nova Scotia. It is likely that the tribes traded with one another at their summer meetings. French merchants from Dieppe and Saint-Malo made Tadoussac their trading base specifically for furs by 1543. Some of these merchants had previous trading experience with the Caribbean Indians. The Montagnais chiefs who lived on the north shore of the St. Lawrence made sure that they gained due respect from these new traders.[3] The French traders were required to make gifts to the Montagnais leaders. France was gaining in the world fur trade. In 1583 Sweden captured the Baltic port of Narva and blocked the Russian fur trade to Europe. France was in an excellent position to profit from the closure of the Russian fur trade. Tadoussac became the leading French trading post until in 1608 the French fishing boats and fur traders outfitted by La Rochelle investors focused their trade at Quebec City.

Large numbers of Mistassini quartz artifacts found at Chicoutimi show that a well-known trail existed between Chicoutimi and Mistassini for the stone tool trade. This later became the trail for the Mistassini fur trade.

Hieronymus Megiser published a catalogue of fifty languages in 1603. One of the five Amerindian languages included was that of the Labrador Indians, probably a category that included both Ungava and Labrador Indians as given by Tadoussac traders.[4]

The Mistassini Indians did not have the sophisticated communication system of our modern newsrooms, but being in the center of a system of hunting territories that radiated like the spokes of a wheel, they became aware of what was going on around them. They were close enough to know what was happening around them, but far enough away not to become any more involved in the outside world than they felt was necessary.

The Mistassini from the northern part of Mistassini Lake took one set of rivers that brought them to Lake St. John and then to Tadoussac, while those on the south end of Lake Mistassini came via a different set of rivers that led them to Lake St. John and then Tadoussac.

Most of the early accounts include the Mistassini and Naskapi as Montagnais tribes, which sometimes causes confusion. Tadoussac was

almost directly across the St. Lawrence River from a major New Brunswick waterway leading from the St. John River to the St. Lawrence River,
a route followed by Maritime and Maine Indians. Great Lakes Indians
were also attracted to this trading hub. Tadoussac was included in the
Montagnais Indians' St. Lawrence River land holdings. Thus Montagnais chiefs claimed the middlemen's role. The ancient Indian Kingdom
of Saguenay received additional titles: The King's Domain, The King's
Post, and The Trade of Tadoussac. The kingdom's lands extended from
the St. Lawrence River to Lake Mistassini and nearby lakes, and from the
Saguenay to the Domain of Mingan, east of Seven Islands.

In 1603 Samuel de Champlain spent forty-six days at Tadoussac. On
June 11, 1603, as he gathered data for his reports, he talked with some
northern Indians about the river systems in their homeland. He found
that the Mistassini Indians were among six Indian nations represented at
Tadoussac. His informants indicated that there was a large saltwater bay
at the northwest end of the trail. They may have drawn the river and lake
trails on birch bark, as Indians did to show neighbors where they would
be camping if they had to change their original plans.

The year 1604 was significant for the French because Champlain
attempted to establish a settlement in the New World, their first
attempt since Cartier's 1534 endeavor. It was a rare, short period when a
Huguenot and a Catholic clergyman lived side by side with royal approval
in the new settlement on St. Croix Island, near Calais, Maine.[5] Although
the settlement was not the success that it was hoped to be, it showed
that winter survival was possible for the French. Those who endured the
first winter moved across the Bay of Fundy, establishing Port Royal. The
following year Catholic missionaries began establishing mission points,
teaching Indians from Nova Scotia to Mount Desert Island, Maine. In
1610 the Micmac mission reaped its first harvest of Christian Indians in
the Northeast.

The year 1604 was significant also for the British because King James
ordered a new translation of the Bible. The translation was completed in
1611 and was the version of the Bible translated into Indian languages
for use by the first Protestant missionaries. The King James version of
the Bible is still preferred by many people. French Catholic missionaries
as well as the Anglican missionaries would find their way to Mistassini.
Religion continues to play an important role in New World history.

In 1615 Champlain brought the first missionaries, Recollect, also
known as Franciscans, to Tadoussac. They lived in humility and poverty.
Their meals often depended on people's donations. It was probably

easier for this group to assimilate with the people of the wilderness than groups who were accustomed to higher standards of living. The first recorded Mass was celebrated in July 1617,[6] although there must have been previous services.

When winter came and the Indians began returning to their winter quarters, Brother Jean Dolbeau volunteered to depart with a family to the interior bush. He soon acknowledged his folly, for he was not up to the rigorous Montagnais life or the harsh winters and joined the other priests who spent their winters in Quebec City. In 1619 Brother Joseph Le Caron opened a school for Indian children at Tadoussac, teaching them reading and writing.[7] It is very possible that they included Mistassini youth among the students.

The French knew that they had to respect the Montagnais middlemen, controllers of the trading, but the French also took steps to establish their leadership at Tadoussac. It was designated a French post, with fort, church, and trading headquarters. Most of the Indian inhabitants at Tadoussac were there for only a brief summer stay to attend to their trading. It continued to be only a summer activity for the French until the post required a year-round core group of settlers and soldiers.

Henry Hudson discovered the bay now known as Hudson Bay in 1610. Seven years earlier Champlain gleaned from Mistassini Indians at Tadoussac information on the trails and important rivers and lakes leading from Tadoussac through Mistassini lands to a great salt sea to the northwest, enabling him to draw a nearly perfect map of the region. Although he had never seen it, the reports of a large salt water bay at the other end of the trail fascinated him. Champlain stressed the importance of sending ships to the bay and strongly recommended to his authorities that they should claim all the area in the name of France, thus locking in this rich fur resource for his country. The Indians told him that the trip from Lake St. John to Tadoussac took ten days, but they did not impart details about the rest of the trails. King Louis XIV evidently saw no need to hurry about appropriating more colonial territory, as no one else apparently showed any interest in it. France was receiving the furs harvested in the region. After Louis XIV died, Louis XV was soon embroiled in a war with Spain, making much greater demands of his time and treasury. It was not until 1632 that they published Champlain's amazingly accurate map of the Mistassini Territory. To Champlain's disappointment the maps did not inspire immediate action to declare the bay and Mistassini Territory a part of the New France.

Tadoussac was a summer mission, manned with a full complement of missionaries, only when the Indians were present. Christianity requires a special structure where its members gather as a community, an innovation for Indians. At first a simple bark structure took shape as a chapel, a fragile edifice requiring many repairs each summer. This type of structure is mentioned in a number of the early missionary reports, leading one to believe that the missionaries followed a plan established by their supervisors. French policy permitted limited interest in the construction of notable church structures in the Indian missions. It was not until 1642 that construction finally began on an attractive, small, brick-and-stone church that included hangings, other church furnishings, and a bell from France. The brick for the edifice was also sent from France.[8]

About the middle of the century, Iroquois war parties extended their raids into the St. Lawrence River Valley. Although the fur trade at Tadoussac was not affected, the trading posts farther up the St. Lawrence River were, since the Mohawk conquerors redirected the trade to the British. At the same time the Seneca were conquering the western fur sources, also sending those furs to the British. Jean Talon, intendant of New France, had reason to show concern. He felt that the French should send someone to the Mistassini country and to the Great Bay to lock in that fur trade by declaring the whole country as part of New France. He began looking for qualified people who could make the trip from Tadoussac to Mistassini and the bay through unknown country.

In the early 1660s there were frequent rumors that the Mohawks, one of the Iroquois tribes, were approaching the Mistassini area. Stories about the fierce Mohawk attacks on Indian villages to the south had penetrated the borders of the Mistassini country, causing the small, remote, defenseless bands of hunters to become very distraught. The Mistassini chief sent a messenger to Quebec City asking for aid against the Mohawks. Two missionaries who had good experiences in the field, Claude Dablon and Gabriel Druillettes were chosen to go to Mistassini. Druillettes had been a successful ambassador to Boston for Maine's Norridgewock Indians.[9] In the fall of 1661, when most of the Indians were traveling to their winter quarters and the priests were returning to Quebec City, the Iroquois attacked Tadoussac. Luckily Dablon and Druillettes were four days' travel from Tadoussac on their expedition to Mistassini when the Mohawks attacked.

Tadoussac was virtually a ghost town with few to protect it. The church was targeted and easily destroyed. It may be difficult to imagine Indian warfare in the north where great armies of hundreds or thousands were nonexistent and there were no large open areas for two armies to face off. When an Iroquois had been murdered, a young family warrior had to show his indomitable courage by going off and killing one of the enemy. It was "an eye for an eye" philosophy that could create heroes. The timing of the Tadoussac event was not aimed as a battle to kill people, but as a means to win the famed fur trade site and become the middlemen of the trade. The population density was extremely low; people were spread out over great distances. It would be impossible to gather a large fighting force quickly for either defensive or offensive maneuvers. A Mohawk force would be small. They would have to attack without being detected, taking their opponents by surprise and then disappearing. Speed was a top priority.

According to the story, a hunter was killed on the edge of the Mistassini Territory. (Today world powers boast about the size of their armies. Current accounts of this and similar stories increase the number of combatants from one to several hundred.) Then the attackers retreated without penetrating farther into Mistassini lands. The Waswanipi, southern neighbors, have a similar story of Iroquois attacking their hunters at Indian Point on the O'Sullivan River. Harry Blacksmith, Bandmaster in 1972, referred to the River as "Pustamaskow" and said that it flowed from a lake of the same name. Close by is a sandy beach where present-day Waswanipi children enjoy swimming.

These raids were power plays, typical fear tactics, and attempts of the Iroquois to become the middlemen of the Mistassini fur trade, not attempts to conquer nations. The oral histories of the Cree living along the Moose River and at Rupert House, Mistassini, and Waswanipi all stipulate that the Iroquois came by way of the Nottaway River.[10] Variations of Nottaway or Nodway, defined as "other kind of people, unfriendly or enemies," are known from James Bay to Virginia and refer to the river that brings Iroquois warriors. In the North it has been also used to refer to the Eskimo. The stories of Iroquois warriors lurking in the forests may have been used to scare children, so they would not stray far from their wigwam, especially in the winter, when the low temperatures can quickly kill one not properly dressed for it. The Iroquois were successful in spreading fear and still worried some Mistassini people in the twentieth century. However, the Iroquois did not win a middleman position with the Mistassini beaver trade.

French missionaries reached the height of land near Lake Albanel, where they met a Mistassini hunting party who blocked their advance. The Mistassini were concerned about the possibility that their Iroquois enemy could be lurking within striking distance of their homeland, and they were afraid of all strangers. Druillettes, the diplomat, proposed that the Mistassini could rely on the French for aid against the Iroquois, but he decided that the hostile atmosphere was not conducive to the French to stay. The group retraced their steps. It was a missed opportunity.

Various histories of the period that I have studied are in exact agreement regarding the major events, but dates and times are often in disagreement. I have taken liberties from my readings and have attempted to correct what may be misinformation. All accounts state that it was the Iroquois who burned the church. Some say that the Tadoussac raid took place in 1671-72 after Charles Albanel left for Mistassini. The 1671 date is too late for an Iroquois raid. The destroyed church had already been replaced by then. I place the raid as taking place in 1661, a few days after Dablon and Druillettes left Tadoussac for Mistassini. Typically, word of tragedies spreads quickly through Indian country. The remote Mistassini hunters had good reason to fear the Iroquois warriors, who had a reputation as being fierce fighters.

Unfortunately *Le Premier Registre de Tadoussac* burned with the church. Father François de Crépieul claimed that the records covered the years 1646–1668. They would have been most valuable documents for the history of this very early period. However, the parish's *Second Registre de Tadoussac* was placed for preservation in the Séminaire du Québec archives and has been published.[11] There is also another Mission of Saguenay manuscript in the Séminaire archives that commenced in 1585. This provides a suggestion that Indians, including Mistassini people, could have been baptized Christians as much as thirty-five years before the Pilgrims arrived in Massachusetts in 1620. More than 250 years later they were still labeled as "savages." All the priests for the Indian missions of New France were trained at the Séminaire du Québec and most returned for the winter to improve their missionary skills. The bishop might make new appointments for them in the spring. For about ten years there was a lull in activity at Tadoussac until the French were satisfied that the Iroquois were no longer sending war parties against French-Algonquian settlements on the St. Lawrence River.

The burned church was replaced by 1668 and is still a picturesque Tadoussac landmark overlooking the St. Lawrence River. The bell from the first church was salvaged from the ruins, hung in the new church, and is still in use. It is very easy to imagine wigwams around it and birch canoes beached below it, while other canoes plied the St. Lawrence River. François de Crépieul was assigned to the mission from 1668 to 1700.

Fortunately he kept baptismal, marriage, and burial records for the many tribes drawn to the Tadoussac trading center and those who gave gifts to the church. However, it is not a record of tribal attendance at weekly church services. The missions at Chicoutimi and Lake St. John were also recorded in *Le Second Registre de Tadoussac*. The first Mistassini sacraments recorded were the baptisms on June 16, 1669, of two Mistassini children, followed by the baptisms on June 23, 1669, of eight Mistassini adults.[12] The last Mistassini entry recorded the death of a twenty-year-old man who died in the bush in 1695.

It was customary for Indians to pay their tithes with furs. On June 12, 1677, at Chicoutimi, the Mistassini Indians gave the church on Lake St. John sixteen moose skins and five beaver skins.[13] This appears to be a tribal donation rather than an individual's gift or memorial, as no family name is mentioned. This method of paying tithes or donations to the church continued into the 1970s. Although some Mistassini people were paid in actual money when they guided or worked for the mines in the 1940s, the Hudson's Bay trader factor still kept the trapper account records for expenditures and credits in furs rather than dealing with them in cash. Hunters, after settling their HBC account, designated some hides to be credited to the church's HBC account for their tithe.

After 1677 Mistassini Catholics went to Lake St. John or Chicoutimi for their church needs. Friendships were made with members of other tribes. Often intertribal marriages were the result. Mistassini marriages between different surrounding groups included both their Indian and Eskimo neighbors.

On April 7, 1686, Father Crépieul, when living in the cabin of Louys Kestabistichit, a Montagnais Chief who must have been baptized as a small boy, addressed a letter to his Father Superior, *Remarks concerning the Tadoussac Mission of the Society of Jesus since 1671*.[14] He mentions three Mistassini chiefs who died without the sacrament of confession, implying that they had the opportunity to become Christians but did not. Wesib8ourat,[15] chief of the great Lake Mistassini, died in the forest near Lake Peokwagany (Lake St. John). The Mistassini said that he was deceived by the devil and perhaps carried off since only his jerkin was found, a story that appears to be a blending of Medieval and Native beliefs. Father Crépieul noted that the Chief had killed his brother but gave no dates or other details.[16] Wesib8ourat's name does not appear in the church records. (The figure 8 was used by early Catholic missionaries with the French to represent an Indian sound which could not be represented by the English or French alphabet.)

In the later seventeenth century, Indians from south of the St. Lawrence started to migrate north of the river. Father Crépieul noted a change in dialect among the southern tribes and took steps to prevent the southerners from migrating north of the St. Lawrence. However, early anthropologists noted that in more recent years several Maine Indians have been accepted into tribes north of the St. Lawrence. Some accepted invitations to join winter hunting groups, and some were granted rights to hunting territories, an act that usually occurred after marrying into a family and hunting with one's father-in-law.[17] Perhaps there were Maine traditions of some earlier marriages to the Mistassini people.

In 1670 rumors were circulating in Quebec City that British fur traders were in Hudson Bay. By 1671 Father Charles Albanel was a veteran Tadoussac missionary of ten years' experience that included several years of successful rugged wintering with families of Montagnais. These experiences had hardened Albanel to the vigorous life north of the St. Lawrence River. He was also considered a gifted linguist who knew several of the area's Indian languages. In 1671 Albanel and another priest were selected with five Frenchmen and an Indian guide to find the trail to Hudson Bay. The group did not leave Lake St. John until September 7, 1671.

On September 17 they met a group of hunters who told them that two British ships were trading on the bay. Albanel decided that passports would be needed, as they would be entering what was considered British territory. He sent two men to Quebec City to obtain them. The group would camp waiting for the return of the men. It was not until October 10 that they returned with the passports. At Mistassini, lakes and rivers are often frozen, and snow is usually on the ground in early October. Albanel opted to stay where they were for the winter. The winter was severe, the hardest that Albanel had ever encountered. His guide left him.

The following May, Albanel found sixteen Indians who would take his party to the lake that was later named after him. When they reached the height of land, the Mistassini tried to prevent the Europeans from proceeding further. Albanel negotiated with them with gifts and a promise of French aid against the Iroquois. The Mistassini, who feared the Iroquois, accepted the terms. Albanel continued to Lake Mistassini and then went down the Rupert River, reaching Hudson's Bay on June 28, 1672, where they saw a British ship. It was the Hudson's Bay Company ship *Nonsuch* that had begun making annual trips to the bay in 1668.

UNMAPPED RUGGED COUNTRY

Albanel was the first European to successfully venture into the entire Mistassini territory from east to west and return. His was the fourth attempt by Europeans to enter that cruel land. The winters are rigorous, the summers are noted for severe thunderstorms and swarms of black flies and mosquitoes. He reported encountering two hundred portages, many rapids and other dangers on the trip. As a missionary, he succeeded in baptizing two hundred Mistassini. No other Europeans were seen, although the *Nonsuch* was observed anchored in Hudson's Bay.

Albanel was hardly back from Mistassini when he was asked to lead another mission there. The goal was to dissuade the Indians from trading with the British and to persuade Groseilliers, the rebellious Frenchman who had guided the British to James Bay, to return to the French and influence the Indians to trade only with the French.[18] At that time Albanel's knowledge of bush travel and woodcraft, combined with his ability to negotiate with Indians, was more important to the French than his ability as a post missionary.

While the French were busy developing their system of forts and trading posts on the St. Lawrence and expanding westward, the British slipped into James Bay in 1668. It was not until four years later that the French discovered the British activity in the bay, something that may be difficult to understand in today's high-tech and super-high-speed world. The vast virgin forests, unmapped rugged country, cold and snow, were like an iron curtain preventing anyone from knowing what was happening on the other side. The Mistassini did not readily pass on information to their non-Indian neighbors.

In 1610, when Champlain was actively exploring and building a French empire in the New World, Henry Hudson sailed into Hudson Bay to explore the economic opportunities it could offer to the British. The ship was frozen in for a winter, providing the crew an opportunity to explore. They found a hunter who was willing to trade only for what he needed at that time. His ideas about trading were quite opposite to those of the trader who always wanted more and more furs. Apparently Hudson had encountered a Mistassini Indian who periodically made the arduous trip to Tadoussac for trading. There was no incentive for the Indian to even consider a huge amount of money beyond what was necessary to pay for his following year's outfit. Money beyond that was of no real value to him. His life was a planned simplicity, centered around food, the knowledge of animals, hunting for game, and the enjoyment of a plentiful harvest feast. If there was a surplus of food, the hunter could give a feast, a happy interlude, creating an image of him as a person of importance among his peers. Encumbering himself with unnecessary material goods could lead to disaster.

# IV

# THE HUDSON'S BAY COMPANY
# BECOMES ESTABLISHED

Hudson's exploration did not set off a rush for others to follow him. By today's standards it seems that so much time elapsed before the next voyage into the bay that any gains that Hudson made would have been lost. Twenty years later, in 1631, the next known person to explore the area was Captain Thomas James, who sailed into the bay now bearing his name. Another long period of inactivity followed.

In 1668 Médard des Groseilliers joined with another rebellious Frenchman, Pierre Radisson, to look for a prospective fur market, from which the British would prosper. Both felt that they had been cheated in Montreal and offered their services to the British. Groseilliers arrived in September 1668 and established the British Hudson's Bay Company trading base at Rupert House, Quebec, a settlement at the mouth of the Rupert River. They proceeded to build Fort Charles there, with cannons facing the ocean. The fort was not for protection from the Indians but for protection from foreign naval forces that might sail into the bay. Rupert House, named for a nephew of Charles I, was one of the Indians' favorite fishing places.

In 1669 three hundred Indians showed up at Fort Charles, with skins to trade, many more Indians than were anticipated. By this time many Indians probably relied on European trade goods and may have lost the art of crafting certain basic material goods, just as Maine Indians lost the art of crafting stone arrow points within a generation or two after receiving guns.

This trading site was a great advantage to the Indians. Hudson Bay's ice often blocks the entrance to James Bay until late July, leaving a short window of opportunity for trading between the British and Mistassini Indians on the west side of Lake Mistassini, before ice begins forming again. In 1670 King Charles II announced to the world that the Hudson's Bay Company was a creation by royal charter, giving Britain authority to trade in beaver skins in all of Rupert's Land. This included Hudson Bay and all its drainage tributaries, about two-thirds of present-day Canada. They enjoyed their monopoly trading there until 1672, when the French discovered the British presence on Hudson Bay.[1]

The Hudson's Bay Company was a business whose primary concern was the making of money. Their goal was to buy as many furs as possible from the Indians. Most of the early reports of Rupert's Land evaluated the area as an extremely high fur-producing country. A few reports were negative about the prospects of a profitable enterprise in Ungava. Enhanced reports sounded very attractive to businessmen who were willing to gamble on a country of which they knew little and had even less knowledge of the local inhabitants.

The Mistassini were certain that they did not want Europeans to enter their territory from either the west or the east. Both the French and the British wanted trading houses closer to the source of the furs at Lake Mistassini. King Louis XIV realized that France needed something more to compete with the British, who in 1670, by a mighty pen, proclaimed the powerful Hudson's Bay Company. With a dip of an equally powerful pen into an elaborate inkpot, the French king directed that all the land on the east side of Lake Mistassini was now part of New France. The king then proceeded to grant land to his patriotic friends. By 1679 they obtained permission to construct a simple trading house at the eastern door of Mistassini. Then the French king's great pen created a royal charter announcing that the Compagnie du Nord had sole rights to trade in Hudson Bay. At least on paper, the French had the advantage of a trading post at the eastern entrance to the Mistassini Territory and the right to trade on James Bay as well.

The Indians no longer had to make the long trip to Tadoussac to trade. Of course the British or French never invited the Indians to negotiate for their land, so they were probably completely unaware of the change in their land's title. Other than the difference of flags flown and languages spoken at the posts, there was little to indicate to the Indians that there was a political change in Ungava. Mistassini people were more willing to deal with the French. The presence of the French missionaries and the French traders had a much longer and stronger influence among the Mistassini than the British did. Also, the Mistassini

Cree knew that the British had supported the Iroquois, a good reason to be suspicious of them.

The French attempts were sudden bursts of energy that were of short duration. They had outstanding explorers, geographers, and mapmakers, but, apparently, they lacked the necessary backup substance. In 1679 Louis Jolliet, famous for his explorations on the Mississippi, was sent to check and map the route from Tadoussac to Hudson Bay. He concluded that the Mistassini country was the richest source of furs and said that whoever controlled the region would be "masters of all the trade in Canada." In 1700 Mistassini was declared one of the French king's posts, but little is known about active, realistic policies to control it.

In 1720, Father Laure was assigned to Tadoussac, a position that had been vacant for several years. He was charged to work especially with the Mistassini Cree, an assignment that lasted for ten years. He became very knowledgeable about the Mistassini people and wrote the first description of them. Their life and beliefs were little changed from 1700 to 1900. The French built a new trading post in 1725, but they soon abandoned it. In 1730 the Mistassini Indians were trading back at Lake St. John. There were years when it was hard to find men to go into the remote, frigid wilderness. Eighteenth-century priests were often reluctant to go to the northern missions. There were short periods when the void was filled. Life was extremely hard for those not accustomed to it. Besides the cold and snow of winter, daylight was much shorter, and one was lucky to find another of his countrymen with whom he could converse. Usually one had to depend on oneself for everything. A few years of northern experience often left its mark on a person for the rest of his life. In the middle of the nineteenth century, Mistassini Indians were returning to Chicoutimi to trade.

The British tried unsuccessfully time and again to gain access to Lake Mistassini. The Mistassini Cree were still determined to prevent strangers from trespassing on their land. However, the British were determined to find their way to Lake Mistassini and build a trading post there. It took a hundred years to gain the friendship and acceptance of the Mistassini Indians. Finally in 1812 their century-old quest became reality.

The governing core of the Hudson's Bay Company merchants were people whose business enterprises depended on ships and seamen. It is not surprising that the company emphasized discipline at all levels and branches of the business. A sea captain had complete charge of his vessel. The success of a voyage was his responsibility. He knew the importance of a well-disciplined crew for a successful voyage. He also served as a church layman aboard his ship, reading Sunday services and if necessary performing a funeral service for a crewman. It is not surprising to find that the authority given to a Hudson's Bay factor was modeled after that of a British warship commander or merchant marine ship captain. The trading posts were just as remote as a ship at sea, perhaps more so. The factor's powers included the discipline of both his staff and the Indians who came to trade at his post.

Only a certain type of person can face the solitary confines of the trading post life during the lengthy, cold, lonely winters. Those whom the HBC sent into the country to work with the Indians would have to respect Indian customs and treat them well. Although the company, on paper, prohibited their employees from fraternizing with the Indians, they usually turned their backs on this rule when a factor married into a tribe, realizing that such a relationship could be good for their business. It was to the advantage of the company for factors to remain at the same post for a long term, because they would come to know their clientele and their needs.

The Hudson's Bay Company needed lower-echelon workers. A recruitment system was developed to attract young men from Scotland's Orkney Islands. Willing employees were found. Orkney people generally agreed that life and the economy anywhere else in the world would be an improvement over theirs. They were accustomed to taking wild winter weather in their stride. France lacked a similar source of hardy recruits for their trading posts. Young men in the British welfare system were also offered a new start in life. They were to sign up for a seven-year apprenticeship. When that contract terminated, they were encouraged to sign a new contract. They gained a great knowledge of the area and the Native people within it. By that time most had adapted to the disciplined Hudson's Bay Company life, and friendships had developed among them. Many did not hesitate to sign another contract. Their memories of life before coming to James Bay held no particular charm for them. Continuing with the Hudson's Bay Company meant stepping up from apprentice to "servant" with an increase in pay. Future factors would be selected from this group. In 1979, I was surprised to find that the Hudson's Bay Company was still recruiting employees. The main purpose of the factor was to make money for the company. He must be able to estimate the quality and value of furs, to anticipate his clientele's needs from the store, and evaluate new products that would improve the Indians' quality of life. Any way that the trappers' lives could be made easier and more efficient would most likely benefit the Hudson's Bay Company as well as the trader.

The James Bay posts, like most of the northern trading posts, received their supplies once a year. In early October, when the trading ship embarked from Rupert House for England, they carried the factor's orders for all goods required by the factor, his employees, other non-Indians dependent on the post, and stock for trading with his Indians. Each European made out a huge shopping list of all the anticipated store goods that he would need in the following year. It included food, clothing, holiday gifts, tools, and any item that a city dweller could purchase at the corner store. It was important for the factor to estimate correctly for the Indians' needs. If several Indians decided to trade at a post where they had not given their order, the factor would probably have to refuse them. Otherwise, a regular customer might have to go without his goods. The factor at the post where the Indians should have traded would have a surplus. That too could mean a loss of money. Indians were encouraged to trade at the same post each year, so all customers' needs would be met. The factor had more control over his Indians' debts and his stock orders when his Indians were encouraged to purchase from a specified post. Posts were set up over an area that a factor could control. Living for the year on one's estimated needs was a form of discipline. The annual order system was still followed in 1970 at Mistassini. The Hudson's Bay Company ship still came into James Bay once a year with the annual supplies. Everyone at Mistassini looked forward to the shipment. In 1970, after the gravel road was completed from Chibougamau to Mistassini, this traditional system ended quickly.

The Christmas-New Year's celebration was the year's dominant social activity at the post. The St. Lawrence River posts, considered the most southern, invited the trappers to come in with their furs and join the festivities. This was not feasible at Mistassini. The round trip between bush camp and post would break into the best season for the trapping of superior furs. The warm undercoat of the fur was in its prime at the beginning of the season. As the winter wore on, there was more chance for the pelt to be damaged in possible fights with other animals or by an accident.

Before the mid 1970s, in the dogsled days, there were trading posts at most of the following sites: Eastmain, Nemiskau, Neoskweskau, Nichikun, Caniapiscau, Waswanipi, and Chibougamau, which together covered an area greater than that of New York State. These posts were of reasonable size for a factor to control and for him to become well acquainted with his Indians. These groups are still decidedly independent, each wishing to retain its own identity. Today the government considers each of these groups as a branch of the present Mistassini family.

Early anthropologists hypothesized that the Mistassini and other northern Cree wintered as isolated families on their family territories. Recently this hypothesis has been questioned. It is possible that before the Hudson's Bay Company arrived, the winter groups consisted of more than one extended family.[2] Emmett McLeod, Jr., the son of a trader, was himself a trader for the Hudson's Bay Company, the French North West Company, and finally a free trader. He lived at Mistassini for many years. When he was young, two to six families, usually related, joined for the winter hunts. The population was much smaller, and the families were also smaller and lacked sufficient hunters for success. The multi-family groups provided a sufficient number of young men for successful hunting. The group camped near sites where caribou were apt to be. A shaman of the camp was head of the hunt.

At that time, the people were dependent on snowshoes. The head of the hunt directed the young hunters to go to a certain locality and arrange themselves in a large semicircle, standing facing into the wind, so the animals would not smell them. Older, experienced hunters would drive caribou toward the men standing in a semicircle. When the caribou came to the semicircle, they were shot.

Apparently, there was a generation or so when caribou did not come to the major Mistassini areas, making it difficult to supply food for a large number of people. As mysteriously as they left, they returned. Perhaps the loss of the caribou stimulated the traders to work with the Indians to establish an improved plan to further develop the family hunting territories. Apparently some family traditions can trace their hunting territory holdings back for considerable time. There was probably a mix of families including those who did not have territories in their heritage and others who had long established territorial rights. The reasons for these rights were long ago lost in time or known only to the Mistassini.

Indian families were close knit, independent, self-supporting groups who needed good reasons to make friends of strangers. They listened respectfully to strangers, making few comments, knowing that most white strangers remained in Indian country for only short periods. The family was the base for most of their social activities.

Food or the obtaining of food was their primary goal in a land where hunger was well known. Before the traders came, the Indians had little use for furs beyond clothing and containers for their family use.

BEAVER SKIN STRETCHING

The animal foods were found in specific environmental circumstances at specific times of the year. They named most of the months for the primary or special food harvesting that took place during that time of year. The family groups changed their place of abode to be at the right place at the right time. Since they moved a number of times a year, they did not encumber themselves with unnecessary material goods. Leaving unneeded material goods cached at a site for use the following year was customary. Their entire goods would be an unnecessary burden as they traveled their complete annual circuit. Theft was unknown. The tribe members understood that it was acceptable for someone to borrow a needed item that his neighbor was not using. Finding a canoe missing upon return to one's camp was nothing to be excited about. The borrower would return it shortly, perhaps with a piece of meat or fish. They cached snowshoes in winter camps for the summer; canoes were left at the summer sites where they would be found in the spring.

From the earliest sixteenth-century accounts of trading, both the Indians and the traders knew their expected roles in the trading venture. When the trader appeared, the Indian was just as happy for the opportunity to obtain goods that would improve his quality of life as the trader was to acquire furs. The common image of trading pelts for beads is exaggerated! The Indian haggler often outdid the European,

IN THE DOGSLED DAYS

but who would admit that the man of the forest outdid him? The Indian speculated that he had negotiated the best deal. He was exchanging some furs, nothing more than commonplace possessions, for copper kettles and iron or steel tools that were an improvement over his traditional tools. The Indian considered the beaver big game. For the average family, a large beaver weighing fifty pounds or more was considered a valuable supply of meat. The fur, often a waste product, became a valued trade byproduct. The traders, who settled into Indian country, gained the Indians' confidence and surreptitiously began to modify the Indians' lives. The trader's life also changed as he adapted to Ungava's conditions.

In the days of the dog teams, before 1975, the number of trading posts was larger, the factor overseeing a smaller area than in recent years. A relationship grew between traders and trappers. Before the Indians paddled off to their winter quarters, they held meetings with the factors. In time, a program of two or three winter factor visits to the Indian hunting camps evolved. This accommodated both parties. The young employees, called the "servants" of the company, were provided with work during the winter: sorting and baling the furs, cutting and hauling firewood by dogsled, or hunting for food. There was always work to be done.

Each trapper calculated the store food and other necessities to supplement what he obtained from hunting and trapping. The standard store food staples were limited to tea, sugar, flour, and lard. In more recent years, the list has become more extensive, especially to fit the change in diet to which the children became accustomed while attending residential schools. The trappers provided the factor with a list of supplies to deliver at each of the three visits that the factor would make during the coming winter. The trapper did not have the burden of storing and transporting his entire winter's supplies as he made each of his moves.

For many years the trader came by dog team and delivered the ordered supplies. This was not just a quick stop and transfer of goods and then on to the next camp. All was done in a prescribed procedure, showing respect to and by both parties. Trading involved a bit of ceremony, beginning with a gift to please the trapper's wife. It has always been a good policy to treat the lady of the house well. It was customary to make a table and chair for the factor who presided over the trading. Often periods of bad weather forced the traders to delay their scheduled drop of supplies. These delays were not good for trapper or trader, since the trapper would stay home rather than check his traps. The fur trade developed into a well-planned and regulated business, using trapping methods that led to a less painful death than the long agony of a trapped animal.

The coastal people were the first to find that the Hudson's Bay Company was becoming the central focus of their lives, but these people still enjoyed the feeling that they were independent and in charge. The annual pattern of wanderings in which hunting had been the primary objective began to emphasize trapping; store food supplemented country food. The hunters acquired more possessions. They gained goods such as camp stoves, steel traps that replaced deadfalls, tinware, copper wire for rabbit snares, duffle, canvas, steel needles, guns, ammunition, steel crooked-knife blades, clothing, fancy colorful ribbons and thread, and much more. The dwellers of the snow-white wilderness could not resist bright clothing or any dazzling item that caught their eye.

Frequently the trader was disappointed in the low number of furs a trapper brought him. The Indian saw little or no merit to trapping more furs than were necessary to pay for the following year's outfit. In his attempts to obtain large fur harvests, the factor often found the Indian code of conservation ethics frustrating. I have heard stories from frustrated Peace Corps workers sent to Africa to train agricultural people to increase their harvests without enlarging the size of their gardens. The people enjoyed the benefits of larger crops in smaller gardens but obviously missed the objective of the project. They saw the benefit of increased production as an increase in their leisure time, oblivious of the fact that the new procedures could produce additional food for starving neighbors.

Southern poachers unknowingly aided the factors, whose jobs depended on their ability to persuade the Indians to trap more animals for their furs, before the southern poachers took them. Indian ethics was part of the Indian oral history passed down from one generation to the next. They obeyed this code of law, although unwritten, without dispute. The trapping process took a familiar step already felt in the east and south. The greed at the top pressured the factor's subordinates until the pressure reached the trapper. Then the Indian conservation code of ethics broke down. When some trappers learned, to their consternation, that southern trappers were encroaching on their hunting territories, the Mistassini felt forced to harvest the breeding stock. Indian ethics for the benefit of future generations broke down. Trappers who fell into the traders' trap found that animals became scarce. Although the trappers received praise, they found that it became even more difficult to pay for their outfit. Soon the beaver were very scarce. Eventually traders and trappers came to their senses and began enforcing the ancient oral conservation laws that Indians had practiced since ancient times. Thus the Hudson's Bay Company and Mistassini survived together through the twentieth century by recognizing the ecological mistakes made by their predecessors and took steps not to repeat them. In the years when animals were scarce and the Indians faced starvation, it was in the traders' best interests to seek out the trappers and provide sufficient store-bought food for the survival of his group. A skilled, dead trapper could produce no furs!

The normal demands of life in the North over the winter period are so great that it is almost impossible for a single man or woman to survive the ordeal of an Ungava winter alone, having to be food provider, cook, dishwasher, laundryman, tanner of furs, tender of fires, water boy, mender of nets, and performer of all the other necessary details of northern bush life. The development of a demeanor for bush behavior was inevitable. A hunter following trails on his snowshoes to his trap lines or hunting with his dog team or skidoo in the bitter cold winds all day could not concentrate on his hunting and trapping if he knew that those left at home were squabbling with one another about their duties. As the provider for his group, he needed to be able to focus fully on his hunting, knowing that all was in order in his tent home, and that when he returned in the evening, often with white spots of frostbite on his face, he would enjoy the comfort of a warm tent and hot meal. From a very young age, children were encouraged to participate in camp duties. Parents also had the philosophy that adult life was hard and filled with responsibilities. Children should enjoy a child's carefree life for as long as they could. There was a balance of camp chores and enjoying life. The family members performing the everyday duties were the hunter's backup team.

Many early accounts of Indians mention, contemptuously, that some hunters had two or more wives. If a hunter died, his widow joined a relative or friend who had a good record as a provider. It was sometimes necessary for hunters of special repute to take under their wing one or more persons besides those in his family. This was their way of looking after everyone, a much condensed version of our modern community service programs. The strong hunters capable of providing for more than their extended family became respected tribal leaders. A young hunter taking over the responsibility of his deceased father was under considerable pressure to prove his leadership qualities during the first year in his inherited position. The headman of each camp had the great responsibility for the welfare of everyone in his camp. Besides providing food, his duties included basic medical care, such as setting broken bones, stitching up ax and other serious wounds, and operating on frozen, gangrenous areas. It was a rare event for a visitor to arrive at a post. However, occasionally one or two showed up, not enough to cause shortages in the post supplies for the Indians. If one happened into an area and required food and equipment, the post store was the only source available. It was not likely that an outsider would request an extravagant order, since he should know that the store's supplies were limited, and they could not fill a very large order.

Although many have criticized the Hudson's Bay Company's profit-making policies that have made it a successful business, most traders did their best to improve the Indians' standard of living. They gave the Indians the opportunity to retain the life they enjoyed, making it less labor intensive. I think of the example of the Naskapi Indian who received what to him was a fabulous $25,000 for leading a prospector to a Labrador seam of iron ore. His lifestyle provided no training or experience for such a windfall. He was not prepared to handle such a bonanza. He probably became notable among his people for a few months from his gift giving and providing feasts. The following winter he returned to his trap line with as little money as ever to continue enjoying the richness of living in his primeval wilderness.

I once met a Moose Factory Ontario Indian who went south and became a successful businessman. He longed to return to his boyhood home and finally retired and went "back home." A winter in Moose Factory disillusioned him. Both he and Moose Factory had changed over the years. All his money could not bring back into reality the wonders of his boyhood on the trap line. The traditional images of the trap line greatly impressed many of the young people who grew up in that lifestyle, and they never forgot it.

# V

## MISSIONARIES

After the posts took on the form of an assemblage of structures, the beginnings of a frontier settlement, European missionary societies became interested in sending clergy to the James Bay communities and Indians. The Roman Catholics began sending missionaries to convert the Micmac of Nova Scotia in 1605. Their plan was to assemble the Natives in large villages, often assigning more than one tribe to a village. A gathering in a community setting would create a parish atmosphere favorable to missionaries but not necessarily to the Indians. The primary disadvantage from the Indians' point of view was that the country food supply would soon vanish.

Forest dwellers did not appreciate close neighbors, many hardly known to them. The settlements became too large for individuals to share the success of their hunts with everyone in the traditional manner. Providing a wedding feast for the total community was not possible for a bridegroom. The congeniality so characteristic of the extended families broke down, especially when strangers from other tribes became close neighbors. Community living was a new experience for forest dwellers. The independent Mistassini gave their early Catholic missionaries no encouragement to develop a community-oriented village. They preferred their roving, bush-camp ways.

In 1822 John Evans arrived in the Canadian north and was hired as a school teacher.[1] Several years later he became a Methodist. In 1828 he accepted an appointment as a teacher for the Ojibwa Indians of Rice Lake, Ontario. He enjoyed languages and was soon understanding and recording the Ojibwa language. He had tremendous energy and did a fine job. However, his strict interpretation of the Methodist rules of conduct caused him to clash with the fur trader leaders who then shifted him from place to place, eventually sending him to isolated Norway House. Now he is probably best known for developing a syllabic script system that apparently was based on an early form of shorthand that he learned in the British Isles. Several other denominations working with Indians adapted Evans' syllabic system to their needs. Later the Evans syllabic system was improved and is still in use today. In 1975 two ordained Indian Anglican priests told me that they would teach me the syllabics in an hour. It is an interesting system. Evans worked hard and deserves much credit for his linguistic work and translations.

The managers of the Hudson's Bay Company felt the addition of clergy would enhance their work at the post settlements. They contacted the Church Missionary Society requesting clergymen for James Bay. In 1840 the British Wesleyan Society sent Rev. George Barnley to establish a mission at Moose Factory. For eight years he worked diligently at the mission, but like Evans he adhered to the strict Methodist rules and regulations. The Hudson's Bay people considered that some Methodist rules such as the declarations against work on Sundays conflicted with the traders' business practices. In that generation, work included travel. A walk was not a leisurely stroll down a country lane. Due to the rigors of the country and the type of business the fur trade was, the traders felt that Sunday travel was often a business necessity and should not be restricted. Sunday travel became a big dispute between the Church and the Hudson's Bay Company traders. The HBC controlled the politics of the north. There were many ways that they could create unpleasantness for uncooperative clergy. In 1847 Barnley gave up and abandoned his mission. The Methodists were unable to find replacements wishing to take on the challenges and rigors of Canada's subarctic. They decided to close their northern Canadian mission and offered it to the Anglican Church Missionary Society, who were happy to accept it.

The Anglican Church Missionary Society advertised the position. There was no rush of applicants. In colonial times, the Anglican Church had difficulty finding men to fill Indian missionary churches in northern climates. Settling in a cold wilderness among "wild men" in a far-off country was not their cup of tea.

In the middle of the nineteenth century, the United Kingdom was a very class-conscious country. It was expected that one would not rise above the status of one's parents. Although John Horden wanted an education, his father apprenticed him to a blacksmith.[2] However, John continued his studies on his own, taking on Greek and Latin. He was hired to teach at a boys' school, where he also continued his own studies.

The Church Missionary Society appealed to him. In 1851 he contacted the Society regarding a position, having in mind an assignment in India. At the time, the Missionary Society's priority was a teaching position at Moose Factory at the bottom of James Bay, where the Hudson's Bay Company had established their headquarters. Although their headquarters has now moved to Winnipeg, Moose Factory is still considered a revered historical site, the foundation of the Hudson's Bay Company. Although disappointed, Horden accepted the challenge. Three weeks before he was to leave for Canada, the 23-year-old convinced Elizabeth Oke to marry him, accompany him to Canada's northern frontier, and share the challenges of his life's work. It was far from the dream honeymoon most women expect.

On August 26, 1851, John and Elizabeth Horden arrived at Moose Factory. They sailed on the Hudson's Bay Company ship *Prince Albert*, which became trapped in James Bay ice for an uncomfortably long time. It was a good introduction to subarctic weather. Horden's primary work was to be a teacher and catechist, just as Evans had been. The churches placed a high priority on education for Indians in the early days, just as they have taken that responsibility into the present. The Hudson's Bay Company leaders felt the missionaries spent too much time with the Indians but not enough with the people of their posts. Horden was forced to change his priorities.

Horden worked hard. Although only 23 when he arrived at Moose Factory, he had work experience as an apprentice for a steel company, teaching experience, as well as a capability of study and planning to see projects through. He had good judgment and could be trusted to make good decisions, probably much better than a committee many miles away. He could distinguish the points of view of the Hudson Bay traders and the Church on such matters as work on Sunday. He was well aware of a discipline to keep holy the Sabbath Day. However, Horden was also aware of the importance of respecting the practical business needs of the fur traders to journey on a Sunday, if necessary. Often weather conditions prohibited travel, so it was necessary to travel when the weather permitted it. He showed flexibility. In the long term, he realized that both the Church and the company would benefit from a strong cooperative spirit and gave in on what he defined as practicality under the climatic conditions.

In 1849 the Anglican Diocese of Rupert's Land was officially created. It consisted of the Yukon, the Arctic, Prairie provinces, Northern Ontario, Northern Quebec, and western Ungava Bay. It was much too large for a single person to administer efficiently, especially in those days when rivers were the major highways of the area, and communication systems were unknown. The bishop's visitations took four years to complete, most by canoe and dogsled. In 1872 the Church Missionary Society decided to split the diocese in two. Thus it created the Diocese of Moosonee, still the second largest diocese in the Anglican Communion; their northern neighbor, the Diocese of the Arctic, is the largest. John Horden was elected bishop of the new Diocese of Moosonee. Among Horden's accomplishments were the translations into Cree of *Pilgrim's Progress*, the *Book of Common Prayer*, much of the Bible, and other religious writings, including hymns. He also learned Ojibwa, Inuktikut (an Eskimo language), Chipewyan, and Norwegian. He encouraged the Indians to become catechists and ordained priests. But when it was time for Horden to step down, he looked at his replacement candidates through the eyes of a British leader of a British system.

Rev. James Vincent was of mixed blood and a thirty-eight-year veteran priest of the diocese. He had risen to the position of archdeacon and had an excellent working knowledge of Cree and English. However, Horden did not support him as a candidate for bishop for excellent business reasons. He felt that a bishop must have some British contacts and know the possible sources for much-needed financial support. Today, such a policy would result in a large outcry of racism.

Although the Cree greatly outnumber the non-Indians in the diocese, a Cree bishop has not been elected yet. However, there has been one Cree candidate who ran, but lost. Most of the diocesan clergy are white, and they can control the vote.

Bishop Horden died unexpectedly on January 12, 1893, thus ending an era. It was not until the end of February that his friends in the UK received the news. A telegram was carried by dog team to Mattawa, the nearest post office to Moose Factory, some four hundred miles away.[3] Bishop Horden succeeded in establishing the Diocese of Moosonee on a firm foundation for others to continue.

# VI

# THE GREAT LONE LAND OF MOOSONEE

I answered the knock on my door to find a casual friend carrying a bundle. He said, "I know that you are interested in the North. Here is Fred Swindlehurst's manuscript of his ten years as a missionary in the North that began in 1897. It is called *The Great Lone Land of Moosonee*. Some years later, Fred became a very good friend of my sister, but he did not feel himself worthy of marrying her. He gave her this document for safe keeping with the words, "They are dead. I soon will be. I am now passing it on to you."

I was overwhelmed by the gift. A week or so later the donor was in the hospital. He could not recognize his closest friend, not even his wife, due to his Alzheimer's disease. I felt highly honored to be the recipient of this document from a man whom I hardly knew. He must have had some hint of what his fate would shortly be. I will quote from this narrative that provides eloquent descriptions of early twentieth-century James Bay life.

The Rev. James Scanlon served at Nemaska on the Rupert River as a student during the summers of 1953 and 1954. He much enjoyed working with the Cree some years following Swindlehurst in what he called "the twilight of the olden days and the dawning of the new."[1] Swindlehurst went into the district, remaining there for eight years without a break. He was stationed at Moose Factory and would sometimes join fur brigades taking supplies to various posts and returning with furs. Fur brigades were groups of canoes manned primarily by Indians taking bundles of furs to a trading post, then returning with supplies. Excerpts from Swindlehurst's narrative follow.

On the morning of Sept 10 [1897] I left Montreal to journey West and take the canoe that was to carry me to my destination.

After traveling for about 18 hours on the Canadian Pacific R.R. we reach a country which indeed savored of a wilderness— Rocks, dead trees, gorges, stretches of swamp, a lake, then rocks again . . . then the conductor shouted, "Missanabie."

Missanabie being translated into English means "the pictured waters" and most of the canoes leaving for Moose Factory, the Metropolis of the North are "outfitted" and started from here. As a fur trading post it does not compare to the Factories of the North, but as a shipping point it is important . . . A more untidy, desolate place than Missanabie as I viewed it in the year of grace 1897 would be impossible to discover on this side of Purgatory . . .

About noon we reached our first portage. We had arrived at the northern extremity of Dog Lake and a narrow path through the forest had to be traversed before we could launch our canoes into the waters of Crooked Lake. Now I must say to the Indians' credit that he exhibits no sign of his native indolence when "on portage." The cargo is thrown onto the beach with a recklessness and rapidity that would do credit to an average railway baggageman. Well indeed is it that our boxes or "cassettes" as they are termed in the Hudson's Bay District are strong as they would be smashed to match wood upon the rocks against which they are violently thrown during the hurried moments of unloading the canoe . . . The Indians after carefully lifting the canoe from the water and placing it on the shore produced their portage straps which are generally tied to the cross bars of the canoe to form a seat. With these straps they tie up the cargo into 200 lb. bundles. Placing the wide portion of the strap across the forehead, they balance the load on their backs "and bear the white man's burden" across the portage path at a fast trot . . . The novice will do his best to help the Indians by undertaking to carry a 200 lb. bundle over the path but after proceeding about 1/2 mile he will drop the burden disgusted. His neck is minus some of the powers of resistance and he will curse the day when he left civilization to become a human derrick. The man who leads the busy procession over a portage must possess the patience of Job or its English equivalent, especially after a heavy rain fall. Swarms of mosquitoes attack him, black flies bite and cause the blood to flow freely from face and hands, he is wet to the skin with only the knowledge to console him, that once his clothes are thoroughly saturated, they will gather no more moisture from the surrounding bushes.

About noon we landed to have dinner my first dinner in the free forest. Paddling and portaging gave one a most ravenous appetite, but that hungry feeling disappears as one is called upon to witness Indians preparing a meal, the prevalent idea of the romance of voyaging in the north remains a rude shock when confronted by reality. The Indian is supplied with pork, flour, tea and sugar, no luxuries it is true, but good substantial provisions. From experience I can vouch for the fact that the Indian likes "strong food." His method of cooking and eating is barbarous, nay beastly to say the least of it. Romantic? . . . A huge cauldron is filled with water and placed over a roaring fire until the water has reached boiling point, pork is cut into large slices with knives that have been used to cut plug tobacco and never cleaned. Of course tobacco is a strong antiseptic and also a flavoring medium. The pork is thrown into the boiling water. Flour is mixed with cold water until it attains the consistency of dough and then with dirty hands it is pulled in pieces and thrown into the cauldron to strike up an acquaintance with the pork. Stray dust, ashes, dead mosquitoes and black flies are never molested if they fall into this Indian stew, indeed so far as I know these may be wholesome. The flour dumplings, popularly known as doughboys or "choke dog" are taken up on sharp sticks by the more genteel or by filthy fingers of the savages who wish to uphold the glorious traditions of their forefathers. Greasy fingers and faces proclaim eloquently when the Indians have dined. The tea they brew is notoriously strong. A kettle is placed over the fire and filled with equal portions of cold water and black tea. This mixture is permitted to boil and when it reaches the thickness of syrup three or four cups of it are drained by each Indian . . .

Night approaches and we prepare to camp. Such gorgeous sunsets as one sees in the North Country. They are not to be equaled anywhere beneath the blue dome of heaven's splendour. The scenery is grand and amply repays one for the struggle engendered by a sojourn in the country of the Woods Cree Indians.

The Indian's camping outfit can be neatly stored in a flour bag, and generally is . . . I watched for the first time, these natives of a wild lonely land deposit house and furniture in a flour bag. Nothing on earth can equal the simplicity of our Hudson's Bay voyageur. Time, weight and space are his first consideration and if comfort has any place at all in his life it comes only incidentally. The rapidity with which camp was erected, supper cooked and everything safely stowed for the evening astonished me. Each Indian seemed to know just what was expected from him and he did it. No fuss and no excitement and goodness knows in a country like Rupert's Land excitement is welcome, but as silent as our gloomy surroundings the temporary homes were erected. The canoe was beached, and the guide with a torch was repairing the leaks occasioned by the chipping of the gum from the seams of the bark craft, caused by rubbing against trees in transportation across a portage and rubbing against rocks when landing. Our baggage was piled on the shore and covered over with waterproof canvas. Some of the Indians disappeared into the silent forest to cut boughs of hemlock to place on the ground and over these was spread a huge tarpaulin. The tent was next erected, a couple of blankets thrown in and our home for the night was complete. Hardship, you say, not a bit of it. Given a tired man, a warm blanket, let him roll his boots in his coat to form a pillow, get beneath his blankets and he can actually enjoy life . . . Supper over the Indians assemble around the campfire and filling their pipes with strong black tobacco, named by Hudson's Bay Traders "black strap," they smoke in silence. The fumes of that awful narcotic are a guaranteed germicide and mosquitoes avoid the vicinity. After the smoke the Indians reverently remove the hoods of their capotes, kneel and the guide offers up prayer in an earnest, sonorous tone and the stanzas of the well known hymn "Jesus breathe an evening blessing On thy children gathered here" broke in upon the stillness of the night. Oh it was sweet, yes sublime!! Never will time, the great destroyer, eradicate from my memory that beautiful night scene witnessed in a Voyageur's encampment upon the shore of Lake Missenabie, the pictured waters.

We had journeyed for fourteen days . . . Sick and weary I was growing as silent as my surroundings when rounding a point in the river the white washed houses of a Company's Post burst upon our view . . . Here at least was a semblance to civilization which had been transplanted in the North . . . From the flagstaff at the Fort fluttered the blood red banner of the Hudson's Bay Co., while the beautiful white ensign with its red cross of St. George was flying from the mission post. It seemed so romantic then and a pleasant break into the monotony of voyaging but I found out later that it was a life we could never learn to love. In the foreground were scattered wigwams of the Cree Indians, the mission house situated upon a piece of rising ground and in the distance gleamed the spire of the Pro-cathedral of St. Thomas the Apostle.

This is the headquarters post of the Southern Department of the Hudson's Bay Co. The bishop of Moosonee has his Episcopal palace here (a log house). To this place mails are brought twice during a year, and the ship brings provisions and takes away the fur. What the Indians and the isolation of the place really mean can be gathered from the fact that the missionary and trader from Rupert's House have to journey a hundred miles for their mail after waiting six months for it to arrive at Moose Factory, or that people of Fort George have to journey nearly four hundred miles by dog sled and snow shoe, but such is really the case. Time is of very little import in that Northern country and mail time by breaking the eternal monotony of routine life is welcomed even if one had to snow shoe a thousand miles to enjoy the party at the post, gayety which is given a free rein during Packet time . . . Life at this post may be more tolerable than at any other post of the Southern Department. Being a headquarter post of the Great Company it could not fail to be otherwise, but a two years sojourn at Moose Factory and a three year sentence in an up to date penitentiary do not differ much, so far as the freedom loving white man can judge.[2]

In mid April 1983, I was invited to Moose Factory to update booths for the Indians to sell their crafts to summer tourists, most of whom arrive by the Polar Bear Express from Cochrane, Ontario. This unique two-hundred-mile rail line was constructed on muskeg, a kind of bog and unstable base until the severe cold creates a firm underpinning. In milder weather the rails continually move up and down with thawing-freezing conditions that limit top speed to 25 mph much of the time. May was the expected time for the ice to go out, a major event at Moose Factory, climaxed by the guessing of the exact time that the ice actually goes out, determined by the downing of a big red-painted tree placed in the middle of the river. The winner receives a large purse. Elders who have watched this spring ritual for many years have developed their secret formulas to estimate the time the river will open. It's a time that has always drawn many people to Moose Factory. Activities include music, dances, card playing, and storytelling. I met two elders who as teenagers had joined the fur brigades, collecting furs from far-off posts, including Mistassini.

Birty was fifteen or sixteen in 1916 when he began working for Hudson's Bay Company. He received eight dollars a month. After working for three years, the pay was raised to ten dollars per month. Birty was sent to Mistassini with others to build a new store. The antiquated pitsaws were still in vogue at Mistassini. Birty, a new man on the pitsaw team, was assigned to the position below the platform on which the log to be sawn was placed. When one in that position perspired, which didn't take long, the sawdust stuck to him. Some streamed into his eyes. He would soon be caked with sawdust. I saw the pitsaw in 1970, the last year it was in operation at Mistassini.

Willie Corston went to work for the Hudson's Bay Company when he was fifteen. He recalled taking supplies to the island posts. There were seventy-five portages the first hundred miles. The longest was three miles. If you could not carry 200 lbs, you received no pay. If you could not do it, you quickly figured out that you could learn to do it. In summer one did not need a tent when traveling for the HBC. You gathered some boughs and spread them on the ground and slept on them. Corston crewed on the voyageur canoes for ten years. In August 1903, Willie and a companion canoed from Moose Factory to Rupert House in seven days on Hudson's Bay Company business. The ship *Mink* lacked crew so was late making the trip. Since the *Mink* had not arrived and Willie's work was completed, he decided to return to Moose Factory by canoe and made the 130-mile trip in three days.[3] Willie was typical of the young Moose Factory men; they knew the bay, the weather, and were expert canoemen.

Willie found fault with the contemporary village young people, saying that they go to school, drop out, and don't know what to do with themselves. He continued, "They are up all night and drum, then sleep most of the day." He added that the drumming at night kept them awake, and it never was like that.

There have been changes at Moose Factory in the sixty or so years since Birty and Willie were part of the backbone and muscles of the Hudson's Bay Company. There is an area hospital for Indians and Eskimos and an area school with dormitories for young people. Each entity is surrounded by a forbidding fence. Each group had non-fraternizing rules, limiting their employees to associating exclusively with those of their own compound. The only unfenced places where all were free to come were the Catholic and Anglican churches and the HBC store. Young medics, nurses, and teachers, enticed by higher salaries, came to gain experience and found themselves incarcerated within the walls of their frigid institutions. Their superintendents were puzzled as to why drugs dominated the lives of so many of their staff. The Natives saw the fenced-in institutions and began to copy them by fencing in their crude abodes. There were so many fences that I wondered why the Cree also felt it necessary to be surrounded by fences. Were they following Robert Frost's philosophy that "good fences make good neighbors," or was it to keep within certain limits, or to prevent the outsiders from crossing the line? Perhaps they were copying a custom established by the white strangers. At any rate, it seemed to me that these freedom-loving people for some reason found that they were forced to show that they, too, possessed a separate entity.

Why was such emphasis placed on education here? There were no businesses, offices, or trade shops requiring educational certificates. Moose Factory is an island isolated by two hundred miles of tundra and has very limited need for positions requiring certifications or exams other than what the government has established there. Although the local employees did not meet the civil service requirements, for years the hospital and school maintenance departments were staffed by local Cree whose performance records were very high. The government's sudden change in its policy of ignoring the regular civil service procedures on the island had resulted in the local people, some who had been employed for years, being forced from their jobs, unable to compete successfully for the economic opportunities that the government created on the island. The former local employees went on unemployment insurance and were replaced by others not accustomed to the cold and isolation of Moose Factory. It seems surprising that the school did not equip the local people with the skills necessary to pass the required civil service examinations for employment in their schools and Indian Affairs offices.

Vehicles required no licenses or inspections at Moose Factory. Most vehicles were owned by people from away. The local people had little need for them. Even when the river froze over, one could only go across the ice to neighboring Moosonee. When the river is free of ice, canoes are the principal form of transportation from the island. For those wishing to drive in Canada beyond Moosonee, it meant purchasing a license, plates, and inspection, then driving to Moosonee and putting the vehicle on the Polar Bear Express that meets the highway in Cochrane.

Swindlehurst often reflected that he never lost the call of the mighty challenging North. The unmatched images of its beauty never leave one, and the powerful challenges met and overcome were blended with the hardships and the very simplicity of the life. The comforts of a campfire lead to the brilliant, sparkling northern lights. Swindlehurst both loved and hated the North at the same time, but his fascination for it always lingered, a typical reaction for many who experience the North.

> There is a something one cannot reason as "why or the wherefore" that is so extremely fascinating about the life in the Far North. A charm broods over that silent land, the spell enters the soul and as soothing as a narcotic, the more one experiences the "call of the North." It leaves one more dissatisfied with civilization . . . and when compared to the artificial life led in civilization, the past experiences seem to be a glimpse into the almost forgotten paradise of the past . . . With a mail coming in only twice a year, only an occasional visitor, no newspaper or telegraph, how can one expect to find this country otherwise than just as it is, asleep, dead, monotonous, just two centuries behind the times . . . James Bay of the Seventeenth Century and the James Bay of today, silent, solitary and almost neglected.[4]

Swindlehurst found that the Rupert House Church records were a shambles, lacking organization. The arranging of these legal documents into a proper system became his first priority. He lost no time in organizing them.[5] Fred was never to know the significant service that he performed, for organizing the birth, baptismal, marriage, and death records was of the utmost importance to establish land claims and inheritance rights in the 1975 James Bay Agreement, and for welfare benefits as well. Swindlehurst knew the Bible stories well and had a knack for storytelling. Both Indians and white men loved to hear him repeat the tales. He took seriously the Biblical command to become his brother's keeper.

# VII

# THE GOVERNMENT TAKES AN INTEREST

Although Ungava was within the geographic boundaries of Quebec, the Indians' welfare was the responsibility of the federal government until about 1950. As the Hudson's Bay Company was the dominant entity in the area, most Indians knew enough English to meet their needs. Mr. H. Larivier, Indian agent for about forty years, visited the chief no more than once a year, but sometimes skipped a year. In actuality the Hudson's Bay Company was the primary overseer of the Indians. Missionaries checked on the health of those Indians who were within their reach. About 1960 federal medical support was provided for about eight weeks in the summer at the tribal summer meeting places.

The French were the mapmakers of the Colonial period. Mistassini appeared for the first time on the Franquelin *Carte de la Louisiane ou des Voyages du Sr. De la Salle et des pays qu'il a découverts depuis la Nouvelle France jusqu'au Golfe Mexique, les années 1679, 80, 81, et 82*, published in Paris in 1684. Fifty years later, in 1731, Father Laure, S. J., Mistassini's first priest, drew the earliest detailed map of the Mistassini country.[1] Although it was very inadequate by contemporary standards, it shows that he had a good knowledge of the region. Mapping their areas was not an unusual task for early missionaries. Early Catholic missionaries were usually assigned to pursue some area of scientific study to increase knowledge of their regions. Several missionaries made such valuable studies of natural history topics of their areas that they are still consulted today.

No attempt to survey the Ungava Peninsula was made until 1870, when the Canadian Geological Survey sent James Richardson to explore the country north of Lake St. John. After surveying thirty miles of Lake Mistassini, his food ran out, forcing him to return to civilization. The following year, Walter McOuat surveyed 150 miles of the shoreline.

Nothing more was done until 1884, when John Bignell headed a joint project of the Canadian Geological Survey and the Quebec Department of Crown Lands to finish surveying the lake. This survey party failed to complete the task assigned to it, probably because they attempted the project in the dead of winter.

McOuat did not arrive at the Mistassini Hudson's Bay post until nearly the end of December, where he met post factor William Miller, who lived quite comfortably with his wife in one of the four company buildings. Miller was adding a church to his cluster of structures.

Bignell noted that Miller raised potatoes and other vegetables, such as cabbages and turnips, successfully. There was an abundance of dogs— beasts of burden in winter, hauling firewood, and going out on the ice to the fish nets. There was six feet of ice on the lake. Fish made up the dogs' primary diet in the winter; in the summer they ate off the land as they roamed free.

A. P. Low, who was in charge of the Lake Mistassini section, found mistakes in Bignell's data. They quarreled. The reports were considered inaccurate and incomplete, but Low's reports were accepted. Perhaps the problem was the fact that the Hudson's Bay post had moved from a southwest outlet of the lake to the southeast, where the fishing provided better results.[2]

Low's reports soon attracted prospectors to the area. In 1903 Peter McKenzie, a fur trader, brought out some ore samples and took them to Joseph Obalski, Quebec inspector of mines. Obalski was so impressed by the ore samples that he ventured into the area. He started with Indian guides by canoe from Saint-Félicien at the north end of Lake St. John. It took nearly a month to canoe and carry over more than fifty portages to reach Chibougamau. Obalski was even more impressed by his own findings regarding the mineral potential of the area. It would soon be a place of interest to prospectors and miners. And in his official 1904 report he wrote that the new district of Chibougamau was "destined to play a great role in the industrial development of our Province." Obalski was followed by John E. Harding, first president of the Canadian Mining Institute, who in 1905 predicted that "the Chibougamau district is destined to have a large and profitable mineral production." A proposal to construct a railroad to the district to serve a future mining community followed. In 1910 J. B. Mawdsley, a geologist for the federal government, pushed for a railroad to Chibougamau. Then the Chibougamau Mining Commission was appointed. In 1911 the commission mapped 1,000 square miles and investigated the known deposits. The commission published a low-key report to avoid a rush of prospectors to the area.

Interest declined, but suddenly blossomed about 1925. Saint-Félicien became the jumping-off place for prospectors going to Chibougamau. The government constructed a 150-mile winter road from Saint-Félicien to Chibougamau, so that prospectors and miners could transport their equipment and machinery by horse-drawn wagons. Prospectors attracted to the area by gold, silver, copper and zinc lived up to their rugged reputation by facing the snow and daytime temperatures of −30°F, −40°, −50°, and colder nights. Wall Street championed Chibougamau mining stocks, and then came the crash in 1929. The would-be millionaires left, drifting south, lucky to have their shirts. The slump was short-lived. By 1934 the miners began a slow return. By 1936 a post office was established, serving a community of more than a thousand people. In 1938 war seemed imminent. Investment funds became scanty again, and miners left. Chibougamau resembled an aging ghost town. When World War II ended in 1945, it was time for the world to regain normality. The Quebec Government began to turn the 150-mile Saint-Félicien-Chibougamau winter road into an all-weather road. Miners returned long before the road was completed in 1949. The new highway reduced what originally had been an arduous month-long canoe trip to a pleasant three-hour journey. Fishermen also quickly discovered this route to significant prizes. An eastern door was opened to Chibougamau, and Mistassini to the north. In 1971 I met one of the earlier indomitable prospectors who remained in Chibougamau and was as hard as the rock that he drilled. He lamented that the city was growing, destroying the pristine wilderness, and that the new inhabitants did not always respect the unwritten law that the owner of a cabin on a lake had sole rights to fishing there.

The intrusion of the miners and prospectors at the turn of the twentieth century had little effect on those at Mistassini. Each group went about its own business, neither interfering with the other. In 1904, Joe Kurtness, chief of a small Mistassini group at Lake St. John and HBC fur trader, accompanied by Gladstone MacKenzie, made a trip by dogsled from Lake St. John to the Mistassini country. MacKenzie left a description of his impression of Mistassini.

> The Mistassini Indians were totally different from the Lake St. John Tribe. Their complexion was much fairer and most spoke English, although they had never left the district and knew

nothing of the outside world. They had learned the language from the Hudson's Bay Company traders.

They were a happy and congenial people, hospitable and gay and during the festive season spend weeks visiting one another. Dances were held every night with a violin and accordion . . .

Some fifty Indian families lived in the Mistassini area and shortly before my departure they gave an Injun banquet in my honour. The Hudson's Bay Factor and I sat at an axe-hewn table as the entire population squatted circular-wise on the ground at our feet.

Some five or six squaws, gaily dressed in beaded costumes, approached our table carrying large birch bark baskets laden with smoked meat—bear, moose, cariboo and smoked fish. Bannock . . . was then served with bear fat . . .

There were only two plates in Mistassini and we were honoured with their use. The smoked meat was served in eighteen-inch strips and, as forks and knives were unknown, the local custom was to devour them in sword-swallowing fashion.[3]

Anthropologist Frank G. Speck visited Lake St. John in the summers from 1915 to 1923. He found a group of Mistassini Indians living on the Montagnais reserve under Chief Joseph Kurtness who, with his father, gave Speck much help.[4] I found that in 1970 there was still a group of Mistassini at Point Blue, Lake St. John. The new road made the 150-mile trip much easier for the related people to participate in family celebrations. The Mistassini Cree have had a very long attachment trading at Lake St. John, yet they have retained their identity.

# VIII

## WASWANIPI

The war ended in 1945. It took a few years for the country to adjust from a wartime setting to peacetime ways of life and work. There was a bigger demand for some metals like copper, lead, and zinc, all metals that prospectors had discovered in the Mistassini territory. A railroad line linked La Tuque and Senneterre to far western Canada. A gravel road extended from Val d'Or to Senneterre. It was now time to extend both the railroad and road to Chibougamau, so the mines could be developed. Work began on the railroad first and on the road a few years later. They were built about twenty miles east of the old Waswanipi Island settlement in Waswanipi Lake. The railroad was finished first; the road was not finished until 1963. In 1964 the Waswanipi Hudson's Bay Company was closed. The glorious years of the Waswanipi hunting society ended. Now new transportation routes stretched into what had been a region almost inaccessible without canoe and snowshoes.

The Atikamekw, formerly called Tête-de-Boule, was the Waswanipis' southern neighbor, living in the heavily forested area between Senneterre and La Tuque. Along with a few Odanak St. Francis Indians, the Atikamekw had winter hunting grounds there. In the mid 1960's the government made what sounded like a rosy offering to Mistassini Indians to move them to sites on the Senneterre-La Tuque railroad line. It included losing all their Indian rights. Work in forest operations was the carrot. The government enticed a few Cree to move from Mistassini, but they have seen few benefits worth the loss of their Mistassini Indian rights.

The Waswanipi territory was south of the Mistassini territory. Both tribes went to James Bay by different rivers that took them to the Broadback River and then to Rupert House. It was a month-long round trip for the Waswanipi, just as it was for the Mistassini. Rev. John Gull commented, "It was a five- to six-week trip to collect our mail." The mail came once a year on the Hudson's Bay supply ship, just as it did for the James Bay villages. I certainly hoped that his mail was much more interesting than much of what appears in my mail box! Both the Waswanipi and the Mistassini knew each other, and there were many relationships between them. Politically they were independent groups. They followed a simple cycle of events centered around well-developed bush hunting activities. The family hunting groups were so spread out that it was impossible to quickly notify each one if there were a tribal emergency.

The Rev. Harry Cartlidge was the first Anglican missionary assigned to Waswanipi, serving from 1914 to 1927. For several years Harry had had an image of being a missionary in Canada's northland. In 1914 he wrote to the bishop of Moosonee telling him of his interest in becoming a missionary. Harry was promised a job. Soon after that he was sent to Waswanipi as a deacon in training. He quickly made friends with Indians and built a church and a house for himself. He seemed immediately to meld into the life of the northern frontier Indians. In 1918 he was ordained a priest for the village. Harry Cartlidge said that Waswanipi received its name from the practice of catching sturgeon at night by the light of birchbark torches there in the rapids in the river below the HBC post. Thus it was named, "The Torch Lit Waters." His heart belonged to the people, who became aware that they could go to him for advice and help on all sorts of problems. He did much for them, and when I asked about him in 1970, the elders lovingly remembered him. Someone recalled that he was now blind and living in a Winnipeg nursing home. The elders had fine and fond memories of his Waswanipi days. Periodically Waswanipi guides paddled him over ancient canoe trails to neighboring Mistassini where he held services.

The selection of chief seems to be an informal affair. "Formerly the chief was the best warrior and most trustworthy man. He was not elected or appointed, but acquired his office by tacit consent at the death of the former incumbent."[1] In 1928 Noah Diamond, chief of the Waswanipi, drowned (Church Records: St. Barnabas, Waswanipi Lake). Chief Diamond must have died shortly before John Cooper, a Catholic missionary, arrived. "The writer was informed consistently and emphatically that the Waswanipi have no chief."[2] Probably Cooper posed questions during the difficult interval before the election of a new chief. Waswanipi has a Hudson's Bay Company trading facility. Diom

Blacksmith's father followed Noah Diamond as chief. Diom's father died at the age of 99. My informants disagreed about whether his wife or his sister followed him as chief, but it didn't seem to matter. When she was near death, the people universally selected Diom Blacksmith chief for life.

Up until the 1960s, the provincial Quebec Government showed very little interest in the Waswanipi and Mistassini people. Apparently the Quebec Government was happy that the National Bureau of Indian Affairs had taken responsibility for them. The primary relations with the outside world had been first with the Hudson's Bay Company, second with the federal government's Indian Affairs department. Both agencies used English as their predominant language. The Waswanipi's second language became English. The Hudson's Bay Company factor, the chief, and the priest had worked together developing an outstanding Indian island community. As an example of their Indian policies at work, the Federal Bureau of Indian Affairs showed it off as a model Indian village.

Chief Diom Blacksmith and the Reverend John Gull, the Waswanipi leaders at that time, realized that their way of life was on the threshold of change. They felt that they were too remote and would be overlooked if they remained at their village. They saw the proposed road as the place for economic opportunity. Tribal members moved down their hunting territory rivers to points where the road would cross them. Chief Diom Blacksmith moved to his territory on the O'Sullivan River at Miquelon; the Reverend John Gull moved to his Waswanipi River site about thirty miles farther north, and others moved to their river roadside sites. For those from the old Waswanipi village, this was their first actual face-to-face meeting with the white culture.

Although the Waswanipi were now located where the work was, they were the low men on the labor totem pole. The contractors brought workers with them. After the Waswanipi departed from the island community, a local fur-trading post was no longer available to them. The closest places to trade were Senneterre or Chapais, a good seventy miles either south or north, to sell their furs and purchase their hunting, trapping, and fishing gear. It did not take the Waswanipi long to realize that they were being overlooked as a potential labor resource. A few of the younger generation were hired at the Chapais copper mine, but Waswanipi life remained primarily that of a trapper on a trap line. The Waswanipi River communities began to take on their own importance. There was no longer a central tribal meeting place. The tribal cohesion began to dissolve.

THE USUAL RABBIT-SNARE TRAINING PROVIDED
TO YOUNGSTERS

The people moved their village to a site with road access, thinking that it would provide many advantages to them. The electricity bypassed them. Among the foremost benefits was that those who needed hospital service would be able to get there and return more quickly and easily.

John Gull was a good example of a Waswanipi Indian who became a respected leader. John's father, Jacob, was born in 1878 and died in 1970 at 92. John was a rugged, respected hunter. He made a good living as a trapper and was a fur brigade leader from Waswanipi to Rupert House. He left with furs and returned with supplies. John had four brothers and a sister. They all grew up in the wilderness, sometimes wintering near James Bay and at other times in the Waswanipi Lake watershed. By the time he was six, he had the usual rabbit-snare training provided youngsters. Often accidents made it necessary for youngsters to be the temporary providers of food to prevent starvation. John was still in his teens when he, like other boys his age, joined the fur brigade, transporting furs to Rupert House. He learned how to carry the two-hundred-pound parcels over the portages by using a tumpline. These robust young men gained their great strength from their daily activities. The brisk exhilarating air and the fragrance of the surrounding spruce were the background for the daily chores. There was no need for a health club!

John cited the year 1927 as the time of change, when the first prospectors came into his country. John, who had some command of

English, was one of the first to meet these strangers. The prospectors needed some help moving a four-hundred-pound pump. Could John assist them? John and a friend moved the machine to the desired site in the afternoon and reported back for supper, not realizing that the move had been considered two days' work. The boss, who had not expected the pump to be moved so quickly, said, "John, you good man, take tomorrow off!" John was paid in actual money! It was the first money that he had ever received.

John and his crew worked and watched the strangers. The prospectors soon had a building where all the workers went at the end of the workday. John and other members of the tribe were curious about what was in the building. Where and why were all these people going to the building? One day they decided to follow the others. They found that it was a bar, another new experience for the Waswanipi Indians.

John said that when the first white people came, the Waswanipi had great respect for them, because they seemed to have so much equipment and knowledge. The first doctors who came told the women that they should go to the hospital to have their babies. They respected the doctors; the women went to the hospital to have their babies. The mothers were told that they should stop nursing and use formula and bottles; the mothers took the advice and stopped nursing their babies.

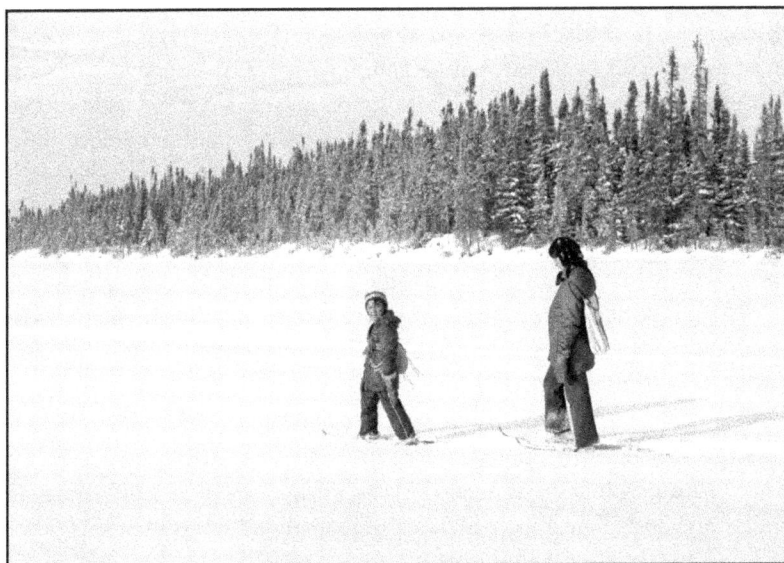

YOUNG BOY LEARNING TO SNARE RABBITS

After learning much from the white people, many Waswanipi began doubting the white man's wisdom. Women returned to nursing, feeling that their milk was healthier than formula. They generally concluded that the bars were detrimental to the Indian. The white ways may be better for white people, but not for Indians. They decided that they preferred to continue living as they had in the bush.

John's grandmother was influential in introducing him to Christianity. She kept her prayer book and Bible in a finely-crafted leather bag tethered to a tall pole, out of the reach of young children for safekeeping, a method signifying that it was something extra special. John enjoyed singing hymns. When canoeing and passing a camp, it was customary to stop, visit, exchange news, and sing a few hymns. The Rev. Harry Cartlidge also influenced John, who began to write hymns on birch bark. The birchbark scrolls were included in his camp gear for his trips into the bush, so that he could sing and teach others he met along the way. The bishop recognized his interest in the Church and encouraged him to become a deacon.

There were never enough clergy to fill all the vacancies of the parishes in the Diocese of Moosonee. John was doing an excellent job as deacon. Could he become a priest? Local Indians would not require as large a salary as the white clergy did. The bishop was well aware that such a recommendation would receive much criticism from the white priests, who have to be willing to serve anywhere at the bishop's discretion. This Indian wanted to serve his people and was not interested in an assignment to a white congregation or other Indian congregations. John had backers, but there were some people on the other side of the question. The Indians wanted one of their own to be their priest. John was willing to take the responsibilities of a priest, and was ordained a deacon in 1946. There was opposition from the white priests, who had to meet much higher educational requirements and be willing to move beyond their home parishes to become a clergyman.

The missionaries from away were always trying to change the Indians. John had no inclination to change the Waswanipi lifestyle. He did such a fine job serving his people as a deacon that in 1964 he was ordained a priest.[3] He was one of their own; the Waswanipi looked up to him as a leader. An anthropologist studying the Waswanipi rated John as the third most important person in the village, after the Hudson's Bay trader and the chief. John's life was little changed from being a typical Waswanipi Cree, but he was very surprised to learn that he could make more money as a trapper than as a priest. The Reverend Gull retained

BEAUTIFULLY DECORATED LEATHER BAG TO PROTECT THEIR PRAYER BOOKS

his hunting skills. Once in the winter when the snow was soft, wolves
came to the edge of the village. He grabbed his rifle, took aim, and
squeezed off three bullets. One wolf lay dead; one was wounded. The
gun jammed! John grabbed a piece of wood, ran up to the struggling,
wounded animal and hit it squarely on the head, killing it. He said that
Indian people become uneasy when they think that wolves are around
and remain uneasy until they know the wolves are killed or scared away.
It was part of the Indian culture to kill bears. One day John and his
brother William were hunting. They spotted a bear's den. The snow
was almost waist deep. John cleared a narrow path to the den with a
snowshoe. They called to the bear to wake him up, as was the custom,
then poked him. The sleepy bear gave a start, growled fiercely, jumped
up, and charged the entrance. John put his gun to his shoulder and
squeezed the trigger. Nothing happened! John flattened himself as tight
as he could against the snow bank and called to William to shoot the
bear. John felt the bear brushing by him. William fired, killing it. Every
hunter has a repertoire of stories.

Another illustration from the Gull family reflects the independence and self-sufficiency of the James Bay people. Five years before John was born, Sam was born in a typical winter bush camp, far from anything that could be called civilization. When Sam was young, the family hunted in the Eastmain area. On a cold winter day, while still a very small boy, one of Sam's feet got wet. He continued on with what he was doing, unconcerned about his wet foot. He did not take the time to remove the wet clothing and exchange it for dry footwear. The result was frozen toes. Jacob, his father, was concerned and checked the foot carefully for several days. The dreaded gangrene appeared. Jacob assessed the situation and knew what he had to do to prevent losing his son. He heated the knife and began the delicate operation of cutting off the necrotic toes with his sharp hunting knife. Jacob had nothing to give his son to block the pain. At that time a doctor was sent to Moose Factory each summer for a few weeks. About a year and a half later, the Gulls were at Moose Factory. Soon the doctor there heard about the boy's foot and asked to check it. The doctor couldn't believe that a person of the wilderness with no professional medical training could perform without other professional assistance what the doctor called "an amazing operation." A hospital would have required a team of several doctors and nurses to perform that intricate operation! Jacob, like all the hunters gained much knowledge about anatomy from skinning and butchering many kinds of animals. The operation saved the boy's life.

People like Jacob can successfully meet the challenges of survival in their harsh life, but they did not have the proper education to pass our I.Q. tests. Sam claimed that he could do what he wished and was in no way incapacitated. After the Reverend Henry Cartlidge and an HBC factor taught Sam some fundamentals of English and mathematics, Sam was hired as an HBC clerk at the Waswanipi Hudson's Bay Company, enjoying the work for thirty-seven years. When he moved to Waswanipi River, he put shelves on his walls like the Hudson's Bay store. Sam stocked his shelves with the goods he knew Indians needed. Like the traders, he prepared the land for a vegetable garden and planted potatoes, perhaps the most northerly vegetable garden at that time.

In 1970 Sam joined some others going out to cut firewood with chainsaws. He ran into a problem, and two fingers fell, causing the snow to become red. One of the men bound up his hand and rushed him back to their settlement. Another picked up the fingers and brought them with him. A taxi was called to rush him to the Chibougamau Hospital nearly one hundred miles away. The hospital was not equipped to handle such a severe problem. Sam was bundled into another taxi and sent to the Roberval Hospital, more than one hundred miles down the Saint-Félicien road, where they were able to attach the fingers so that he could regain use of them, which he slowly did. What a change in medical care during Sam's life!

Roger Ratte was a French Canadian who during the 1929 stock market crash went north to trap. He had other versions of his story, all showing marvelous creativity for his change of residence. Since meeting Chief Diom Blacksmith's daughter Mary, he has had close ties with the Waswanipi. When Mary married Roger, government regulations terminated her Indian rights and changed her citizenship to French Canadian. Her children also were officially French Canadians. The children were not permitted to attend the Indian school with their cousins and friends but had to go to the small French Miquelon school, where only French was spoken. Government laws may affect one externally, but Mary's heart was still that of a Waswanipi.

About 1961 Roger and Mary Ratte moved out to the O'Sullivan River Miquelon site. They both applied for work on the railroad, hoping to get jobs as cooks for road crews. Roger was hired as a cook; Mary was assigned to an outdoor construction crew. It was winter. She dressed in warm clothing that included a hood snug around her head. She dared not speak, fearing that the men would discover that she was a woman. After about three months, the boss came looking for Mrs. Ratte. He was horrified to find that she was working as part of the outside construction crew, doing the same rugged work as the men did. However, he did not transfer her. The next day Mary went to work as usual. All the men whistled at her. She quit the job.

When the road was finished, the Rattes decided to build a camp for hunters and fishermen. They purchased a parcel of land adjoining the Indian reserve at Miquelon. They had no heavy construction equipment for cutting down trees, pulling stumps, or building cabins. Mary helped Roger with the rugged outside work. They worked hard and established a good business, much of it with American sportsmen. About 1971 Mary had a freak accident. She was hanging out wash on a metal clothes line. Bits of rust blew off the line, sending some razor-sharp filings into one eye, causing loss of sight. She became limited in what she was able to do. The accident forced the children to take more responsibility and do more of the home chores. Mary made it her responsibility to check up on the health of everyone in the small community.

Those who moved into drafty, small shacks tended to be almost continually sick during the winter. It had never been like that in the canvas or bark domiciles on the trap lines, where common colds and sore throats were rare.

In 1970 Diom Blacksmith had been chief for thirty-five years. Many Waswanipi people had known no other chief. He was born in the birch era and lived to see and adapt to the canvas and motors that replaced birch bark. His children, grandchildren, and neighbors admired him as a provider, teacher, and counselor of great wisdom.

Suddenly the Quebec Government wanted to take responsibility for all the province's Indians. Diom faced incomprehensible problems stemming from Quebec Government actions that interfered with Cree life. Diom's Cree life background failed to prepare him to understand these problems. In the mid 1960s, without warning or negotiations with the Cree, the Quebec Legislature passed laws limiting the terms for the Waswanipi and Mistassini chiefs to two years and setting the dates for their elections. The Quebec Government no longer recognized the existing chiefs.

These actions reminded me that in 1834 the Maine State Legislature

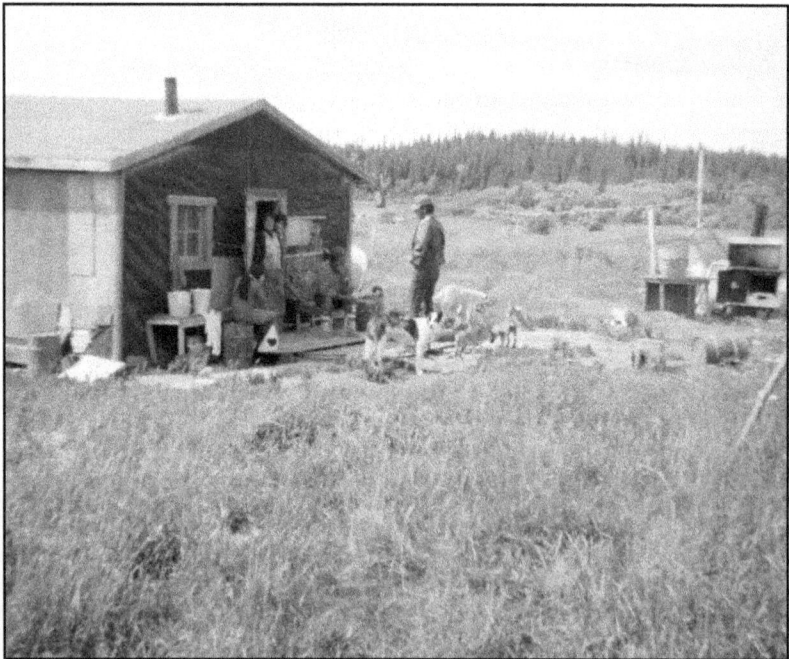

WASWANIPI LAKE SETTLEMENT HOME

took similar action changing the terms and dates for the election of Indian chiefs and establishing political parties on the reserves, without negotiating with the Indians.[4] In both the Maine and Quebec situations, the white men's governments were meddling in private Indian matters, without negotiating with the chiefs. They took the Indians completely by surprise. However, the Cree, like many Maine Indians, felt that they had no recourse but to follow the orders.

The Mistassini and Waswanipi chiefs, elected for life, realized that they and their people were not prepared for the Quebec decisions. However, the elders agreed that younger people, who had been to school in the white man's cities and had acquired a better knowledge of the white man's ways, would be nominated for the positions of chief. Both the Mistassini and Waswanipi chiefs recognized their inadequacy to deal with the provincial government and agreed in principle to the new rules. However, Quebec did not understand Indian ways. The newly elected chiefs were only the spokesmen and negotiators for the tribes; the traditional chiefs and elders actually made the tribal decisions for the newly elected chiefs. The new, young chiefs acted as the intermediaries between the tribal elders and the Quebec politicians.

A younger school-educated Indian was selected to be band manager, a paid position similar to that of a town manager. Government departmental office buildings sprouted on the newly created Indian settlements. Harry Blacksmith, Diom's oldest son, was in the first group of Waswanipi children to attend school and was the first Waswanipi band master. Harry Blacksmith, like most of the young Indian band masters, had never handled the large government budget for running an Indian reserve.

The first Waswanipi chief elected under the new regulations, not a paid position, was Peter Gull, a young man who worked in the Chapais copper mine. Peter depended upon the mine for his income; the mine took precedence over the chief's responsibilities. Much of the time he was not available on the reserves to attend to tribal business and problems. The two-year term made it easier for disgruntled followers to replace him. Although the Quebec Government recognized those chosen in the biennial elections as chiefs, the Waswanipi recognized Diom Blacksmith, whom they elected for life as their leader.

In 1962 Waswanipi leaders had observed scientists arriving with instruments for measuring the river currents. It was no surprise when years later workmen began ravaging the land. The elders became deeply involved in planning a new reserve that would be satisfactory to all

Waswanipi. The government offered three proposals. The first was for the Waswanipi Cree to join the Ojibwa Rapide des Cèdres reserve. The Cree rejected this on the basis that historically Cree and Ojibwa placed together had never integrated on a common reserve. Success would be impossible. In simple terms, neither the Ojibwa nor the Cree would want a chief from the other's nation as its leader. A second suggested site was on a high bluff overlooking Waswanipi Lake. This proposal was rejected after engineers feared that the James Bay Hydroelectric Project's predicted rise in water level could create an unstable area resulting in landslides. It would be an unsafe area. Another Lake Waswanipi site was rejected also because of unsafe conditions that the James Bay power project would create. Several years later Waswanipi River became the accepted site as the home of the Waswanipi Cree. In 1972 the government built an office building when Harry Blacksmith was band master. It was the first building to have electricity at the Miquelon Indian settlement. Harry was Diom's eldest son and was a member of the first Waswanipi group to attend school. The Waswanipi people had no electricity until the Waswanipi River site became the official reserve. At that time Roger Ratte, Chief Diom Blacksmith's son-in-law, was the only person connected to the Miquelon reserve to have electricity installed in his house.

Louis Blacksmith, Diom's brother, had a camp on a small point near the mouth of Pusticamica Lake about two and a half miles east of Miquelon. Both Louis and his wife, Mary, enjoyed the bush life. About 1971 Mary had a heart attack in the bush. Louie rushed out to Miquelon to obtain help and Mary was rushed to doctors who were able to control her situation. The doctors told her that she was lucky to get to Miquelon so quickly and receive attention. She should move to the settlement and give up the bush life. She might not be as lucky the next time. Mary hated the thought of settlement life. She was born and raised in the bush and would die there just as her ancestors did. She still appeared very able and wanted to show us her camp. We decided to go. Shortly before our arrival she had shot a seagull on the lake with one bullet from her .22 rifle. Several of her grandchildren proudly told us how she shot the gull, killing it with only one bullet; they doubted they could equal her prowess as a hunter. Her eyesight was still excellent. The elders enjoyed having visits from their grandchildren, who were given a marvelous introduction to bush life, the way life should be. It was a joy to see grandparents and grandchildren relating to each other in a bush camp.

About twenty years earlier, about 1951, Minnie Paul of the Woodstock, New Brunswick, Maliseet reserve demonstrated to me the extraordinarily creative art of birchbark biting. A very small, thin sheet of birch bark was folded into several square layers, placed in the mouth and bitten, so that the canines and molars made impressions on the bark, creating fascinating designs. The person knows exactly what designs she will impress on the bark. While in this forest scene, I asked Mary if she knew birchbark biting. Her face lit up, and she quickly found a proper piece of bark for the craft, folded it, put it in her mouth, and began biting. She retrieved the bark, unfolded it, and showed off her talent, creating delicate snowflakes. Then more intricate patterns followed, a string of geese, and finally a row of children with outstretched arms. I since have learned that the mothers within the birchbark region taught all Indian children this craft.

It was time to leave. Mary gave us several birchbark packages of fish and rabbit to give to some people in the settlement who were no longer able to procure food for themselves. They always thought of their old

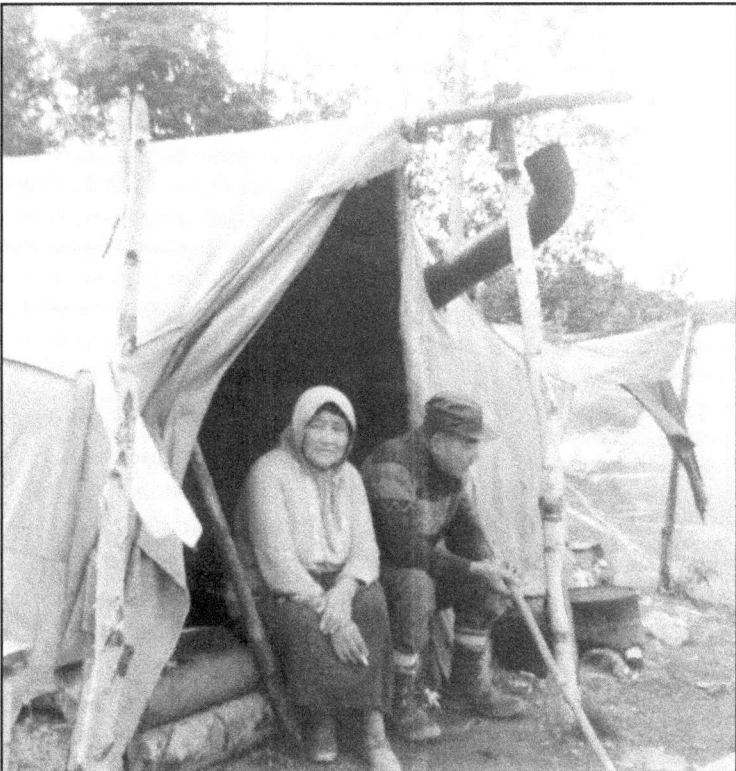

MARY AND LOUIS BLACKSMITH LIVING IN BUSH AFTER HER HEART ATTACK

friends in the settlement and how much they would enjoy country food. This practice was in keeping with the ancient, unwritten principle of sharing, whenever they could, with those less fortunate among them. In this time when their culture was breaking apart, they were the generation with the heavy burden and important task of keeping and imparting the age-old ethics and traditions of their great tribe for the younger generation, just as elders on other rivers were also preserving their heritage.

The hunters still sometimes employed traditional methods to obtain food. Once when I went to see John Gull, I could not help but notice that on his kitchen table a moose scapula supported his pipe. John Gull was still a hunter as well as a priest of the church. He kept the moose scapula for use as a divination tool to tell him the moose's location. Close by was a piece of quartz which he used to demonstrate how to strike a spark by hitting his steel pocket knife against it. Diom Blacksmith had also demonstrated this technique for starting a fire by holding a piece of flint against a punky piece of birch and striking his knife against the flint. A spark quickly ignited the dry, decayed wood. I concluded that these hunters still used this method for starting a fire. They knew where they could easily obtain the proper stone to create the spark. It reminded me of 1952, when a Passamaquoddy hunter demonstrated what he called a "strike-a-light," consisting of a flint and the metal of his knife striking it to make a fire. The strike-a-lights were important trade goods in the seventeenth and eighteenth centuries and were still in use here in the twentieth century.

Diom lived in the largest frame house at Miquelon. When he was younger, the birchbark tepees were customary. He said that the fire was in the center of the tepee, and the smoke went up through a hole at the top where there was a flap that could be moved in any direction as the wind changed. He added that it was bad luck to count the number of tepee poles. Frank Blacksmith, son of Harry Blacksmith and oldest grandson of Diom Blacksmith, described the ancient method of netting beaver. Although Frank was a young man in his early twenties, it was apparent that this procedure was well known and still employed by both Waswanipi and Mistassini. Comments concerning details were added from time to time by others ranging in age from a teenage schoolboy to Frank's father and uncles, men who had considerable trapping experience. The method is the same as Alanson Skinner described in 1911.[5] The major change is in the netting, which in 1911 was homemade of bark, but now is substituted with a store product.

The hunters, working as quietly as possible, drove a row of stakes around a beaver house. It was important not to talk, so that the beaver would not detect the people. I learned that a combination of sign and body language was used in such situations. The net was attached to the stakes, preventing the beaver from fleeing. Then the beaver house was dismantled. The scared beaver fled in a hurry and became entangled in the net.

If the beaver house is in a small pond created by a beaver dam in a small stream, the hunters will go at dusk to break the dam, so that the water level in the pond will soon fall. A net was set across the stream to catch the beaver when they came to make repairs. There were two other ways of trapping beaver, with steel traps as described by Rogers.[6]

Once in late winter when the snow was deep and soft, Louis Blacksmith was hunting. He came upon a fresh moose track, ideal conditions for hunting moose because it cannot travel fast, since each step breaks through the deep snow. Louis cut a sapling, sharpened one end and attached his knife firmly to it. He followed the track. He ran with his snowshoes, soon caught up to the floundering moose, and thrust his spear into its shoulder. The moose staggered, went down, and Louis killed it. It is interesting that these descendants of generations of successful hunters provide images of earlier methods of procuring their food.

I knew that something sad had happened when I returned to Miquelon after taking some Waswanipi River children home after that day's summer Bible School program. The silence was so intense that it announced the death of Diom Blacksmith, the beloved chief who had been sent to the Amos hospital eighty miles away. The official age given for Diom at death was seventy-nine, but that was based on his baptismal date. Elders surmised that he was eighty-three. No children were playing outside. Harry Blacksmith invited me to attend the men's all-night ceremony. The singing of death songs started promptly at sunset to the accompaniment of a small drum, continuing until sunrise.

Each man sang a song beating the drum and then passed the drum to the next man without missing a beat. Each song was ten to fifteen minutes in length in the singer's rhythm and cadence. Apparently, there was no special way to hold the drum; each man held it as it was most comfortable for him. The vibrations from the beating of the drum powered Diom's spirit to the Milky Way. His spirit would fall backward if they missed a beat. The spirit should arrive at the Milky Way at daylight and take its place among the brightly lighted spirits there.

The hearse carrying Diom's body arrived about 4 a.m. Roger Ratte

JOHN ICEBOUND SINGS THE DEATH SONG TO CHIEF DIOM BLACKSMITH.

asked me to help him carry Diom to the church in the welfare casket that the government had provided. Diom reposed in the church until his funeral. It was daylight, and I welcomed Roger's invitation to join him for breakfast. The hearse driver and Roger were acquainted. I presumed that the route was well known to the driver, who it appeared had stopped at nearly every tavern along the way. He recounted gory stories about some of his past customers, not the most tasteful breakfast companion.

The next day's silence was uncanny, so different from the typical exuberance of the children's voices. A sport fisherman arrived from Pennsylvania and thought the village was deserted. He asked me where everyone was. I passed along the sad news, and he understood. In the evening the family held a wake. The people expressed their mourning for the chief by a quick, strong, warm handshake with Mary, his widow; then each said two or three words and passed by. Lingering and more conversation would be indiscreet. The Rev. John Gull, a close childhood friend of Diom, asked me to lead the singing of the 23rd Psalm in English while he led the singing in Cree. We both ended simultaneously!

The next day John rose early, checked his fish nets and brought in his firewood, before dressing for the funeral that he had planned. It was an ecumenical service with both Anglican priest John Gull and the Catholic priest officiating. Both Anglicans and Catholics lived in the Waswanipi area. John Gull reasoned that it was only fair to have both Catholic and Anglican priests participate in the two-hour service, since Diom was chief of all the Waswanipi.

Before the service, Roger Ratte set up chairs in the church. As the mourners arrived, he ushered them to their proper places. The immediate family sat in the front row. Other family members sat in a semicircle in the front, facing the congregation. The Indian community sat behind the immediate family, and non-Indians sat in the back of the church. The casket was at the rear of the church.

At the end of the service John Gull thanked the many white people for coming. Some had driven more than a hundred miles to pay their respects to this fine person. It was an honor to have them present.

Harry went to the casket, picked up and put on his father's headdress, then his drum, and circled the casket three times while beating his father's drum in a slow, somber cadence, before leading the pallbearers in a procession from the church to the river, where the casket was placed on a boat for the chief's last ride upriver.

I joined the Indian gravediggers in the cemetery. Two men worked for about twenty minutes, and then two others relieved them. The two teams finished the grave rather quickly. They had cut a sapling and placed marks at 3 feet 6 inches and at 6 feet 8 inches, the measurements for the grave. It was a good six feet deep. The men had used long steel probes to push into the soil, checking for large rocks that would prevent them from digging the grave. They found no obstructions. The diggers showed no fear about getting into the grave. Apparently thoughts had changed since Skinner's visit in 1911: "Persons never get into a grave while digging it, only taking out as much earth as they could reach, for if any one went into the grave it was thought that he would die in a very short time."[7] When one of Diom's sons thought it was finished, he jumped into the grave to inspect it. When he was satisfied that it was perfect, he said, "You know, this is going to be his home forever."

The entire community followed the casket upriver to the cemetery. The Rev. John Gull presided over the interment service, standing at the head of the grave; the Catholic priest stood at the foot. After the casket had been lowered into the grave, it was time to throw a handful of dirt on it. John signaled to his counterpart and both threw dirt on the casket simultaneously. The widow followed, throwing her handful next. Like the others, it made a hollow thud when it landed on the casket. The chief's children took their turns filling the grave until others relieved them. Each member of the tribe proudly took a turn filling the grave.

Diom Blacksmith was laid to rest. The people started returning to the village in their canoes. I returned in a canoe with Harry Blacksmith, who pointed to a place where the trees were grown up quite tall and close together. Harry pointing said, "I was born in a tent over there." He continued that in the 1960s and 1970s babies were born in the bush, but nurses strongly recommended that the women go to the hospital to have their babies. Most families had a family midwife who would arrange to be at the camp when she was needed for the delivery. The prearranged birthing with a midwife took place in a separate, temporary tent that was off limits to men.

Everyone was expected to be present for important tribal community events like this funeral feast. However, one prominent member of the tribe missed it. The following day he provided a feast for the village. I was told that he would not be in good standing in the community until he gave a feast. Everyone had donated food for the feast that followed Diom's burial. The occasion seemed to set a happier tone to the affair. John Gull, in an aside to me declared, "For us this is the end; it's all over after that." He is expressing that the public, emotional displays are over, although the mourners' sadness is present but not shown.

The mourning family returned to the settlement from the cemetery, and in the evening gathered for a private ritual dinner together and smoked the old, traditional tobacco, an important element in many ancient Indian ceremonies. Two or three days later, Mary, Diom's widow, distributed the chief's possessions. Obviously she carefully considered who should inherit each of the chief's possessions before making the weighty decisions. Although some disagreed with Mary's judgment, her word was final. Later, family members set a wooden cross and marker at the head of the grave and built a grave fence protecting the remains from ravenous wildlife. From time to time, people would tie bundles of tobacco to the fence or cross for the departed one.

In time I asked several people what factors were important in selecting a chief. Strength and prowess as a hunter were always at the top of the list. These two words probably best described the characteristics of the leaders. Community members said that Diom never walked if he could run. He enjoyed swimming in the cold rapids of the O'Sullivan River, even as an elder. The Waswanipi have honored Diom by bestowing his name on their community building.

From time to time John Gull made comments regarding Indian burial customs. The Waswanipi cemetery was about a mile up the river in the bush. He said that most Indians who lived in the bush wanted to be buried in the bush. There was no cemetery by the Miquelon church. He added that there was no problem being Anglican and being buried in the bush. However, Roman Catholics had to be buried in their consecrated cemetery. If a Catholic died in the winter when he was in the bush, someone had to haul the body out on a toboggan. That could take several days of hard work that took time away from hunting and trapping. A plane sent into the bush to recover a body would be very expensive. Selecting a burial place made safe from animals was customary for Anglicans, when burial had to take place in the bush. The following are procedures that both Catholics and Anglicans were likely to follow.

If a Catholic priest was not there, then the Indians could perform their burial service. The grave was dug, and then it was lined with logs. The Indians washed the body. In former times the body was wrapped in birch bark. Later, a wooden box was constructed in the manner of seventeenth-century seamen's caskets, most likely learned from seamen who came to James Bay. The Indians could perform their burial service. In the old days, they covered the top of the grave with birch bark and spread rocks over the bark for protection from wild animals. At a later convenient time, the body might be removed to a family burial site. If the body was buried in a church cemetery or where people were present year round, the Indians probably did not have to take all the precautions against wild animals disturbing the grave.

Once I arrived at Miquelon in the midst of a very sad discussion. The body of an eight-year-old boy had been returned from the hospital. He had been buried the day before I arrived. The family was faced with a bill of $160 for transporting the body. The bill was enormous for this poor family. If there had been no road and they were back at their island home, the boy would not have been sent to a hospital; he would have died surrounded by his family. The family would have attended to his last rites and burial, simple, solemn, meaningful observances. With the new road an old law now applied to the Indians: only a funeral director could transport a body by road. The Indians interpreted the law as another way to take away what little money the government gave them. The Indians looked at the government expenditures on the road construction as extravagant, making rich people richer. Why couldn't the government pay the transportation cost for this poor family? The bill was another hardship for a bereaved family to face.

The Waswanipi have had a fine relationship with the land and the plant, animal, and stone resources that their Creator gave with the land to sustain people. A set of long-established ethics ruled their life, honoring the land and all the life within it. As long as their laws were not abused, there would have been enough for everyone.

# IX

# MISTASSINI, A HUNTING COMMUNITY

The story of Mistassini in the last half of the twentieth century is the story of the transformation of a fur-trading post into a contemporary Canadian town in the subarctic wilderness. The self-sufficient extended families living remotely from one another were to be brought together into a central location where the people could benefit from all the services that a modern city, town, or community provides. Officials in far-off Quebec City were planning a transformation from a post to a typical twentieth-century Canadian town. They had no actual experience at the place called Mistassini, nestled on an isolated bay, deep in the black-

MISTASSINI AERIAL VIEW, 1979

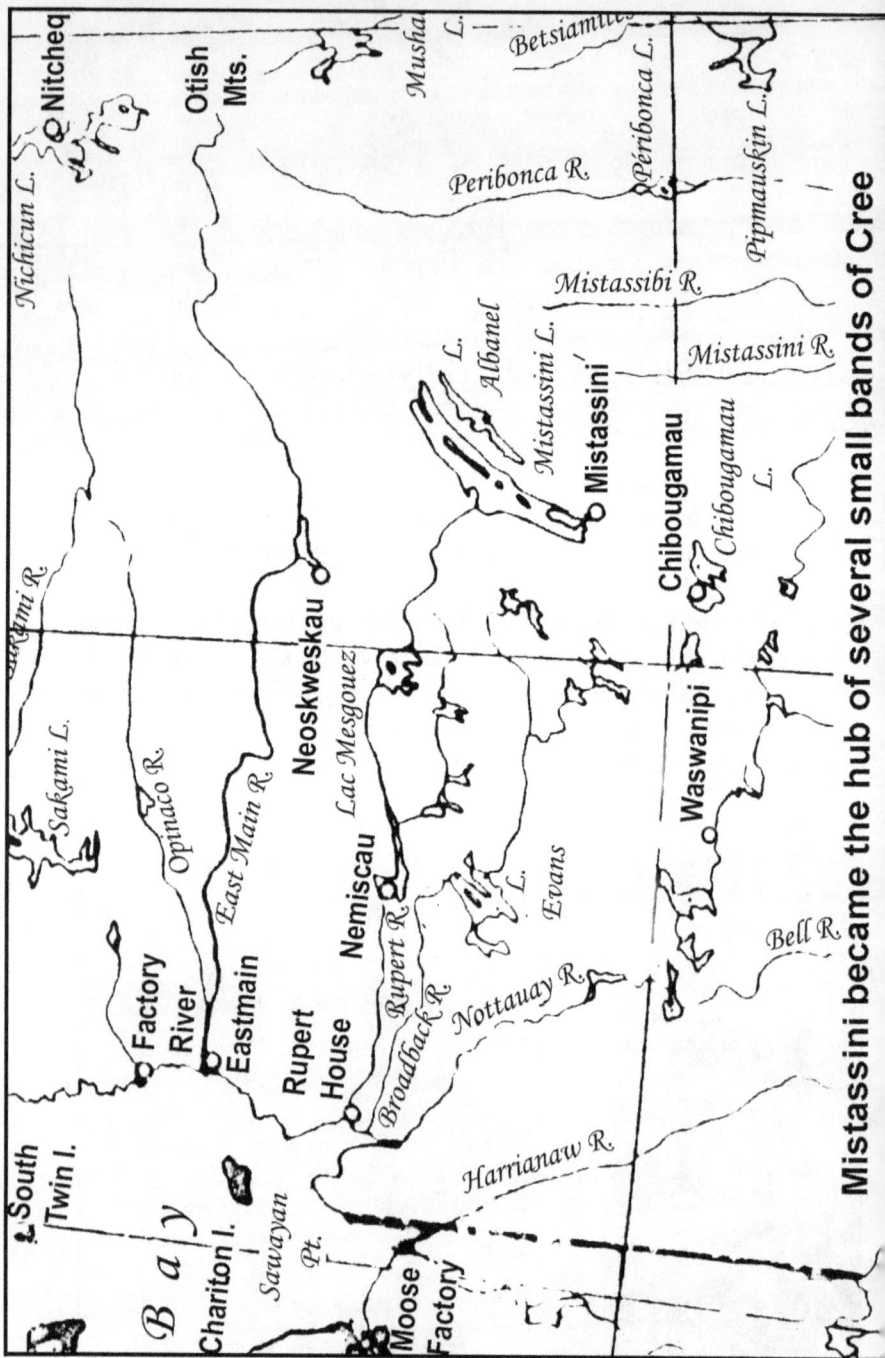

Mistassini became the hub of several small bands of Cree

Drawn by Ed Casw[...]

**Labels on map:**

Nitcheq

Otish Mts.

Nichicun L.

Musha[...] L.

Betsiamii[...]

Peribonca L.

Peribonca R.

Pipmauskin L.

Mistassibi R.

Mistassini R.

L. Albanel

Mistassini L.

Mistassini

Sakami R.

Chibougamau

Chibougamau L.

Neoskweskau

Lac Mesgouez

Sakami L.

Opinaco R.

East Main R.

Factory River

Eastmain

Nemiscau

Rupert House

Rupert R.

Broadback R.

Nottauay R.

L. Evans

Waswanipi

Bell R.

South Twin I.

B a y

Chariton I.

Sawayan Pt.

Moose Factory

Harrianaw R.

PATH LEADS TO ISOLATED WINTER BUSH HOME.

spruce wilderness of Northern Quebec. The town planners were using the term "village" for the gathering place of an informal aggregation of several hundred local people. However, these people returned annually only for several summer weeks to "the post" for the business of trading, social activities, and knowledge of weather, life, and job opportunities at Mistassini. The rest of the year they were spread out in isolated hunting camps in sixty thousand square miles of Northern Quebec. A description by Jacques Rousseau in 1949 shows that there had been little change since trading posts had first been established:

> The location of the post is best described as a clearing in the subarctic forest by the shore of a bay. Until breakup, it is merely a desert where old beddings of rust-colored spruce and fir boughs, and the remnants of old campfires, bear witness to the throngs which formally dwelt there. The Hudson's Bay Company store, the house of the manager, the house of a free trader, two or three tents of Indians who wintered on the spot, are the only dwellings which show any sign of life, as can be judged by the smoke issuing from the chimneys.[1]

As time went on, it appeared that for a number of years a plan had been formulated to make Mistassini a centralized village for the James

SMOKE RISES FROM THE CHIMNEYS OF A HUNTING CAMP.

Bay Island Cree. Although the civil servants denied it, it seemed that changes in policy were made to fit a plan. The Hudson's Bay Company closed the small surrounding trading posts at Chibougamau, Nemiskau, Neoskweskau, and Nichikun. The Quebec Department of Indian Affairs designated that the Chibougamau, Neoskweskau, Nichikun, and

ISOLATED CAMP AREA

ENTRANCE TO WINTER BUSH CAMP WELCOMES WITH EMBROIDERY.

half of the Nemiskau people trade at Mistassini. The other half of the Nemiskau families were to trade at Rupert House. In its paternal manner, the government listed which families would go to the two posts. Some friends who were hunting partners were separated. When the authorities became aware of this problem, they quickly resolved it. Each group from

A TYPICAL ISOLATED WINTER BUSH CAMP

the neighboring closed trading posts was given its own camping area for the summer trading event at Mistassini. Among the groups there was little socialization or mixing. They preferred to retain their allegiance to their traditional group.

Primitive food-gathering society was a face-to-face system, where everyone interacted with everyone else. Economic, political, family, social, and religious systems were subsystems of the one system in which all participated.[2]

The extended family provided two major resources for individual and family sustenance. One was affective support, that is emotional involvement, personal interest, and psychological support. The other resource was instrumental, that is the supply of money, food, clothing, and assistance with daily living and work tasks. The extended family system not only provided these resources, but also defined identity, created values, and specified goals.[3]

Such groups had low population densities. Mistassini fit this description well. The 1952 population density average for Mistassini was one person to every sixty-six square miles, which fits the population definition for wilderness. The extended family represented a small community entity where every member had specific duties that, when combined, made the hunting camp a viable situation. They gave young children much freedom, which encouraged children to enjoy that period of their life. They began to participate in adult work when they passed into manhood or womanhood at the age of twelve. By the time they were sixteen, the men were experienced hunters and trappers. Adulthood was synonymous with hard work. The hunting camp was a united, happy unit.

Social opportunities were few for the people who lived so far from one another. A rich variety of feasts developed around family camp accomplishments, beginning with the birth of a baby. Each ceremony had its significance and included a characteristic feast with an abundance of food available for all. A feast was a time when all had plenty to eat. The Cree rated food as the item of the highest value and the most meaningful in their way of life. Most families are trying to keep the ancient traditional family ceremonies, although they are no longer dependent on hunting for food. The ceremonies done for the first six years of a child's life are the easiest to retain. Everyone enjoys seeing young children dressed up and applauded for their progress.

The Walking-Out ceremony is of ancient heritage. The children did not leave the tent or wigwam on their own until they were about two years old and could walk. Babies remained in cradleboards, papoose bags, or cradles most of the time. This custom prevented the youngsters from kicking or bending their legs, a method that was thought to make the legs strong for when the time came for them to learn to walk.

They dressed boys in traditional costumes, usually of the finest tanned skins, for their Walking-Out ceremony. Each boy had a small hunter's pack on his back and a quiver with arrows for his bow. The father may have made a wooden gun to substitute for the bow and arrows. A spruce-bough path to a nearby tree decorated with colorful strips of cloth made it easier walking for the youngster. In the spring, when there is melting snow, the spruce boughs spread on the snow perform similarly to snowshoes, creating a firm foundation, preventing one from sinking deep into the snow. The child "shoots" towards the tree and then the child is directed down the path and around the tree in a clockwise direction where he finds the goose or beaver, the object of his "hunt." His father triumphantly picks up a carcass and puts it in the boy's backpack. The boy is led back into the tent, signifying he is now ready to start learning his important role as a hunter and provider.

The girl's ceremony was similar, but she carried a small wooden ax and found wood, which she chopped under the spruce tree and brought in for the fire. This symbolized her duties in the family daily tasks. There was a feast, and they complimented the children on their good work. They generally performed these ceremonies in the spring or summer.

When the children turned six, the parents taught both boys and girls how to snare rabbits. Rabbits are an important food source. Their skins are valued for their warmth and other uses. They gave the six-year-olds the responsibility of securing easy-to-catch foods, in case some emergency prevented their father from providing food. Children received their first snowshoes when they were two, the first winter that they could walk. When they were six, they were very proficient walking with snowshoes. The rabbit snares might be set a mile or more from camp.

Twelve was the age when boys usually shot their first moose, an event that signified their passing from childhood to manhood. As with the Rabbit-Snaring ceremony and the Walking-Out ceremony, close relatives who lived as neighbors would be invited guests. On this joyous occasion, while everyone was enjoying the feast of the moose that the boy had killed, the young hunter was not permitted to eat any.

What may be a recent custom is the celebration of children's birthdays. They are generally celebrated in the summer, when families are gathered at the village, no matter when the actual birth date falls, so that they can invite more of the child's friends. They invite friends to a feast that concludes with lighted candles on a cake, a ceremony adopted from Europeans.

The thirteen-year-old boy would begin to accompany his father hunting and trapping. The number of these trips would increase when he was fourteen. When he turned sixteen, he participated in hunting on a regular basis. A well-trained lad could go out alone on some better-known trails. This was the age when one could kill one's first bear, another symbol of manhood. Grandfather might teach the sixteen-year-old the fundamentals of shamanism.

Some parents arranged marriages when their children were infants. When both families agreed that the prospective bride and groom had sufficient training to become a successful hunting family, they organized the marriage ceremony. Traditionally the groups were small, and it was not a hardship for the groom to provide sufficient food for all those attending the ceremony. Today the high concentration of people at Mistassini makes it impossible for a single hunter to provide food for the entire community.

The groom hunted and brought his kill to his beloved who cooked it for all to share. This was symbolic of the groom's hunting prowess and the bride's culinary arts, the skills required of a couple ready for marriage and the start of a new family. Traditionally, boys had little opportunity to see girls or associate with them, except for the few weeks in the summer at the Mistassini trading post. Hunters had responsible hunting friends and arranged marriages. Children were told the families with whom they should become friendly. Marriage customs began to change with the development of the community and school education. As village populations increased and children were sent away to school, they associated more with other children. Traditional rules broke down, and young men began to pick their brides themselves. There were special feasts for the hunters. The first animal killed after the move to the winter camp required special preparation meant to bring good luck to the camp for the year. The first kill of each major game animal also received special preparation. Some of these traditional feasts, such as the well-known Bear Feast, were only for the men, a precedent that is usually still respected.

They respect bears, and the killing of them is required to be done in an honorable manner. The hunter speaks to the bear, telling of his need to kill him, before actually killing him. The bear responds by allowing himself to be killed. In the 1980s, the Indians were actively trying to keep these traditions, especially for teaching the young people who were school educated. These are my reminiscences of those times.

The successful hunter provided a feast for the men and boys. The hunter butchered the bear in a special way. The skull received special treatment and was attached to a tree far out of the reach of dogs. The forearms, considered as the source of the bear's strength, were wrapped in birch bark and hung high in a tree out of harm's way. They put the bear fat into a specially decorated birchbark container. At the end of the feast, the container and uneaten contents would be thrown in the fire to be consumed by it. John Gyles described a similar Maliseet men's bear feast, experienced when he was a captive of the New Brunswick Maliseet Indians, near the end of the seventeenth century.[4]

Sometimes hunters had a men's feast after killing moose or other big game. However, the bear feast is best known and has much symbolism attached to it. The bear required special respect because of its trait of standing up straight on its hind legs, creating an image similar to man. The legs also symbolized great strength, a trait respected by Mistassini Cree.

When the development of the Mistassini village was in its early stages, a civil servant commented that the village would be an excellent site for

BEAR SKULL AND FOREARM BONES WRAPPED IN BIRCH BARK AND ATTACHED TO A TREE TO HONOR THE BEAR

their tribal powwow. An elder asked, "What is done at a powwow? We never had one."

The Quebec Government representative replied that all Indians have powwows with dances, sports and games. Since then there has been a tribal powwow every summer. A feature of the powwow is a tribal feast with all kinds of meats and fancy bannock. Hunters are designated to kill animals in the correct season, and the meat is placed in freezers for the next powwow feast.

Certain bones of all animals, birds and fish, are treated in a special manner in reverence to the animal. It is bad luck for a hunter if a dog defiles the bones. The skull is the usual bone placed on a wooden rack. As store-bought canned goods became more popular, cans were used instead of the wooden racks to hold the bones. The bone cans were hung on trees out of the reach of dogs. In more recent times, plastic containers have replaced cans and are now the common bone receptacles.

A burnt offering of food was placed in the fire as an act of thanksgiving before a meal. A bit of the animal was returned to the spirit world with the smoke of the fire in the balance between hunters and animal spirits, thus permitting hunters and animals to continue to inhabit the land.

Generally the men ate first, then the women and children. There were special feasts or times when all ate together. The hunters returned cold and hungry in late afternoon, ready for a hearty meal soon after their arrival. The women and children had their own schedule, usually eating after the men had finished. I noted that some Maliseet retained this unwritten rule, and I believe some still keep this ancient tradition.

Hunters abided by strict rules, part of Mistassini ethical conduct. A hunter carrying a loaded gun was not being fair to the animal. Some hunters said they carried the gun in its case until they spotted the game. These regulations must also have reduced the possibility of injury to the hunters. I am unaware of a shooting injury suffered from a Mistassini hunting accident.

Relationships between people and animals developed in which a specific animal spirit became a shaman's spirit helper in procuring food and a protector when in conflict. They restricted some hunters from hunting spirit animal-helpers. A rich symbolism and oral tradition were developed into rituals that included religious significance. These regulations were required as they controlled this hunting culture's dependence on successful hunting for their primary food resources. Poor luck was blamed on improperly caring for an animal while killing it, preparing it for food, or breaking some taboo knowingly or unknowingly.

The hunting community depended on seasonal cycles, animal cycles, natural phenomena, weather, a vivid knowledge of animal characteristics, and hunting prowess. One was never to abuse one's powers and ability to kill. Killing was the necessary process for the hunter to sustain his life and the lives of those under his care. However, the power of killing was never to be abused. Sons and daughters had followed the traditional, oral, ethical behavior of their forebears for centuries under the premise that parents know best.

# X

# SCHOOL NOT A COMPLETE MISTASSINI EDUCATION

The government presented a school-based education plan in their typical paternalistic manner. Education would improve Indian life. Some, but not all parents, concluded that school would improve their future. The reserves were notified to have their children ready to go to school at a specified date and place. A plane would pick them up. They were flown a thousand miles to Sault Ste. Marie, Ontario. Most remained there for nine years without returning home. The government presumed that the children would have lost their culture and bonding to home in those years.

In 1963 the children were sent to Brantford, Ontario, or La Tuque, Quebec, rather than Sault Ste. Marie. Both school sites were closer to home but too far away for easy visitations. A school bus came in the fall and took the Waswanipi and Mistassini children to the Anglican residential school in La Tuque. It was said to be the best school building in La Tuque, the only school having a swimming pool. The students were bussed home for a Christmas break and again for the summer at Quebec's expense.

As I am now beginning to learn, there was much alleged abuse in the schools. Few people if any visited the schools to check on their children. A goal of the schools was to "take the Indian out of the man." The Waswanipi and Mistassini concluded that school was not the answer for all their children.

I feel that most school administrators were sincere in attempting to offer the students a practical education to prepare for changing times, but they had little practical knowledge about the Indian people or culture. The school was typical of city schools across Canada. Teachers came with little or no introduction to Indian culture. The school was often an opportunity for those who had not found a teaching position elsewhere to obtain experience. It must have been a difficult encounter for many beginning teachers to find themselves suddenly a minority in a culture far different from their own. Apparently lesson plans followed those of the Canadian educational system, ignoring the fact that much of the education would be of no value on the reservation.

Children growing up in the bush were rather free to play within the forest limitations, often developing a keen sense of creativity. It was not unusual for a child to have no playmates. Knowing that adulthood comes all too quickly and with it hardships, parents wanted their children to lead a free life. Strict discipline was almost unknown. In one situation a father brought his wayward son to a priest, asking him to punish the lad. The upset father couldn't bear to strike his son. The usual punishment that I observed was a gentle slap on the forehead that was more of a way of saying, "straighten up and fly right." Young people received much love from parents, grandparents, and other relatives.

School was an entirely new experience. It was regimentation, discipline, strange food, and the close association of dormitory life. The new student was seen as one whose development was behind that of a white child of the same age brought up in a society where the emphasis of learning was on reading rather than oral tradition. In contrast, Cree children generally knew how to listen much better than white children did. The home environment of the white children was much more oriented towards preparation for the school education process. Radio and television opened new worlds for city children. On the other hand, the bush children were much more prepared for an adult approach to calamitous situations in upsetting circumstances than were white children. The introduction to school life must have been very difficult for the Indian children, who had few relationships beyond the extended family. The sudden break from the closeness of the family situation caused many children to wonder why their parents sent them away to school, a strange new life. Children made many friends at school whom they otherwise would seldom see or have the opportunity to know. A camaraderie must have quickly developed among the students as a means of survival.

Both tribes were losing their traditional artistic designs, music, and language, basic factors of cultural identity. School had become a medium for culture transfer. The children were losing their culture while learning another. Typical Canadian foods replaced their traditional bush foods, known as "country foods." Children's artwork imitated the characteristic Canadian homes with deciduous trees (always apple trees), scenes they had never encountered and probably never would. Art teachers were suppressing typical native art forms for the stereotypical images taught throughout Canada, just as their native language and music were being suppressed. It was obvious in our summer Bible school that children drew what they thought we wanted to see. When we interacted with the children coming to the Bible school, we convinced some that it was all right to draw what they wished to draw. Soon children were enjoying drawing familiar scenes from their lives.

As I mentioned previously, only in recent years have I learned of the terrible abuses that the children suffered through the forced education system. School education was another way that Indian students were losing their identity. It is no wonder that the Cree people wanted to take over their school system, return education to their villages, and place their own people on their school boards and as dorm supervisors. They knew what was best for their children.

A story made up by the first graders at Baie du Poste School, Mistassini, 1973–1974, was called *Bumpidy, the Skidoo Who Wanted to Go Into the Bush*. And is as follows.

> The skidoo started for the bush. Soon he came to a big hill. It was so big that he couldn't get up, so the fox pushed him up. But when he got up the hill, he fell backwards and fell in a big hole in the water. A beaver saw him and took him home. The beaver gave him something to eat. He was all right so that he was able to go on his way into the bush. He got home and lived happily ever after.

During the summer vacations, if parents remained in the villages, often grandparents invited their vacationing grandchildren to their camps, where they received love and cultural training. Grandparents accepted the responsibility of teaching children their culture and heritage. Most grandchildren enjoyed the privilege of being invited for a few days to the grandparents' remote camp. The Mistassini developed a program whereby children could visit parents or grandparents in the bush for a week as part of their school program and learn the traditional ways.

Some older children were on drugs when they returned from school for summer vacation. Their parents were appalled. These parents soon learned that the best cure for this situation was taking them into the bush for the summer, where there was no opportunity to obtain drugs. Busy camp life offered plenty of work and a plan for a useful life. When the batteries for their tape machines wore out, they lost what had become their favorite music selections, their biggest connection to their school world. This appeared to be a successful cure process for many.

In some instances a student who had taken a preliminary course in a subject like mechanical drawing felt that his training was equal to that of one with an engineering degree. He might be given a job on the reserve that really required someone who had additional courses. A high school graduate with a course in mechanical drawing was assigned the task of designing the water system for Mistassini. It was no wonder that some projects ended with problems.

Adult-education courses were also provided at the Indian villages. The Quebec Government sometimes encouraged basic instruction in English, French and math by offering cash stipends. Some interpreted these programs as encouraging people to have an easier winter village life by learning a language and then having some extra beer money.

Waconichi Lake is about ten miles north of Chibougamau. Canadian and American fisherman know it for its fine fishing. A government fish camp with cabins for fishermen and guides was situated on an island not far down the lake. A narrow outlet at the northern end of the lake flows

MISTASSINI SCHOOL. THEY KNEW WHAT WAS BEST FOR THEIR CHILDREN.

over rapids and into Lake Mistassini. It was the gateway to Mistassini until 1970 when the government built a road into the Indian village. Before that, a person radioed from Lake Waconichi to Mistassini, asking for a canoe to be sent down for the visitor. Allen Iserhoff was in charge of the fish camp. A few Indian families and guides reside on the island in the summer, but Allen was the only winter resident.

Several years before, a civil-service clerk discovered that in the early 1800s the James Bay ice had sunk a Russian whaler. A crewman named Iserhoff had escaped and joined an Indian family. In the twentieth century the Mistassini people considered the Iserhoffs members of the Mistassini tribe. Matthew, Allen's fourteen-year-old son, had always attended the Indian school. Now a civil servant told Allen that, since his son was not an Indian, he could not attend the Indian school. This was very upsetting news.

A sport fisherman from Massachusetts, who had been spending his vacations at Waconichi for several years, had a son the same age as Matthew. The youngsters had built up a fine friendship. The fisherman offered to solve the problem by taking Matthew back to Massachusetts with him where the two boys could go to school together. He would return him in the spring. That worked out very well, and the two families bonded together quite strongly. Matthew was graduated from school with high grades and then went on to college. His goal was to return to Mistassini and help the people there. He earned his teacher's certificate from McGill and applied to teach at Mistassini.

The Mistassini School Board wanted to hire him but did not have that authority. The Quebec Department of Indian Affairs selected and hired the teachers. They considered that it was only fair to wait for a complete list of all unemployed teachers in the province to make their selection. This system would give all the unemployed teachers an equal opportunity to apply for the Mistassini position. Usually the Indian Affairs Department hired teachers in May for the following school year. Indian Affairs finally notified the Mistassini School Board just before school was to open that they had hired Matthew. Matthew was thrilled to again be a part of his boyhood community, this time in the important role of a teacher. They also hired five other Mistassini boys for the school. These were the first college-educated residents of Mistassini to have professional positions when they returned home.

In 1972 Stephen Neeposh was a typical seventeen- or eighteen-year-old Mistassini man. He had attended school off and on since he was seven or eight. Although his family's moving about hindered his formal education, Stephen had taught himself and kept up with his grade level. In 1971 some upperclassmen became aware that they lacked knowledge of their Mistassini heritage. They asked one another what it meant to be a Mistassini Indian. They found that they lacked the fundamentals of hunting or trapping. Their vocabulary in their first language was limited. The everyday language used in a hunting camp was almost lost. The charm and creativity of Mistassini stories, oral history, exploits, and the practical craftsmanship for the essentials of bush life were also missing. The young men questioned their purpose in the Mistassini setting. Most of the trappers claimed that one had to live the rugged hunting-trapping life to be an Indian. The Indian community classified as "white men" the young Indian people who had only a school education and lived like the white man. Stephen was one of those who decided that it was necessary to go into the bush with his parents the following winter to learn his heritage as a Mistassini Cree.

The following winter Stephen joined his parents in the bush. He found the food palatable and pleasant and the work invigorating and meaningful. Stephen enjoyed being with his family and accompanying his father on the trap lines and learning the traditional trapping and hunting techniques.

Now that he had found the missing part of him, Stephen felt like a real man. He learned that the Mistassini Cree had a large repertoire of popular folk stories, such as Memegwecio, the Keeper of the Bears, who lives at the bottom of lakes and rivers. Once the bears decided that they would take all the fish. Soon the fish became scarce; finding enough fish to eat was difficult for the Mistassini people. They realized that the bears were taking all the fish so the Indians were not able to catch any. The people were suffering much from hunger. They realized that something would have to be done soon, or they would all starve to death. Finally a brave, strong shaman decided that it was necessary for him to visit powerful Memegwecio, Keeper of the Bears. He went to find Memegwecio. When he found the ugly Memegwecio, who was covered with hair, he was very much afraid but could not show his fear. He offered Memegwecio some tobacco for making the bears release the fish, so that the Mistassini Indians could also enjoy some fish. There had always been enough fish for both bears and people. Surely there was enough for all now. Memegwecio agreed that there was enough for all. The bears would soon set the fish free, so Indians could also catch them. To express their appreciation the Indians were to make tobacco offerings when they came to rapids.[1]

The decision to go into the bush to learn their heritage from their parents for a year was a necessary and enriching experience for those who, like Stephen, were to seize that opportunity. At last these young men felt that they had found and accepted what they were missing and were now more useful people in their community.

In spite of all these improvements, Mistassini could offer big challenges to a young city man who accepted a teaching position there. So it was for a young new teacher who was hired from Montreal. He arrived at Mistassini on October 27, 1980. The temperature had been below freezing all month. Snow came early. Roadside snow banks grew as the young teacher proceeded north on the Saint-Félicien road. He lacked experience driving on snow-covered roads. Before he knew what had happened, the car skidded off the road into the ditch near Chibougamau Park, still some distance from Chibougamau. The front end received some damage, but the teacher was able to get the car back on the road and continue on fifty miles to a Chibougamau garage where repairs could be made. Then he called the Mistassini school, telling them of his predicament; they kindly sent someone to pick him up. Upon arrival at the school, he was given a mobile home. He unpacked his food but found that the refrigerator did not work. He thought that should not be a big problem; he hung his meat up outside. When he went to retrieve the meat, it was not there. Hungry dogs had enjoyed it. The teacher decided that he wanted to see what teaching materials were available in his classroom. He tried to find the custodian who had the key to his classroom, but the custodian was away. This was one young teacher's introduction to the North in 1980.

# XI

# PAVING THE WAY

Chapais and Chibougamau were mining towns (no longer considered mining towns) separated by twenty-five miles of virgin forests in the Chibougamau Lake and Chibougamau River region. Mistassini lies fifty miles north of Chibougamau. In the summer of 1929, Charlie Dixon was looking forward to hunting moose in the section of his hunting territory that now carries the name Chapais. He could not have been more awestruck if he had seen green Martians or a herd of mammoths grazing on his land. Buildings and people were on his hunting territory! Dixon thought, "What are they doing there? No one has asked for my permission to build and dig up my land."

Also in the summer of 1929 Carl Springer and Lloyd Rochester had discovered copper at Chapais. Work started on what was to become the Opemiska Mine but was soon suspended due to the stock market crash. World War II further curtailed the mining. Although Dixon was ignored regarding his tribal holdings, the mine manager asked him to be caretaker of the mine buildings during the suspension of work that lasted until 1952. The men reestablishing the mine found everything just as it had been left. Even the canned goods were untouched, although Charlie had experienced several "very lean and hungry" years. Charlie was rewarded with a house and pension for life.[1] The town of Chapais grew around the mine.

The mine drew Indians in need of jobs. They came from Rupert House, Mistassini, and Waswanipi. Fred Cooke, the manager of the mine, developed the Opemiska Experiment, a program by which Indians worked and lived in mine housing, side by side with the white strangers. The Chapais schools were among the first to provide orientation to the teachers about the special problems concerning educating Indians. The

Cree wanted their children to benefit from the white man's education system and after graduation to be on competitive terms with white students in the job market. The Opemiska Experiment was at first a great success, becoming a model for the district, but in recent years as the white population grew, Cook's "experiment" was forgotten, replaced by an age-old reluctance to include Indians in the job force or have them as next-door neighbors.

Chibougamau is in the southern limits of the Mistassini territory. It is the dividing line between Waswanipi to the south, and Mistassini to the north. Chibougamau means "meeting place,"[2] or "place where the two groups meet." Chibougamau, like Chapais, sprang up in the middle of a hunting territory. Jimmy Mianscum and other owners of the hunting territories were uprooted and sent to several different sites before finally ending at Dore Lake, a beautiful bay of Lake Chibougamau, about six miles south of the Chibougamau line. What a contrast between these two mining towns and how they handled the former inhabitants and owners of the land!

Chapais had good housing for the Indians in a typical town setting, whereas Dore Lake was a magnificent, undeveloped timberland setting hidden from the town's view, an "unserviced section," composed of a few shacks and tents; they were completely ignored by the town fathers who felt no concern for the Indians living there. Dore Lake's umbilical cord to town six miles away was an undependable taxi service, which did little credit to the Indian settlement. Civilization had confused the people, and everywhere there was evidence of their lack of faith in the white man. It was a most disappointing reflection of the white man's attitude. The white man just pushed the original inhabitants out of his way and closed his eyes to them as if they did not exist, while churches raised their steeples in each town, an ethical backbone, calling people to treat their neighbors as themselves.

The Diocese of Moosonee, the second largest diocese in the world, included the ancestral lands of the Mistassini and Waswanipi and had become stronger. There were a few young, reliable men who became catechists to promote the faith in remote places like Mistassini without a resident priest. Joseph Iserhoff, one of three second-generation Iserhoff brothers who became Hudson's Bay Company managers in the James Bay area, managed the trading post at Mistassini. Another brother, Charles, read services regularly on Sundays at Mistassini. John, a brother, was manager of the Waswanipi Hudson's Bay Company. He had a son, Samuel, who became a devoted priest visiting many Indian bands on James Bay and Hudson Bay. His name was still spoken in hushed, reverent tones in 1970.

In 1954 Mistassini had a beautiful log church built by the late Bishop Neville Clarke, with the help of Canon Sam Iserhoff. Bishop Clarke had a fine reputation for building churches around James Bay. When a visitor approached the church door and looked up at the steeple, he probably wondered why the Indians angled the cross so the arms were not in line with the front of the church. The Indians set the angle purposely so that returning canoeists paddling on the lake to Mistassini could see the outstretched arms of their church cross. Many Mistassini Cree visited the church before leaving the village and again when they returned. The clergy were like the other professionals (doctors, dentists, nurses) who served the Mistassini Cree in earlier days only on summer assignment to Mistassini.

The diocese assigned a young man, Rev. James Scanlon, to the area. He was considered as being one of their own since he was born in Geraldton, Ontario, within the boundary of the Diocese of Moosonee. He attended Queens University in Kingston and had a deep interest in Canadian history. While James Scanlon was still in training for the clergy, the bishop sent him to Nemaska for the summers of 1953 and 1954. He was thrilled to see the fur trade in action first-hand. He found that being among the Hudson's Bay Company trading society was a stimulating and happy experience for him. It was even better to feel that he was a part of it. While in Queen's University in Kingston, he met Doris Wiskin, a librarian at the Royal Military College, where northern and fur trade history were prominent subjects. Jim and Doris were married, and she went north with him. She enjoyed the James Bay frontier as much as her husband did.

In 1957 the bishop assigned James Scanlon to Chapais, where the Indians were Anglicans. Scanlon persuaded the Opemiska Mine manager to provide a vacant mine building for a church. Several years later, Scanlon's clerical duties included Chapais, Chibougamau, and Mistassini on a regular schedule. He also provided support to Waswanipi. He interpreted much of Anglican Christianity into a more meaningful religion for the Cree.

In the early 1960s, there were so few moose killed at Mistassini that the Anglican Church imported moose skins from Newfoundland, Labrador, the west coast of James Bay and northern Ontario for the James Bay Indians. In 1965, soon after the bishop assigned Rev. James Scanlon to establish a church at Chapais, the priest suddenly found himself swamped with many moose skins. Scanlon wrote:

On a cold February morning, the Canadian National Railways express truck rolled up to my back door and neatly deposited a ton and half of moose hides on the step. For some reason my training in theology had not prepared me for this kind of occurrence and, as my wife refused to let me bring them into the house, I had to devise another plan. I simply told the driver he had the wrong address, and would he please take them all out to the Indian village at Dore Lake.

The Indians, needless to say, were very surprised when I arrived with three thousand pounds of frozen moose hides. My stock as a hunter went up about a thousand percent, but soon came down again when I told them where the hides really came from. The bishop had a brother in Northern Ontario. His name was Lou, and he lived in Geraldton which was right in the heart of Ontario's moose mecca. Every year, in Fall time, Geraldton was invaded by an army of moose hunters from all over Canada and the United States. If there was an opportunity to cash in on the skin business, this was it![3]

Without realizing it, Doris made history one day. The Scanlons flew into Mistassini one Saturday, where James was to hold Sunday services. No one had told Doris that Mistassini tradition was that the men sat on the right side of the church and the women on the left. On Sunday morning Doris took her customary seat up front on the right side of the church. The people entering the church could not help but notice Doris in her pink dress. They stopped at the entrance, as if not sure what to do. More people came. Then one or two elders decided that if sitting on the right side was acceptable for Doris, sitting together as family on either side should be all right for families. Ever since Doris Scanlon's historic visit, the Mistassini Indians have sat together as families in church.

In the early 1960s it was very apparent to the Indians that they needed more hunting territory. An attempt was made to negotiate with the Lake St. John Band to hunt some of their unoccupied northern territory that adjoined the Mistassini territory. The Lake St. John Band rejected the proposition. It was also known that there was vacant land north of the Mistassini territory in the Caniapiscau Region. Sam Rabbitskin, a concerned hunter, volunteered to survey the northern lands. He took a teenage son with him. It was winter, the area's open season. They hauled a toboggan with their supplies, a custom when moving to a different camp. They were hunting for their food as they progressed. When they crossed the Mistassini border, they entered an unmapped, unknown district. One day, as they were plodding through the snow, the father, who was leading, slipped off the side of a ridge and broke his back. He quickly analyzed his problem, concluding that his back was broken. He knew that there were more than three hundred roadless, wilderness miles to the nearest medical service. He also knew that he could not remain where he was while his son went for aid. Thinking clearly, he ordered his son to rearrange things on the toboggan and bring it to him. Somehow the injured man had the stamina in this upsetting situation to withstand the severe pain. He instructed his son to roll him on to the toboggan and tie him on, so that he could not move. They needed to cooperate for the return trip to Chapais. The father provided directions for the three-hundred-mile trek home. The son hauled the toboggan with its precious load, built the campfires for each meal and warmth for the cold nights, procured and cooked game, built the shelter each night, packed it the following morning, and did whatever he could to comfort his father on the painful journey to the hospital. Some days the travel was short, because the son had to hunt for sufficient food to last for several days. The trip was an example of the discipline and capabilities of these self-sufficient people, educated to persevere under duress and hardship in the solitary bush. Both father and son were well trained for the task.

When they returned to Chapais, the father was taken to the mine hospital, where it was hard to convince the nurses that their story was true. The nurses came to know the stoic Sam Rabbitskin, who never showed any sign of pain or discomfort, never complained about his treatment, but often had a comical story for the nurses. The entire nursing staff came to love him during his long healing process.

Three independent, self-sufficient Rabbitskin families moved to the northern hunting territories and were quite successful hunting and trapping. Ironically, they were the first families to be displaced by the James Bay Hydroelectric Project.

In 1965 the bishop appointed James Scanlon to be the archdeacon of James Bay. Scanlon supported the Indians in the days of change, replacing outdated Victorian ideas with more meaningful policies for the twentieth century. He made a lasting impression on the Indians. His daughter Jane's health failed, causing the Scanlons to return to Kingston and take St. John's parish there. He continued to support the James Bay Indians whenever the opportunity offered. In 2007 the Waswanipi community arranged for James and Doris to return for a visit, honoring them, a most meaningful event to them all. It was heartening for them to see so many of their old friends who still remembered them.

The establishment of the two towns of Chapais and Chibougamau, with their mines, healthcare services, and churches, brought these Indians closer to the white man's culture.

# XII

## MISTASSINI:
## A NEW VILLAGE AND ITS PRIEST

It was customary to place a missionary in an Indian village not only for religious purposes but also to educate the people to accept the European way of life. Planning for the new Mistassini village continued in Quebec City. The planning passed from the general stage to the more specific details. The new village required a full-time minister. A search committee was charged to find the right person to fill the position. A candidate came to their attention who was a young mining engineer at a gold mine in Pickle Crow, Ontario, and a lay reader providing services for the neighboring Ojibwa. Would he be interested in taking the required clergy courses and then filling the Mistassini position? In 1966 the Rev. Kenneth Blaber, his wife Joyce, and their three children arrived at Mistassini.

Ken and Joyce[1] seemed to have an easy time adapting to the hardships of Mistassini. They were both born in Eastbourne on the southeast coast of England near the Kent coal mines. Ken was too young to enlist in the military during World War II,

THE BLABER FAMILY AND MISTASSINI CHURCH

but he would have been called up if the war had lasted a bit longer. He did get a taste of war from the German bombers who frequently attacked the area. At sixteen Ken took an apprenticeship in the Kent coal mines. Several years later he married Joyce Lee and continued working in the Kent mines until 1956, when he was recruited as a mining engineer by the Kerr Addison gold mines, and Ken and Joyce moved to Pickle Crow, Ontario. In 1966 he became a missionary for St. John the Evangelist Church, Mistassini, then one of the largest Indian Anglican churches in the Diocese of Moosonee, where winter began in early October and lasted until late May.

Earlier missionaries Fred Swindlehurst and Harry Cartlidge knew when they went into the Diocese of Moosonee that it was going to be years before they would get away for a vacation. One of the greatest concerns in their time was the shaman who used his magical conjuring powers as fear tactics against his "competitor shamans." In 1924 Cartlidge went to Mistassini, a ten- to twelve-day canoe trip from Waswanipi. F. Macleod, the Hudson's Bay Company manager, reported that the Indians were very upset and stressed by the conjuring. MacLeod asked Cartlidge to convey to the Indians that the conjuring must stop. Cartlidge had a good understanding of the Indians. He attended a meeting of the men and was asked to be the first speaker. The Reverend Scanlon related Cartlidge's story:

> I told them the story of the early Britons and the worship of the Druids; of the Saxons and the fear of spirits, about witchcraft in Medieval times; that through all these times, the white men were growing up from being children to fuller manhood, and the changes had come about when the Church came to teach the

KENNETH AND JOYCE BLABER

Gospel of Jesus Christ, and filled the men's minds with grown up things which left no room for witchcraft and conjuring. The next speaker was Solomon Voyager, the guide and Chief. He said "It is the first time I have heard a white man talk like that. No one ever told me that the white people were once children like we are. But if the church filled the minds of the white man with good things to make him fearless, then the Church with the Gospel of Jesus will do it for us. There will be no more conjuring in my band". Then the floodgates were open and I probably heard more about this practice than any other missionary has. When I saw these people again in 1927, I was told that Solomon and his people had no more fear of conjurors.[2]

Harry Cartlidge humbly opened a smooth path for both Mistassini and missionaries in the years that followed.

In 1964, as the first full-time priest, Father Kenneth Blaber accepted the challenges that Mistassini's 64,000 square miles of wilderness parish offered. The parish included ninety miles of road, mostly concentrated at mining communities and provincial sports fishing camps. Only water and air routes connected Mistassini with the outside world. Most travel was by canoe or dogsled in winter, on the many connecting lakes and rivers. He knew he was entering a country that had had a Christian presence for nearly three hundred years. There was probably a larger percentage of pagans in any large city in the U.S. or Canada than in Father Blaber's parish territory. He was not there to cast the Mistassini into the white man's mold. The Mistassini people and their culture were to be respected.

Mistassini Cree were not "Hollywood Indians." They had never engaged in warfare in historic time or in heritage tales other than defending themselves from an Iroquois attack. Life spans were generally much shorter than the Europeans'. Murders were almost unknown, occurring only in very unusual situations. The last one seemed to have taken place about 1885 but was still remembered because murder was rare. Today murders taking place daily in Canada's large cities are something foreign to the Mistassini Indians, something they fail to understand. The child mortality rate was high. Life was precious, special, to be respected and preserved.

The Mistassini people had a good basic understanding of Christianity as it fit their way of life. The summer clergy had built a foundation for Father Blaber to continue building. Ken found ways to continue to develop and weave Christian ethics into accepted images of traditional Indian ethics as he learned more about their heritage. The Mistassini Cree were notably a deeply spiritual people. They could easily understand many chapters of the Bible and easily transfer Biblical images as happening in their own bush-camp lives. The tent-style peoples who knew where to hunt for specific species differed only slightly from those shepherds of Biblical times who tended their flocks.

When accidents such as drownings had occurred in the bush camps, the family took care of the funeral and burial in the bush. Gradually as such news became known, and the police became aware of deaths in the bush, they felt it necessary to investigate these deaths as suspicious. They sent investigation crews by plane to question the family and even exhume the bodies, checking them for signs of violence. These incidents have been very difficult for these peaceful Indians.

When a white man kills a Mistassini person, the police investigate the Indians first, not believing that a Quebec man would be guilty of such an act. I recall several times waking up about 4 a.m. in the Voyageurs' tent, hearing a Toronto radio news program describing horrible crimes against another human being. I could feel my Indian friends staring at me, wondering how our society could permit such atrocities.

I recall a teenager who, traveling to visit friends on another reserve, stopped at a restaurant for lunch in a town. He wore a sheath knife, part of his regular dress. The manager made him leave, giving him no reason. The young man asked me why the manager would not serve him. These actions by the white strangers have done nothing to improve relations between the groups. This indicates that the white immigrants are not knowledgeable about the original inhabitants and have done little to learn about the people whose land they occupy. There is a great need for people to learn more about the First Nation's residents and respect them. It is time to suspend criticism and obtain a true image of our neighbors.

A prefab log rectory was sent up from Toronto, completely wired for the usual appliances, normal home lighting and electrical outlets, and also set up with plumbing fixtures ready to be connected with running water. It was assembled in the romantic North Woods setting beside the log church that Bishop Neville Clarke had built in 1948, overlooking Mistassini Lake. There was an understanding between the Church and Indian Affairs that water and electricity would be supplied for the rectory under the same plan that Indian Affairs supplied it for the teachers' housing, the school, the nursing station, and other Indian Affairs buildings. Upon the arrival of the log rectory, which was built on the same plan as the teachers' housing, it was understood that electricity and water would be supplied. The Blabers were to be the first family to live in the rectory on a full-time basis, year round. Mistassini was a wilderness Indian settlement that lacked not only electricity but most of the services that one assumes are part of a community. When the Blabers were ready to arrive, no provisions for electricity or running water had been made for the house. Major renovations had to be made to the "electric" house. A woodstove quickly replaced the original oil heating system. Appliances fueled by propane replaced electric ones. As winter proceeded, other modifications had to be made to the building so that the woodstove heat would circulate beyond the living room. The summer supply priests had lived in a small, log cabin with an outhouse and without running water or electricity. The building was suitable for a few summer weeks but not for winter use.

Ken had some knowledge of Ojibwa. He quickly began learning the Mistassini version of Cree under the tutelage of an eager group of lay readers. Ken advised me that the best introduction to the language was through the hymns. Volunteers, including Chief Smalley Petawabano, graciously translated the sermons, thus presenting Ken's message in Cree.

Many Indians were eager to welcome their new spiritual leader and his family to their new village. Some were active members who held various positions that kept the church functioning during the long interims without priests. Other people were curious to see the priest who was to be in their land for a long time. There were those who were suspicious of all strangers who came to their land. A few were well aware that Mistassini needed a counselor to help them understand the many legal documents that Quebec required, such as the necessary data to receive Quebec's welfare funds.

Ken was an active person who enjoyed life. On many days his splendid blending of British humor with the Cree humor was necessary. The mining culture was deeply embedded in Ken, and he quickly became acquainted with the Chapais and Chibougamau mine administrators. At times Ken needed the mine administrators' help for projects, such as the loan of tools and equipment to make the necessary alterations for the Toronto log rectory. There was no electrical or water access available. A twenty-five-foot well had to be dug by hand in the shifting sand and lined with wood. It was, in Ken's terms, "a WGD job," one accomplished "with great difficulty." Ken needed to tackle many such jobs to prepare the rectory for habitation. Some Mistassini men had experience working at the mines and were very helpful and capable regarding the rectory and other problems.

The area Anglican churches combined in a cooperative system, so Ken was sometimes involved at Chibougamau, Chapais, Dore Lake, and with Rev. John Gull at Waswanipi. Ken became familiar with a huge section of northern Quebec. He cooperated with the nursing station and went into camps when the nurse was performing health checks of the Indians. Ken celebrated the service of Holy Communion, and the nurse checked each family's health. On one such trip, when the temperature was very low, Ken discovered that the Communion wafer disintegrated at -40°F. His theology training had not prepared him for that!

In the summer Father Blaber tried to keep a schedule of services for the guides at the government fish camps. Two fishermen had hired guides to take them farther into the wilderness, away from those fishing close to the provincial fish camp. They were enjoying good fishing, when in the middle of the afternoon one of the guides announced, "Our priest will be having a service at five o'clock just a few miles from here. We're going to it. Do you want to go to the service or stay here and fish?" A strange look passed over the fishermen's faces. As they considered the validity of the guide's question, they thought, "We are way out in the bush. How do they know that a priest has come to provide a service for Indians? Are they tired of us and want to dump us and leave us alone in this vast wilderness to try to find our way out?" They concluded that they would go with the guides.

The fishermen accompanied the Indians. About two hours later they were astonished to see a large gathering of Indians and a priest. A service soon started. After the service, the fishermen asked the priest how their guides knew about the service. Ken Blaber replied that it was impossible to have a firm schedule, due to weather conditions and the availability of a plane, so he came when he could. Later Ken told the story to me and asked the fishermen's question, "How did they know that I was coming?"

My answer was that Indians have developed a communication system that we don't have or need, since we resort to other means of communication. I have known their system to work in Maine, the Maritimes, and here in Northern Quebec. Just how, I don't know, but it could be a type of mental telepathy.

No air navigational aids existed for pilots in the area. Air navigation was primarily by looking at familiar landmarks below and at maps with the camps and safe landing places marked on them. It was usual for the weather to be excellent at the camps that Ken was visiting; however, a blinding whiteout or severe thunderstorm could be raging in the Mistassini village area, forcing the pilot to fly just above tree level. There was no way to communicate to the pilot to warn him of the changing weather conditions. Joyce remembered one of Ken's winter trips when the returning plane came right over the house, sounding close enough to hit the roof, yet she could not see it, and it landed safely on the lake. Once, one not-so-lucky pilot landed on Emmet McLeod's roof, an unsettling experience for those inside the house.

Since the Bibles in Mistassini were Bishop Horden's James Bay Moose Cree version, in 1970 Father Blaber wrote to the Wycliffe Bible translators for help translating the Bible into the Mistassini dialect. The translators needed to know the number of people who would use the Bible. He said that the Mistassini Band population was 1,281, plus forty non-treaty Métis. The Cree used their own language everywhere except at the Indian Affairs Day School, Hudson's Bay store, the Band Council Office, and the nursing station. Local telephone operators used Cree and seventy-five percent of the church services were in Cree.

Once in the spring of 1970, the Blabers had been away for several days. When they returned, Ken found an invitation to a bear feast. It coincided with his Sunday services. The Indian host emphasized that they wished him to attend. An Indian catechist could take his services. Ken was honored to attend.

The mine operators tried several times to employ Mistassini men in the mines. The attempts were often short-lived. Quebec miners did not easily accept competition with Indian work partners. The miners vastly outnumbered the Indians and were belligerent toward them, constantly belittling them. The French criticized the Indians as lazy and poor workers. The mines had a far different atmosphere from that of the trap line camps. There is no darker workplace than mines when the artificial light is extinguished. Blaber knew the Indians and the miners. He knew that the Indians were good workers. He suggested to mine administrators that the Indians might do better if they were in a group by themselves, not a mixed group. Finally the Campbell Mine operators reacted favorably to the suggestion and worked out a plan as an experiment.

The program began on July 23, 1973. The Indians had to go to the mine office to complete job application forms. Once the Indians were hired, the mine bus would stop at the Chibougamau Indian Friendship Center, a home operated by Mistassini Indians for Indian people wanting to continue the traditional Indian-style home life while in Chibougamau. The first day of work, two men did not report for work. One man's father-in-law had died, and the would-be worker had gone home. The other man was on fire duty and had been called to fight a forest fire burning out of control. Those on fire duty were obligated to go when called. Fortunately, those at the Campbell Mine understood the situation. The Cree teams would be compared with a similar Quebec team. Father Blaber gave a mining-fundamentals course to prepare the young Mistassini men who wanted to try the mining occupation. It was popular; a sufficient number of potential miners turned out to make up at least two teams of workers.

After several weeks they compared the production of the two groups with startling results. At the midday break the Quebec workers led, but at the end of the day the Indians regularly showed greater production. The French worked hard in the morning but could not keep up their pace all day. Their afternoon production decreased as the afternoon progressed. The Indians began at a slower pace but retained their pace throughout the day, thus outproducing their competitors. The record of absenteeism and length of employment for the Indian workers was the same as that of the French miners in the Chibougamau mines. The Patino Mine became interested and developed a similar plan. They instituted a course in mineral exploration in the Mistassini Adult Education Program. Two more mines asked to hire Indian workers. The program became one of the biggest success stories between industry

REV. KEN BLABER TEACHES MINING BASICS TO MISTASSINI YOUNG MEN.

and Indians. I had the pleasure of visiting two of the Indian teams at their mine jobs. Indians took pride in their work; shift bosses were happy with the Indians' work.

Mining in the region was not dependable. The mines were modern, but the high-grade copper veins were few and soon ran out. One mine after another closed. It was another blow to the Mistassini economy. In 1970 the provincial economists concluded that the Quebec province would benefit most from the development and manufacture of electricity, the biggest economic resource from the Mistassini Territory. The James Bay Hydro Project left little room for other enterprises.

Over the years, Ken shared with me some of his many experiences. Radio communications with the medical planes was not reliable due to the powerful summer and winter storms. A child was very sick, so they called in a medical plane to take him to a hospital. The plane landed and picked up the child. A quick but severe summer storm arose. Ken decided that the plane should not chance taking off in the storm; he would drive the child to the Chibougamau hospital. He radioed to the plane about to take off just as the radio antenna blew down. Communications with the pilot were lost. Ken helplessly saw the plane take off. The plane did not survive the severe winds of the storm. Both the pilot and the child were killed in the crash.

In another situation, a young pregnant wife in a northern winter camp suddenly became very sick with appendicitis. Her husband snowshoed to the next camp, delivering the news. Such relays continued from camp to camp until the message was delivered to the Mistassini nursing station. Ken was at the radio, trying to alert the Air Force radio station at Nichikun about a violent winter storm. The storm hindered the radio reception, but finally word got through that two people needed medical attention. About the same time and near the same location, a prospector had a broken leg. Due to the poor reception, the message was garbled, and the medical personnel understood that the woman had a broken leg and the prospector appendicitis. It was Ken Blaber's persistence in getting the message through that saved the young woman. Later, when her baby was born, she gave Ken the honor of selecting a name for her little one.

The Christmas season came quickly to Mistassini. Ken Blaber asked his Indian church leaders to help with church Christmas decorations. White birch trees were set up in the church. It was a bit different from green spruces, but Father Blaber respected their custom. A few years later, after Ken had a new assignment, the young replacement ordered the Indians to cut green spruce trees for the Christmas decorations. The Indians did as they were told, but it was not the same for them. One of the faithful young women had hand sewn some very colorful hangings for the church, using materials sold at the Hudson's Bay store. The maker's magnificent craftsmanship was lost among the garish inharmonious colors. However, it was a fine piece of Cree craftsmanship, done as a gift to the church. The new, young priest, dominated by a European point of view, quickly replaced them with hangings that he felt were more appropriate in a church setting. The faithful, willing worker was deeply insulted. Others became reluctant to donate their craftwork to the church. It seemed that the church image was losing the unique characteristics of an Indian church, as it took on the appearance of a typical Canadian city church.

A few years later, on a trip visiting winter camps, I happened to see a store-bought, synthetic Christmas tree stashed in a corner of a storage tent. "How ironic," I thought. "Here were excellent spruce in the vast forest scene surrounding the camp for a fine Christmas tree." Then I caught myself making the mistake of thinking like a white man in an Indian setting. This bush person was attempting to symbolize the acceptance of the other culture at Christmastime. Therefore it was fitting to have a white man's synthetic tree for the festival. There had to be a balance between "Indian-ness" and European lifestyle. A change in culture had to be accepted by them, not forced on them.

When Father Blaber was at Mistassini, the North had its own form of investing. The stock market was far away. Communications were poor and unreliable. It was impossible for an active investor to follow the market's daily activity. Investing in furs became popular, replacing stocks. In 1970 polar bear furs were said to be the best investment, because the polar bear population around James Bay was beginning to diminish. Winters were still long and cold in 1970. People did not consider global warming to be a reality soon facing them. It would be about twenty years before some scientists claimed that the polar bear was a global warming indicator. As usual, the Indians were the first to be aware of animal population changes but had no answers to the problem other than man's abuse of the earth.

What was happening at Mistassini in the 1970s reminded me of the building of the Mactaquac Dam on New Brunswick's St. John River above Fredericton in the 1960s. The dam backed up a large reservoir to create water power for the production of cheap electricity to attract business to the province. The water, which filled the large reservoir in the fall and winter, froze in the winter but gradually rose. In the spring when the ice broke, many fish were floating belly up on the surface, surprising all but the Indians. Their cultural hero, Kuluskap,[3] had warned the Indians long ago that if two of the river's islands, known as "Kuluskap's snowshoes" were destroyed, the fish would die. The high water backed up by the dam inundated the islands. The toxins flowing downriver accumulated in the water held back by the dam, whereas previously the toxins flowed down to the sea. The fish and other wildlife depending upon the St. John River reservoir for drinking water died as the toxic content increased.

Missionaries frequently refer to the people with whom they work as, "my Indians." A missionary who is placed in a situation where he is living among his flock twenty-four hours a day should become well acquainted with the group. A trusting relationship should grow between them, and he should become a good advisor to them. He has the opportunity to see them firsthand as they go through their annual cycles, and to learn their values. He helps families welcoming a new member, young couples entering marriage, and families suffering the loss of one of their members. The missionary is there to offer what he can to the people in both good and bad times. He sees the people as they react to all sorts of circumstances and observes their traditional approach to their daily problems. A missionary who performs well with "his" people becomes a trusted and knowledgeable person in relation to the group.

An anthropologist who comes with specialized training to study the culture of a group soon has the attitude that they are "his" people. Many anthropologists consider the missionary as an enemy who wipes out a fundamental element of an ancient culture by substituting by force his religion on the people. Dr. Frank G. Speck, who founded the University of Pennsylvania's Anthropology Department, fostered the hypothesis that missionaries suppressed traditional religious beliefs of the Indians so basic to the study of their culture. Speck blamed the early Catholic missionaries for obliterating the Indian's ancient, traditional religion.

The missionaries' primary purpose was to save souls and ban native religions. Indian religion was forced to go underground; much was retained but performed in secrecy. The white man and often even tribal members were not aware that it existed. The early missionaries were judged by the success of their efforts to convert pagans. Whether they succeeded or not, they had to convince their superiors that they had successfully suppressed pagan worship just as their neighboring missionaries did. Hunting societies like the Mistassini found it easy to preserve their religious traditions when in their solitary camps.

In the latter part of the twentieth century, northeastern Indians made a successful effort to resurrect the Pan-American Indian religion as part of an Indian resurgence movement to recover their lost culture. Young northeastern Indians from Maine to Moose Factory questioned the superiority of values established by the Western world. Many went west to learn and reestablish their Pan-American Indian heritage. They returned inspired and passed their lost culture on to their friends. Their traditional religion served them when they were in the bush. Christianity served those who substituted village life—under white village circumstances—for that of the bush.

Ken compiled a Mistassini newsletter that Glen Speers, the manager of the Hudson's Bay company, sent to the camps with his deliveries. It was printed by using a Gestetner printer of World War I vintage. It contained family news, such as marriages, births and deaths, a church calendar, and village news. When I visited the people with Ken, I usually noted that the church calendar was pinned to the wall of the tent. Calendars served to mark the significant religious holidays as well as to note the days of the fur trader's visits.

As a spiritual people, each family owned their own church prayer book and hymnal and used them on a regular basis. It was customary for the headman to lead his extended family in a service each Sunday. Beautifully decorated leather book bags were made to protect their precious hymnals and prayer books. Bush people had very little actual cash. They supported their church by directing Glen Speers to credit certain furs to St. John the Evangelist Church's HBC account.

One day, to my surprise, I discovered Fred Swindlehurst's prayer book in a distinguished leather protective cover as he had left it some sixty years earlier in the Mistassini Church of St. John the Evangelist. Like the Maritime and Maine Indians, the Mistassini had a custom of hiding a paddle or some article that belonged to a visitor they liked as a means to delay his leaving. I like to think that the hiding custom was the reason that Fred's book was left behind and still in use in the Mistassini church. His journal relates traveling with the fur brigades to Mistassini, where I'm sure that he made good friends.

One day a plane landed at the Mistassini waterfront bringing an unexpected CBC news team to the remote village. The news crew disembarked from the plane with their TV camera ready to shoot. Word quickly passed through the village. To the photographer's delight, there was much activity in the Hudson's Bay Company post. Weather-beaten hunters were carrying out huge sacks of bulk supplies such as flour and sugar, and they walked up a trail. Ken was unaware of the presence of the filming crew. His propane tank was empty. He carried it to the store for a replacement, and he saw the activity and the photographers. He grabbed another empty propane tank as if it were a full replacement tank, hoisted it to his shoulder, and started back to his cabin. The image of the village priest carrying a full propane tank on his shoulder impressed the news team and made the photographer's day. One of the members of the team turned to a nearby girl, saying, "Your priest is strong too."

She replied slowly with emphasis, "Veeery strong, veeery strong!"

A photo of the priest with the caption below it related that even the priest had to be a rugged individual in a northern Indian settlement. Later, when aired on television, the finished film confirmed that the Mistassini priest was "very strong," drawing peals of laughter from the Mistassini community.

Blueberries vie with black flies for being the greatest crop at the territory! The children were very much affected by the black-fly bites. The scratched bites had a tendency to develop into impetigo. As children matured, it appeared that they developed an immunity and were less bothered. The children often wore hoods for protection from the biting insects. Netting placed over the blanket cradles protected infants and toddlers.

The Indians always harvested large quantities of blueberries, drying them in the sun for winter use. The Lake St. John Indians found them

to be a valuable commercial crop. They learned how to make both rakes and mills that separated the berries from the chaff. Some Lake St. John Indians came as far north as Chibougamau Park, harvesting the berries. A truck came by every day, purchasing the previous day's harvest. The word drifted farther north to Mistassini that blueberries were a money crop. Several Mistassini decided that they would go and learn from the

MISTASSINI CHURCH (OPPOSITE) IS OFFERED CREDIT FROM CERTAIN FURS.

Lake St. John people how to harvest them for the market. In 1973 the Mistassini Indians started harvesting blueberries for the commercial market.

The village obtained an ancient, unreliable telephone system that served only the village proper. (A single-sideband radio was still the only connection to the outside world). This ancient telephone system was constantly in need of repairs. Father Blaber became the respected chief repairman of the important communications implement. He gained the respect of many people. Father Blaber was deeply involved not only with his congregation but also with improving the quality of village life.

Joyce Blaber was a substitute teacher in the village elementary school. Her two boys, Paul and Andrew, attended the school. The new Mistassini elementary school followed the Indian Affairs policy, placing children together by age, not by grade or ability, beginning when Andrew was to enter fourth grade in 1969.

It was rare to find a child entering the school from the bush knowing any language but Cree. The entire teaching staff spoke only English. There were no interpreters. Children's books in Cree did not exist. The children's entire preschool world was their northern bush, Cree hunting-camp life. Many parents cut their Mistassini trading visit short, rushing back to their camps before the roundup of school children took place.

When Andrew Blaber was nine years old and at the fourth-grade level, he was put in the nine-year-old group, some of whom were still on the grade-one level. Although it was a difficult educational beginning for an inquisitive mind, Andrew today has a successful career, having earned a PhD in kinesiology. He currently is an associate professor working in the aerospace physiology laboratory in the School of Kinesiology at Simon Fraser University. The fact that Andrew had to attend a class that grouped students according to their grade level contributed to the Blaber family's leaving Mistassini for Chibougamau.

The young Indian child's world was the bush camp, where there were limited opportunities with the written word. Parents were often away doing their chores during the day. There was no television or radio to bring marvelous children's programs in the Cree language to the youngsters in the village or the bush. The older children had the responsibility of watching over the younger ones and were expected to perform helpful duties in the life of the camp. It was a balancing act between performing grownup activities and enjoying a free childhood that would soon be over. There were no Cree storybooks for the children. When I visited camps, I took *National Geographic* magazines to give to children. They enjoyed sitting and looking at the colorful animal illustrations for some time. I hoped this would be an opening to a broader world for them, an introduction to the exciting world of published material that could extend their knowledge of the world around them.

The only school at Mistassini was the elementary school. When the Blabers' eldest boy, Paul, was ready for high school, the Blabers had to make arrangements to send Paul away to school in Arvida the first year and to Chibougamau the second year. When attending school in Chibougamau, Paul could return home for weekends and holidays. The Chibougamau Anglican priest moved in the same year both Paul and Andrew were to attend high school. The bishop thought it would give some continuity at Chibougamau if Ken were to move there. As a result, the Blaber family could be together, and the children could attend schools there. Blaber retained some Mistassini responsibilities until the Mistassini opening was filled. Both Church and community benefited greatly from Kenneth Blaber's hard work and understanding of Canada's Native people. As the Anglican priest in Chibougamau, Ken was appointed chaplain of the Chibougamau Canadian Air Defense Facility on the early-warning Pine Tree Line. He had responsibilities also in Chapais and Dore Lake.

A strange example follows of just how little we have observed or know about Indians after three hundred years of settlement in their land. The Blabers' daughter, Sharon, entered kindergarten in Chibougamau. In Mistassini, outside of her family, her playmates were all Cree Indian children. She had difficulty adjusting to a class with a French-speaking teacher and a mixture of English- and French-speaking children. It was a huge culture shock. Up until then, Sharon didn't realize that she was different from the other children in Mistassini. The Chibougamau teacher's topic was "Indians." She asked the class to sit like Indians. The other children sat on the floor with their legs crisscrossed, tailor style. Not realizing that Sharon sat the traditional Cree way, the teacher did not understand why Sharon could not follow directions.

The new pupil was sure that she was sitting in the proper Indian fashion and did not understand that her teacher was making a fuss because Sharon did not conform and sit like others in the class. Sharon became confused. It was a poor introduction to the white community. The Indian way did not make a public display of one who did things differently.

About twenty-five years later I was attending a meeting of anthropologists. Near the end of the meeting, one retired professor asked, "How do Indians sit?" No one replied. He thought that it was a

good topic for a paper. In due course I received a query from the editor
of the paper asking, "How do Indians sit?" I sent an explanation with
several photos showing how Indians sit. They did not publish the paper. It
appears that learned anthropologists who have worked among American
Indians have never taken the time to observe the traditional way Indians
sit, whether it was in Maine or in Northern Quebec. If the simple action
of sitting causes such perplexity, this leads me to wonder how much

USUAL SITTING POSITION OF A CREE WOMAN ON A SPRUCE BOUGH FLOOR

misunderstanding there has been with more intricate problems between the people of different cultures.

Some years before 1970, signs of rot showed up here and there on the logs of the old church. The Mistassini Cree knew that soon they would have to have a new church. They established a building fund. In 1970, when about half the building fund's goal had been reached, the Indians learned that the neighboring church at Eastmain had burned, leaving their neighbors with no church. The Mistassini people took up a collection for Eastmain Church. Even though it had taken several years of hard work to raise the money for the future Mistassini church, the church elders decided to give their building funds to Eastmain, so they could quickly replace their church. The decision was based on Mistassini logic that their church was still usable, but at Eastmain they had no church and needed one.

The James Bay Hydro Project plan placed the estimated new high-water level of Mistassini Lake at St. John's door. Therefore, the new Mistassini church was to be located in the village area next to the new Hudson's Bay Company store. The new Hudson's Bay structure would no longer be a trading post but a fine modern department store offering a large variety of merchandise.

The church elders knew that it would be several years before a new church would be completed and ready to occupy. They voted to electrify the old church, and on Christmas Eve 1973 the lights were turned on for the first time. While most of the outside world greeted the birth of Christ with the soft glow of many candles, Mistassini, whose source of light had always been candles, rejoiced at their electrified church. At that time Reverend Tom DeHoop was in charge of the Anglican mission. He told me how wonderful it was to have the lights turned on at the Christmas Eve midnight service. The bright lights were an exciting experience after so many years of weak candle light.

One Sunday I was asked to help at the Church of St. John the Evangelist, Mistassini. My good friend Philip Voyageur was the lay reader responsible for the services that day. It happened to be the day that the Anglican Church of Canada collected money for their annual campaign for the world's needy. The appeal mentioned the starving children in Africa who needed food. Philip told me how much money the Mistassini parish raised for the Annual Appeal. I was surprised by the generosity of this small mission parish that also received funding from the Annual Appeal. It was a larger donation than I have seen some big-city churches raise where people have so much more than those of this small fur-trapping community. I praised Philip for their generosity. Philip said that the people had known what it was for helpless parents to hear the children cry from hunger when there was no food for them. This unhappy memory inspired them to give generously for the starving children in Africa. These northern people had endured hunger like that in Africa, conditions that the richer people of the cities just read about, but had never experienced. They didn't feel the severity of the situation. The Mistassini people are very charitable and concerned about their fellow man. When the great ice storm of 1998 blacked out the lights and heat of many Montreal homes, several Mistassini men filled trucks with firewood and sent them to Montreal. The Mistassini also took care of their own who had physical disabilities and were unable to provide for themselves.

# XIII

## OUR INTRODUCTION TO MISTASSINI AND OTHER NORTHERN CREE COMMUNITIES

In 1970 my wife, daughter, and I were among those who came over the new gravel road to Mistassini. The Indian camps that we had seen on our brief trip the previous year had whetted my enthusiasm to see more of these Indians, whose camps appeared to be much like the descriptions of the 1850 Maliseet camps. I had contacted the Reverend Kenneth Blaber and told him of my interest. We were invited to be his guests for several days.

We later learned that Ken and his wife Joyce were concerned about how the people from New York would react to the primitive accommodations and lifestyle in the Mistassini village. City people from the south, in general, had the reputation of being critical, knowing better ways for improvement, while not attempting to understand the situation.

We were directed to a small log cabin (sometimes used as a morgue) that overlooked the lake. A heavy shower broke out a few minutes later. Water dripped down through the roof in several places. We found containers to catch the water and then sat near the door, enjoying the view of the lake. A few minutes later there was a most dramatic scene of storm clouds being chased over the lake. The storm was of short duration. The rector came to see if we were ready to return to New York but found us looking quite comfortable.

He invited us to the rectory to meet Joyce and have tea. We found a couple who appeared to be starved for conversation in English. They started relating their Mistassini experiences, hardly stopping during the few days that we were there. In reality, the Blabers were so enthusiastic about their new way of life and the tasks ahead that they wanted to share it with anyone who would listen. We were good listeners.

Certain events were well remembered by the Blabers, such as the following. One Christmas many schoolchildren returned for the holidays, bringing fine gifts for their families. A student on vacation was looking forward to flying into his parents' camp for the holiday. He had a warm snowmobile suit as a present for his father. His flight took off on Christmas Eve, shortly before a heavy storm set in. Snow had come early that fall, before the lakes were properly frozen. The snow insulates and, when covering open water, prevents proper freezing. Open spots in the lakes are undetectable.

Early afternoon darkness set in even earlier due to the storm. The plane had not returned; there was no word from it. As it was time for the midnight Christmas service, Joyce looked out at the fierce storm with winds that were driving snow horizontally into huge drifts. She wondered whether anyone would come to the service. She was lucky; she lived close to the church. She went out and almost instantly leaned forward at 45 degrees as she faced into the blizzard. She could barely make out blurry figures laboring across a trail. The church filled. The congregation prayed for those on the missing plane.

A cold, crisp Christmas morning dawned with a dazzling, bright sun rising in a light-blue sky. The people knew the planned route taken by the plane. It was imperative to find the crash victims quickly. They could not survive long in the cold. It was an unwritten law that all available bush pilots would help find a lost plane. Another bush pilot set out following his experienced impulse and sighted the downed plane and men about midmorning. He landed, picked up the men, and returned them before noon to the village, where word quickly spread that all the missing people were safely back.

The plane had hit a soft place in the ice, created by an unfrozen pocket, and nosed over. The people had gotten out and saved their gear. As the plane had slowly begun to sink, it was impossible to coax the dogs out into the blizzard. They felt safer in the shelter of the cockpit, away from the angry wind and snow. The men then started a fire in the $-40°F$ blizzard. Several of the men's clothes were wet. The rugged Cree rigged a shelter by the fire, and they dried their clothes and warmed themselves. Those who had wet clothes took turns sharing the boy's new, warm, dry snowmobile suit. There were other less dramatic stories. Mistassini was still a rugged place for Indians and white people.

Ken had a plan for me to meet some village people and then accompany him to some nearby, easily accessible camps, a test of my reaction to this culture. When our visit neared its end, Ken said that he had to fly into the bush to see a very sick man. He asked me whether I would like to accompany him. He would be gone overnight. I agreed to tag along. I left with a few brownies in my pocket that my wife, Edyth, had given us. Ken assured Edyth that we would find food in the bush, so she need not trouble herself to provide more.

As we flew to the camp I looked at the beautiful, rugged country. Then I had an afterthought: it was not such a happy place for an emergency landing. Cree men were rugged enough to match the Cree country.

The camp of tribal shaman William Edwards was northwest, near the government fishing camps at Louis Jolliet. When we walked to the ailing elder's tent, my shoulder brushed Edwards's medicine bag that was hanging on a pole near the tent door. The Mistassini tribal shaman greeted Ken, "I knew my priest would come to me."

A tribal shaman has strong supernatural powers that extend his presence to the animal kingdom and has the ability to detect the intentions in the minds of other tribal members. A tribal shaman is usually selected on the basis that his occult performances will be used to benefit the tribe. This shaman supported the church, was a good friend of the priest, and like many other hunters, contacted spirits for knowledge about game

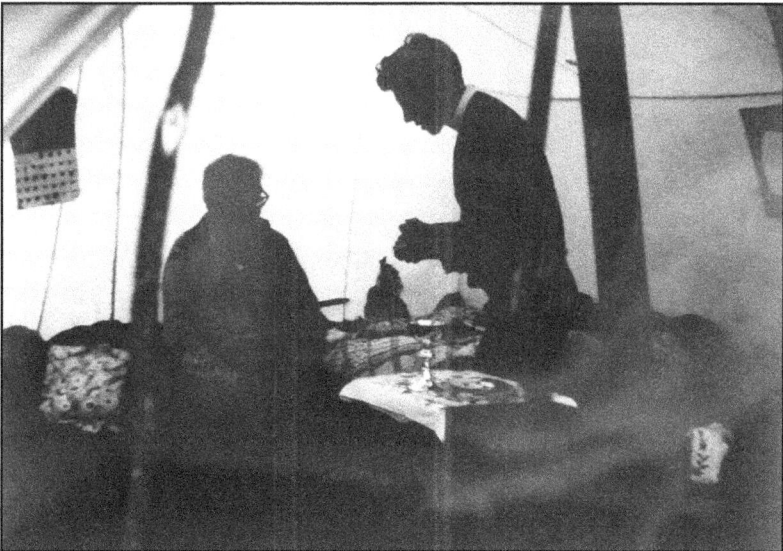

"I KNEW MY PRIEST WOULD COME TO ME."

and where to find it. The neat and uncluttered tent impressed me. A calendar was pinned to the tent wall. Without delay an altar was prepared in the center of the tent, and Edwards was ready for the Service of Holy Communion.

After the service, we saw the camp activities. The men were returning from fishing. The teenage schoolgirls home for summer vacation were cleaning the fish. I asked a few questions. Edwards asked a young man to interpret, and then he answered in Cree. I was surprised that I recognized some of his words and asked another question before his interpreter began translating. I translated Edwards's reply into English. A surprised Edwards asked in English, "Does this man speak Cree?"

I was just as surprised that my knowledge of Maliseet enabled me to understand him. Algonquian languages are very similar, and it should not be difficult for one who knows one form to get at least a gist of a conversation in a different Algonquian language.

There was a sweat bath behind Edwards's tent, his method for curing himself.[1] He said that the sweating made him feel much improved.

We were invited to the government fish camp for dinner, where the chef was waiting for us. I expected fish, but the Quebec chef said, "No, no, no!" and produced the finest of steaks for the missionary to the Mistassini and his friend. I thought of Edyth back in Mistassini, as she had been wondering what we would find to eat in the bush.

We returned to Mistassini. My reactions to the Indians must have impressed Father Blaber. At supper he proposed that if we would come the following summer and do a Bible school for the children, I could accompany him on several visits to bush camps, thus increasing my knowledge of the Cree. Edyth and I agreed to do a children's summer Bible school in 1971. We did not realize what Ken had in mind.

A church-school program had been started many years ago by two Anglican English ladies from just outside Eastbourne, East Sussex. In summer they had traveled to remote parts of Canada to provide this popular church-school program for children. Mistassini had been included in their itinerary. (Joyce happened to meet the "van ladies" in Eastbourne when she was fifteen or sixteen years old. At that time, Joyce did not have an inkling that she would ever end up in Mistassini.) Now the Blabers wanted us to continue the program. Although we did not realize the full scope of what we had committed ourselves to undertake, we later discovered that we were to cover the major Indian settlements over the two hundred miles of gravel road between Miquelon and Mistassini. Our time in each community depended on the size of the settlement. Chapais and Dore Lake, the settlements for Chibougamau Indians, were included. This gave us the opportunity to see first hand how these woodland Cree were adapting to the changes in their land. A short summer visit to compare Mistassini Cree life in the twentieth century to that of Maine maritime Indians of the nineteenth century became an extended study. The advance of civilization into their wilderness had caused a forced change in lifestyle on the Mistassini of the twentieth century.

For several summers our life was oriented around summer programs for Cree children. Our program consisted of Bible stories, crafts, baseball, volleyball, games, and movies. The younger children enjoyed putting up the felt board figures as Bible stories were told; older ones enjoyed drawing with crayons on paper; the oldest enjoyed the sports. Everyone enjoyed singing and the movies.

We applied for and received a grant for a movie projector and a portable generator. Films were borrowed from the Canadian Film Board. Topics included animals, Indian and Eskimo titles, and children's stories like *Paddle to the Sea*. We provided snacks consisting of crackers and bread spread with peanut butter and jelly. Fresh milk, sold in plastic bags by the liter, was scarce and expensive. We served the children reconstituted powdered milk. The children enjoyed the milk and had no trouble finishing large pots of it. Refrigeration space was not required since there were no leftovers.

Churches, both in our hometown area (Ogdensburg, NY, on the St. Lawrence River) and Kingston, Ontario, had teenagers interested in traveling with us to help with the Bible school. Since there was no available housing on the reserves where we would teach the Bible schools, we towed a travel trailer to live in with the teen helpers. The Indian children loved the program and wanted to be around us all the time. When we returned to our travel trailer and closed the door behind us, the children knew the Bible school day was over. It was the first time that the teenagers traveling with us had an opportunity to interact with the Indian culture. It was apparent that both groups were having an enjoyable and gratifying experience. The young volunteers adapted well to living in a very small space and without modern amenities. They all did a marvelous job.

At Waswanipi we heard about the old village of Waswanipi on Waswanipi Lake and decided that we wanted to see it. Diom Blacksmith arranged for a grandson to take us all there by freight canoe. The canoe was the largest one in the village, about twenty-five feet long and four

THE CHILD HAD MANY DOGS FOR PLAYMATES.

feet wide in the middle, equipped with a ten-horsepower engine. It was a pleasant day, but the water was a little rough. When we arrived we found that St. Barnabas the Apostle Church was still there, as well as the old Hudson's Bay buildings. Only one family was living there. It was a Gull family who trained dogs for dog teams. Their young daughter, about eight years old, the only child in the village, had many dogs for playmates. We went into the church. A wooden cross was in its place; its outstretched arms still welcomed the rare person who ventured in. I offered to take the cross and give it to the diocese for preservation. The guide refused, saying it belonged to the church. I did not want to be accused of stealing their church cross.

On the return trip the wind was up. The water got really rough. Then we realized why we had the large freight canoe. Waves frequently broke over the bow, spilling a bit of water into the canoe. The Waswanipi had their version of the Mistassini story of not looking back at an object or the water would become very rough. The girls thoroughly enjoyed the rough water. Our guide told us that some baseball players from a national team had come up for fishing. The water was not as rough as what we were experiencing, but the sportsmen refused to go in the canoe. For us it was an adventure that is still well remembered.

The Waswanipi lived closer to white culture and apparently trusted us more than did the Indians living further north. Usually, for the last session at a village, the women made special treats. Each led us to feel that our work was appreciated.

Dore Lake was primarily the home of the Mianscum and Bosum extended families. Some children, even the youngest toddlers, challenged bees from a nearby nest to sting them, so they could show off their stalwart courage to us. Were they showing us a tough personality that would not flinch under the strict discipline and abusive behavior that characterized their image of schools and churches? A thirteen-year-old boy, who completed the third grade, boasted that he was going into the bush in the winter to learn hunting and trapping rather than return to school. Bush life offered a greater challenge and a greater respect for him than did the school. These young people were tough; they were taught to "take it on the chin," but keep going. The bush education was practical teaching about survival.

The Indians had never worked for money. They knew nothing about wages or workmen's rights. Mine managers took advantage of their ignorance and hired them at a much lower wage than the French Canadians were offered. The Quebec laborers felt that the Indians were filling jobs that rightfully belonged to them. Their organized labor unions protested the hiring of Indians. There was an easy way to replace the Indians. Mine policy required that their employees pass a physical exam

St. Barnabas the Apostle

FIRST BIRTHDAY FEAST FOR THE TWINS

and have written proof, a new concept to Indians. Replaced Indians had no jobs and no incomes. The Indians were forced to rely on country food and their old ways of procuring it.

We also learned why we were not always given a hearty welcome. It was not easy for many to believe that we were giving our time and efforts to provide recreational activities for them and received no money for this service. There must be an ulterior motive! Several young children saw safety flares in our vehicle and hooted, "Now we know why you are here, dynamite, dynamite, you are prospectors!" Why would anyone come to give and not take something more from them?

The same three-hundred-year-old mistakes made with New England and maritime Indians were now being repeated in Quebec. Lawmakers far from the scene with no knowledge of the actual situation found it easy to pass a law similar to those passed in early New England and the Maritime Provinces. Unemployed Indians were not given an alternative source of money to purchase food. Another new law was passed prohibiting the Indians from subsistence hunting and fishing. It is so easy to take away, yet difficult to provide a substitute. The laws prohibiting or restricting hunting and fishing, the activities that were the Indian's major source of food, were unrealistic! When similar action was taken in New Brunswick, about 1925, a Tobique Maliseet woman reacted with, "Why don't you send soldiers to shoot us, killing us quickly rather than give us the slow cruel death of starvation?" A Maine Passamaquoddy Indian said, "I never knew hunger until we went on welfare." The same men who took the jobs away from the Indians began hearing stories about Indians killing moose and began protesting that the Indians were poaching.

Soon game wardens were checking the Indians. Two Dore Lake families went together to their winter hunting territory. The hunter killed a moose to feed the families. A game warden flew in to have a look around. He asked to go into the tent. The hunter would not permit him to do so. The game warden said that he would have to take the two men to a police officer. The hunters agreed to go in the plane, but added that the game warden would have to stay in the bush and look after the Indian families! They could not go away and leave the women and children there alone with no one to provide food for them. The game warden left the bush without taking them in. The member of the group who enjoyed telling how their leader outwitted the game warden did not indicate whether the warden would have found the evidence in the tent needed to prosecute the case. The game warden represented to the Indians a system that imposed standards that would annihilate Indians. They were sure that if the game warden had entered the tent, he would have fabricated some excuse to make an arrest. The Indians had survived over many centuries by killing no more than what they needed for food. They did not abuse the right to kill animals and did not kill for the sake of killing, only to feed their families. The government's game Laws were an overreaction and did not provide an alternative source of food. The result was that people were forced to break government laws just to survive. Arresting a man who had always hunted for food and lacked other means to feed his family was not an act that showed respect to a caring family provider.

We had finished our Bible school programs at beautiful Dore Lake and had enjoyed our time with the people. Living here in the trailer was an experience different from parking in a campground with hookups and electric facilities. Our refrigerator, stove, heater, and lights were fueled by propane gas. Now we were preparing to move on to Mistassini.

I answered a knock on our trailer door. Jean Mianscum, whose father John was the band's leader, had come saying that her father wished to invite us to a feast in honor of the twins' first birthday. Twins were a hardship for these forest dwellers. New babies take a great deal of time. Before going to winter camps, one twin would be given to a relative to care for him. Thus the mother's work was shared. Since one-year-old children are not permitted to leave their tent, we were not previously aware of them. The feast would be "right away." By Indian time that meant sometime soon! It was a gala event for all at Dore Lake. There were chicken, potatoes, canned corn, peas, orange juice, sandwiches, followed by cakes and candy for the children. All was served on colorful plastic plates, plastic "silverware," and paper cups.

Each twin was given a cake with a lighted candle for him to blow out. In honor of the twins, cigarettes and cigars were distributed. Children aged ten and up were given cigarettes. At age fourteen, boys were encouraged to smoke. Traditionally, feasts ended with smoking by all, but that was a different style of tobacco.

There were few who could provide a feast of such magnitude. It was an example of John Mianscum's power to do so. The feast was a pleasant deviation from the normal day's activities for all. A few days later, I took John and his family back to his home and hunting ground at the closed Ikon Mine, where he was the watchman. They were happy to return to the pleasant bush atmosphere that they much preferred to Dore Lake.

One winter day there was a fierce snowstorm with howling wind swirling snowflakes into large drifts. One of Robert Bosum's grandchildren was sick. The infant had difficulty breathing. The concerned family stoked their fire in the stove, keeping their small house warm in the raging storm. It was overly hot for respiratory problems. The heavily-wrapped child's temperature kept rising. There was no improvement in his breathing. Robert took off for the hospital with the baby well-wrapped in warm blankets against the sub-zero weather. The doctor examined the child, declared that there was nothing wrong with him, and sent the baby home. He died before morning.

A few days later another big snowstorm blew in. Another small grandchild became sick. Again the Bosum family had great concern. A plow had cleared the highway, leaving a big drift at the entrance into the unplowed Indian settlement. Robert Bosum called his priest, Father Ken Blaber, to report the problem. Father Blaber called the city manager and told him that the road needed plowing. Father Blaber would meet the plow, follow it to Dore Lake and take the baby to the hospital. Soon after the baby arrived at the hospital, it died.

The doctor did not want to release the body. Again Robert called Father Blaber to arrange for the release of the grandchild. The school children were to be home for vacation in a few days. The family wanted to arrange for a funeral for both deceased children when the school children would be home. The hospital released the body, and the family scheduled the funeral as a complete family affair. They buried the bodies in graves chopped in the frozen ground. The following spring the loving grandfather roamed the forested area in the vicinity searching for the perfect materials to construct protective grave fences for the two youngsters.

Strange as it may seem, the "higher" civilization that moved into the Mistassini territory did little to uplift Indian life to Canada's higher standard of living.

We were scheduled to be in Chapais to meet Joe Weistchee, a Rupert

ROBERT BOSUM MAKING GRAVE FENCE FOR HIS DECEASED GRANDCHILD

House Cree and a driller in the mine. He was also the caretaker of St. Alban the Martyr Anglican Church. Joe and his wife Helen lived in the rectory and had the responsibility of taking care of that building also. It happened to be July 26, 1971, the day of the scheduled Apollo 15 moon landing. Joe surprised us by having a battery-powered TV set up for the unprecedented three-day manned mission to the moon with Lunar Rover explorer to investigate the geology of the moon's surface. Joe invited us to watch the event with him. We had thought that we were going to have to miss it. Now Joe, who had broken the Cree tradition that forbade working underground, had crossed the threshold into the age of massive machines and had braved the depths of the earth, was fascinated by a traditional Cree story about a shaman who had gone to the moon and returned with his interesting face-to-face account of the event. Joe was now eager to compare the ancient medicine man's description with our scientists' findings. He joshed about how much longer it had taken our scientists to get to the moon than it did for their shaman. At last he could compare the Cree account with that of the scientists. They were surprisingly similar.

We found that our programs were generally well-accepted by all the Indian groups. The second year the school children were told when we would be coming to their reserve during the summer, so that they would be prepared for us.

# XIV

# THE CHANGE FROM INDEPENDENCE TO COMMUNITY VALUES

Mistassini is named for a large rock that is plainly seen from almost anywhere in the lake. The first French missionary-explorers to enter Mistassini territory were told that if they looked or pointed at the rock, the water would become so turbulent that canoeing would be impossible for the day. Fishermen and newcomers are still warned about looking or pointing at the rock.

In about 1950 the Quebec Government began planning for a Canadian-style village for the Mistassini Cree. It also appeared that the Hudson's Bay Company was coordinating their plans to close the four Hudson's Bay trading posts at Nichikun, Neoskweskau, Nemiskau, and Chibougamau to adjust to a larger provincial scheme to move the Indians of these posts to Mistassini or Rupert House. The Hudson's Bay Company denied that they had prior knowledge of the provincial plan; it was a coincidence that both plans came into fruition about the same time. Glen Speers was to remain manager of the enlarged Mistassini post. The Quebec Indian Affairs plan was to transfer the Indians served by the four posts encompassing Mistassini to either Rupert House on the coast or to the newly planned village to be constructed at Mistassini. The Quebec plan was not made public until the government was ready to act. Planners realized that coming together in a village community posed a different set of values, relationships, and problems for the independent hunting societies.

One of Rev. Kenneth Blaber's first assignments was to provide orientation programs presenting the community as a family-oriented social organization. The self-sufficient Mistassini Cree hunters would no longer be responsible for certain services that were community responsibilities. Many old established traditions would break down due to the increase in population.

It would soon become impossible for the bride and groom to invite the whole village to their wedding. It was too difficult to procure enough food for all. It was a recent innovation to have a priest available in the summer when the people gathered at Mistassini. Usually there were three to five couples who decided to be married at the trading post gathering. Early in the twentieth century, when Mistassini was served only by a summer priest, it became the custom for all the couples who were ready for marriage to be married in a single ceremony. A popular story circulated

DOUBLE WEDDING FEAST

about a young summer minister sent to Mistassini to obtain experience. He had difficulty with the Mistassini names, but had compiled a list of all the couples to be married in the service. He became mixed up and married two brides to the wrong grooms! Since they were married in the eyes of God, they couldn't become unmarried. As it turned out, the mismatched couples got along very well and everything turned out satisfactorily. The old custom that parents made the agreement about whom their children would marry was still alive. Marriage agreements were sometimes made by the parents when the children were very small. Some teenagers still felt that their parents could make the best decision about who would be a good helpmate. They were perfectly satisfied to abide by their parents' decision. The bush life left little opportunity for girls or boys to have contact with the opposite sex outside the extended family. Sometimes the bride knew the groom hardly or not at all before the wedding. Both parties were trained in the duties expected of their roles, and usually everything worked out for the best. The primary standards set for bride and groom were based on the ability of each to perform the tasks that a hunter and his spouse were expected to fulfill. Parents attempted to match couples who had abilities equal to those of their children. The newlyweds remained with the bride's family as part of the extended family. The young man joined his father-in-law's hunting party.

The Cree hunter lives in such a delicate balance with nature that in 1960, when the families returned from the winter hunting camps, they reported that the snow was no longer white! Unfortunately it has been many years since an unblemished, white snow has fallen on our cities; those in our big population areas have probably never experienced a truly white snowstorm. The Mistassini people were curious about the change. At the time, storm patterns were carrying our city and factory pollutants encapsulated in raindrops and snowflakes to the virgin, subarctic forests.

The Canadian Department of Conservation had tested some caribou carcasses and determined that their death was due to toxins. The caribou consumed the waste when they ate the mosses. The atomic toxins were passed on to the Indians who unknowingly ate the tainted caribou. Indians were tested for the dreaded toxins. Mercury was found in Mistassini waterways from newly constructed paper plants two hundred miles away.

About 1972 a very concerned Rev. John Gull informed me that several Indians had died of mercury poisoning by eating fish. Indians had been warned to watch for the symptoms of the deadly toxins. A

Quebec Health directive instructed Indians to stop eating fish. The advisory prompted John to think of some very practical questions about the situation. He sent the questions to the Health Department, but they went unanswered. I was not qualified to answer them. Since fish is a primary food for the Cree, what is a substitute for them? All animals go to the rivers and lakes to drink. Won't they also become infected with mercury poisoning and pass it to Indians, just as the fish do? Indian Affairs did not offer an alternative food or money to purchase safe food. What were they to eat?

In 1970 the road from Chibougamau was pushed through to Mistassini. How convenient for government employees and school teachers to be able to drive there rather than rely on bush plane or boat. Younger people rejoiced, for it meant easier and quicker access to that other world beyond the horizon. Elders held opinions entirely opposite to those of the young people. The elders saw as it as a path of evil; now the beer and drug peddlers and other unwanted people had easy access to their door. The previous lack of a road hindered the evil influences of the other culture from making an easy entrance to their village. The road brought both the good and bad. It took several years for those tempted by the bad influences to realize the harm of their over-indulgences.

The road also brought various missionaries, some thinking that they were the first to arrive to convert the Indian nonbelievers. One came by airplane and settled on the village outskirts. Only twenty years before that, Mounties were quick to enforce a law that prohibited influencing an Indian's religion. In a short time the village of less than two thousand people could select any one of five variations of the white man's Christianity. These new converts came from the two established Mistassini churches, not pagan Indians. It seems strange that there are so many missionaries in the outside world who can't find pagan people to convert. Apparently, their only recourse was to convert Christians of other denominations, when it became easy to enter an area.

The new ministers gained the curious and disgruntled Indians. Some wondered why there was so much competition among people worshiping the same God. Why couldn't they worship together in the same building? Usually each group considered his way the only way. Summers brought special missions to Mistassini, where people saw "miracles" in action, as some denominations tried to impress the people with their superior power. One summer a Southern Baptist school group arrived to convert the "pagan Indians." The group leaders let off two of the youths every five miles and directed them to walk down the road and talk to everyone they saw. One of the teenagers approached the Rev. John Gull and declared that the reverend was worshiping the Devil! The only true way for John to be saved was by going with the teenager into the river to be baptized. Unlike southern rivers, Waswanipi rivers were very cold and never became warm.

A very disturbed Christian priest came to me, asking me to explain what that man was saying. John was fluent in English and was an ordained Anglican priest. How could he be worshiping the Devil?

Another group learned that the Anglican Church had prayer books and hymnals in the Cree language. They sent their Indian converts to the church to steal the books, telling the Indians that since the books were written in Cree, the books belonged to the Indians, not the church. Indian ethics taught Indians to be honest and not to steal.

The Mistassini people could not financially support one church or one clergyman without mission funding, unless the minister's salary was based on the Mistassini economic system. One church would have been ample for the size of the community; soon the missionary societies of five competing denominations were sending funds to duplicate, not extend, what the others were doing. The village that had once been united for religious purposes became divided. A young person who wanted to marry someone of a different denomination usually found it did not lead to harmony. Some said that there was no divorce in the village until the influx of churches came to the village. Others claimed that the divisions influenced people to return to the traditional Indian religion. The various churches remain, but now the people know that they have to respect one another.

Indian people were very spiritual, with a deep faith and fear of the various spirits in their domains. Most northeastern Indian spirits were vengeful and demanding. I know of only one that spoke in the Indian's language, and then only after seeking him through the proper procedures of the shaking tent would he offer his advice as to where a hunter could find game. This spirit was only contacted when a hunter needed him. He, like the other spirits, was not worshiped on a regular basis, but was only contacted when needed.

Water spirits were given tobacco for safety before shooting rapids. The spirits demanded respect through donations of tobacco. The earth was greatly respected as Mother Earth, the life support for all existence, but not worshiped. Some, it was said, included the sun as a deity and looked to it in the morning and said a prescribed prayer in thanks for sharing light and warmth. The Creator of all things had no name other than Creator and was highly respected and sometimes was called upon in prayer.

Indians did not make images of the spirits or highly regarded beings who gave them food and water. I find it hard to believe that their spiritual world was an authentic religion. The spirits offered to protect and provide for the Indians. The dead went to a spiritual world of the deceased, where they looked down on their loved ones and tried to protect them from any approaching evil.

The Christians saw the Indians as bundling all the gifts of the spirits and Creator and attributing them to the god figure whom they respected, worshipped, and glorified. Both groups recognized man's humble nature and the need for something mightier than they were. I feel that contemporary Indians looking for a heritage religion have added to their findings features borrowed from Christianity. I have been told that Indian languages do not include profanity. They do not blaspheme any of their revered beings.

A nursing station was one of the first government community institutions established. At first, medical and dental services were only available in the summer. The transition to the white man's medicines seems to have happened rapidly. The nurses were compassionate people and well liked. They were required to perform many things that city hospitals consider only as being among a doctor's duties. The nurse had to be able to assess the situation to determine whether the patient should be flown to a hospital, whether a doctor should fly into the bush, whether the family would be able to care for the condition, or whether the problem was within the nurse's sphere of medical care.

One of the early nurses was Noella Roussell, a small but energetic woman who seemed to enjoy her northern assignment as director of Mistassini's nursing station. She was a dedicated nurse with an outpouring of sincere warmth to her patients. Everyone loved her there. In winter the village was compact, but it greatly expanded in the summer when the various bands came in to trade. Each band had its own camping area. In the summer Noella drove a tractor to visit her patients. She was remembered best for her winter exploits with her dog team that she managed very well. Later a skidoo for winter travel replaced her dog team.

Evadney Gunner was a young woman who was an early village leader by 1964 and recognized the important work that Noella was doing at Mistassini. About twenty years later, Evadney became very sick and was sent to a Montreal hospital. She thought that she recognized a small, familiar figure rushing about the hospital wards. Then she was sure that she recognized the voice of her old friend Noella, who also recognized Evadney. It was a marvelous reunion for both. The knowledge that Noella was Evadney's nurse in this bewildering, large hospital lifted Evadney's spirits and surely helped her recover much faster. Germ diseases, whether viral or bacterial, were not a common problem in the bush. Germs do not like the cold weather; they prefer to live and multiply in warmer, moist conditions. There are few visitors who might carry germs to the camps, especially in winter. Broken bones, severe lacerations from an ax or knife, birthing difficulties for both mother and child, burns, and pulmonary problems were among the common complaints.

There was a tenuous communication system between camps and nursing station. If a problem occurred in a camp, they told the symptoms to a teenager who would run or snowshoe as quickly as possible to the nursing station, if it were within close range. The camps that were farther

EVADNEY GUNNER WITH A WELL-TANNED MOOSE SKIN

away depended on a runner going to a neighboring camp where another runner would be readied to take the message to the nursing station. There might be several runners involved before one reached the nursing station. The nurse would then decide if they just needed medicine and give written directions for the runner who would then retrace his steps. The nurse decided her options: to hitch up her dog team and take her medicine bag to assess the situation first hand, or to turn the situation over to a doctor who would need to fly in, or to have the patient flown out to a hospital. When the small battery-operated tape recorder became popular, the pertinent information was taped and sent to the nurse; then the nurse knew that she was receiving the message directly from the scene. Later they established a two-way radio system that was very efficient. Hospitals or doctors could be reached immediately and could fly to the patient in a short time, if necessary.

It was difficult for many Indians to adjust to the white man's pill system that typically limits the number of pills for each dose and the number of doses per day. Indian medicines were given liberally under the hypothesis that the more one took, the quicker one would be cured. Although the nurses firmly stated the instructions, there was always someone who returned, due to an overdose of pills. I had found that the New Brunswick provincial nurses had the same problem with maritime Indians in the 1950s. Indian doctors agreed that their own medicines were better because there was no limit to what a patient could take. The more the patient took, the quicker he would be cured. It was difficult for the Indian patient to understand that serious problems could result from pill overdosing.

By 1972 the tremendous improvements in health service at Mistassini could be measured by the sudden increase in population. Large plastic bags, pink or blue, were used for layette gift bags given to new mothers. Some mothers preferred the traditional ways and would not accept the gifts.

Juvenile respiratory ailments were still very common, traditionally the biggest cause of juvenile deaths. One August day in 1972, I saw two people come in from Lake Albanel, each carrying a baby who suffered from a respiratory ailment. There were three other Cree babies in the hospital with pneumonia. Now the total was five. All these babies had a good chance of being cured, whereas a few years before all would have most likely died. The birth rate was increasing, and the death rate for all age groups was decreasing, resulting in an increase in a population explosion. In 1972 Rev. Tom DeHoop of the Mistassini Mission gave me the following statistics: seventy births; only three deaths, of which two were babies. The increase in population resulted from an improved nursing station and the new road to Chibougamau providing a quick, direct drive to the hospital.

The Cree, like other Indians, have a marvelous sense of humor. There is much happy-spirited, supportive humor; derisive humor is almost unknown. All is done to give support to those having difficulty with work assigned to them. Indian societies were not competitive. Each individual was encouraged to do his best. No one would publicly show that he could outdo the chief. That would be severe disrespect to the chief. Happy laughter is the best ingredient for a successful camp. When people come together, a key element is humor that often sounds like the hearty laughter of a group of people who are attempting to top one another's stories. That is exactly what is happening. Almost every camp has one who is exceedingly creative in concocting tall tales and enjoys challenging another when an occasion occurs. Humor is most important for the pleasant health of the camp community throughout the long winters. No one laughs at or criticizes a poor job, since everyone does his best. Everyone receives support from all the others in the camp. Children had been attending school long enough that by 1971 some high school graduates returned to the village. Indian Affairs was slow to establish their offices in the new village. There were few employment opportunities available for high school graduates. But there was always a need for children in their early teens to help in the winter bush camps. Those were the training years for future hunters in the traditional lifestyle. Parents selected certain children to accompany them to the winter camps, while they sent others to school.

The school children were introduced to quite a different world, one where electricity seemed to be king. School meals offered varied menus and an introduction to unfamiliar vegetables. In the bush all meals were primarily meat or fish with fried bread known as "bannock." Often students returning to the bush camps found hunters' fare was a difficult adjustment to make. The aromas of wild meat and smoked leather that permeated everything in the camp were quite different from anything at school, as was arising on a –40°C morning and running to the outhouse. A large variety of taped music was replacing traditional Cree music and stories. There were no stores to run to for junk food or some of the top-ten musical tapes and no electricity in the bush. The long hours of darkness did not help. Some did not know how to react to this strange, seemingly incompatible life, for which school did not prepare them. Soon, some just wanted to remain in bed. They felt incapable of performing properly, lost faith in themselves, and usually were considered to be mentally ill, uncommon conditions for young people brought up in the bush. Adults had full work schedules, making it impossible for them to spend much time with the indisposed youth. If there were relatives in the village, they might arrange to take them. For some it meant a trip to a Montreal hospital.

In former times there was a mental illness known as the "windigo malady," described as a form of "famine cannibalism" when one's heart apparently became a chunk of ice. It was often a man's malady. If not curtailed, it was believed that the person afflicted with windigo malady resorted to killing and eating other Indians, usually in a neighboring camp. The illness was known in various forms in northern regions from coast to coast and occurred near the end of winter. In Maine and the Maritimes it was prevalent in the maple syrup camps; in the north the windigo came to the spring goose camp, or just before the move to it. The geese returned in early spring and were the only food available for several weeks while snow and ice melted. Indians moved to places known for the migratory waterfowl. People looked forward to seeing friends they had not seen since the previous summer. Some anthropologists conclude that the malady was caused by food deficiencies suffered near the end of the long winter.

The Cree treated mental problems such as this in a way almost entirely opposite from the methods performed in the hospital. The traditional care for a mental breakdown was for a friend to sit close to the patient and clasp his warm hands over the patient's hands, but say nothing, thus emitting a feeling of total understanding and sympathy through nonverbal communication. It was a quiet session supporting the afflicted one, so that he was assured that someone cared about him. It was a calming and bolstering treatment.

The Mistassini nurses were not trained in this area of medicine. Their recourse was to send the patient to the hospital in Chibougamau. The patient was placed with others who were of entirely different background, way of life, and first language. He was encouraged to tell the group his problems, so the group might help him solve them. It would be very unusual for another in such a group setting to relate to the Indian's problems. It was a cold response for the Indian. This type of therapy emphasizes language. The Cree are not as dependent on language as the Western world is; the Cree have much difficulty in responding to this type of therapy. This treatment is more likely to deepen a Cree's psychosis than to cure it. The result was that when the patient's condition became worse, they sent him to a large, Montreal hospital. Even when one made every effort to go along with the procedure, it was difficult for the Indian patient to react in the expected way with the intended results. Usually the Indian regressed further in the unfamiliar atmosphere. Some psychiatrists began to recognize that the poor results with Indian patients were a cultural problem of which the profession had limited knowledge. The cultural psychiatrist Wolfgang Jilek concluded, "When I started to treat Indian patients, I soon became painfully aware that my therapeutic armament of Western psychiatry was insufficient equipment to meet the needs of the Indian clientele."[1]

The hunters residing in the bush changed little, while the villagers adapted to many changes in several decades.

# XV

# GLEN SPEERS AND THE
# ROLE OF THE HUDSON'S BAY COMPANY

Glen Speers could be considered the king, or at least the squire of
Mistassini. Hudson's Bay Company assigned him to the James Bay area
in 1944. He matured with it as the Hudson's Bay Company changed to
meet the modifications demanded by the business world. His immediate
position before being assigned to Mistassini was at Fort George on James
Bay. A typical loner, he found his place in the company. Until 1965 he
was well protected from direct contacts with most of the white man's
world. I do not believe anyone was really well acquainted with him or
knew anything about his boyhood. While still in his teens and living in
British Columbia, he applied to the Hudson's Bay Company for a job.
He never mentioned having any relatives, not even parents or siblings.
He was friendly to everyone, whether they were his business associates
or customers.

J. W. Anderson, a fellow James Bay fur trader wrote:

> It is my opinion that there is an optimum period in the
> relationship of any primitive people in their dealings with the
> white man. This might be described as the period of time when the
> aborigines have sufficient of the white man's material civilization
> to ease the burden of life, but yet not enough to disrupt their way
> of life.[1]

This hypothesis was probably the key to Glen Speers' successful fur
trading operation at Mistassini. Glen tried to create a balance between
gain for the company and an improvement in the standard of living for

the hunters and trappers. He stocked his store with improved goods that would also make his clientele's work easier and more efficient. The expected result of this policy was more furs for the company.

In 1970 Glen was probably one of a kind. As manager of his trading post, he had the powers of a ship captain. He offered the highest prices that he could for furs. In his later years, when souvenir-hunting visitors were looking for Indian handicrafts, he gave Indians good prices for their craftwork and then made a respectable profit at the store. He made good judgments regarding the products that Indians would buy and priced them fairly to the Indians. His fine reputation with the Mistassini Cree became known to neighboring bands, but he discouraged them from doing business with him, because Glen's supplies were not unlimited, and they were for the Indians at his post. This was made plain to me once when Indians thought that I had purchased too much there. A bush person might go without for my excessive purchases. Mistassini people often went to him when they had problems or needed information. Glen also had a fine reputation for sewing. If anyone suffered a bad laceration, Glen often stitched up the wound.

Glen was probably the last Hudson's Bay Company manager applying the old company rules to his staff until he retired in 1980. The young men sent to his trading post were forbidden to fraternize with the Mistassini girls. No non-Indian girls were there for them to date. If one attempted to outfox Glen and date an Indian girl, he was never suc-

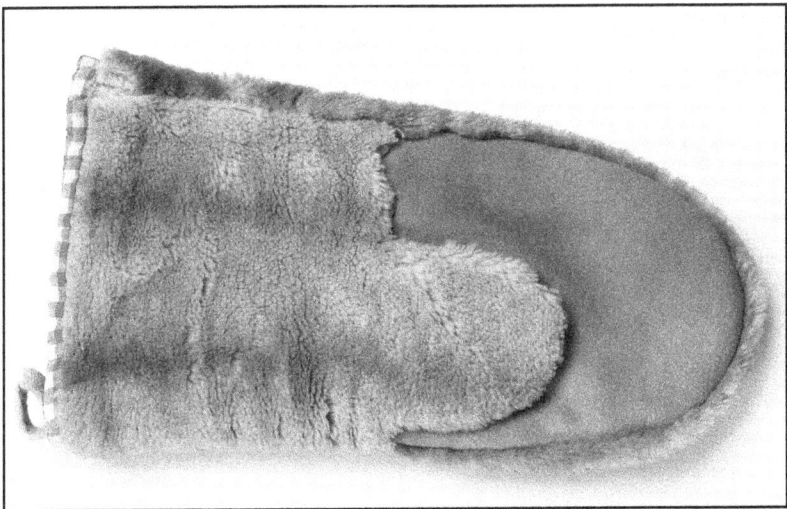

HANDMADE MITTEN

WORKING WITH BEADS

cessful. Glen always learned about it and the employee was punished. Young employees dreaded the assignment to Speers' kingdom. Glen provided the young clerks with rooms in his house. He had the latest available Hudson's Bay TV and radios set up in his living room. Although English-speaking radio stations were available in Mistassini, only French television channels were available. TV signals, having no obstructions, came through very strongly down the lake, providing excellent video. On *Hockey Night in Canada*, the French TV picture version was presented in Glen's living room, while a radio station in English provided the commentary. Glen's house was a popular place for the few English-speaking people to meet for *Hockey Night in Canada* on winter evenings. Mistassini's English-speaking men spent many winter evenings watching hockey. Glen required his staff to ask permission to come into his parlor. He had a demerit discipline system for the staff, which deprived them from parlor use or gave them unpleasant duties. Although they received excellent training for the fur trade, the young men dreaded Glen's old-fashioned disciplinary system.

Glen kept his store open Tuesday through Saturday, closing Sunday and Monday. He maintained Eastern Standard Time all year round. His hobby was filming bird life with a 16 mm movie camera. On his weekends he went to his bush camp located in an ideal spot for making his bird movies, which he sold.

When miners and prospectors began coming in, he outfitted them. One miner gave him two beagles. Some wondered if they would survive the cold. The low temperatures were not a problem for the beagles. They were quite a contrast to the large Indian sled dogs. He trained one beagle to find gold, the other copper. He was well aware that there were rich mineral deposits in the huge Mistassini Territory. Gold nuggets were found in several rivers, but no one had located the source.

Glen had little knowledge of mechanical problems that occur in the various motorized devices that are common in our society, such as canoe motors or cars. He never applied for a license or attempted to drive a car, but was impressed by how such modern innovations could make life easier for Indians. Speers was credited with bringing the skidoos to Mistassini. ("Skidoo" is the term used at Mistassini for snowmobiles.

FINISHED PRODUCT

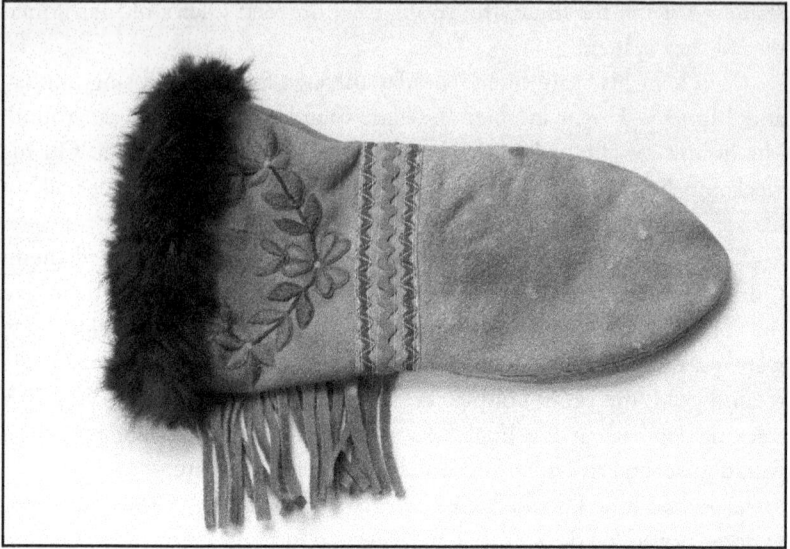

BEAUTIFULLY DECORATED MOOSEHIDE MITTEN

Mistassini Cree defined snowmobile as an enclosed vehicle provided with tracks or skis instead of wheels.) His speech was often difficult to understand, since it was nineteenth-century fur-trading lingo.

Glen hired a teenage Mistassini girl to do the household chores for him, such as cooking, dishwashing, housecleaning, and washing laundry. They became very good friends. Her father hoped that Glen would marry his daughter. The girl became a young woman. Since there were no signs of marriage, the girl's father made preparations for his daughter to marry one of her own people. It seemed to be a case of following company rules, prohibiting fraternization. He wished to honor the company regulations. In many situations the company encouraged its traders to marry Indian girls, believing that it made a stronger company tie to the fur sources. Glen realized too late that he had lost his opportunity to marry his former housekeeper; he remained a bachelor.

Trappers spent the long summer evenings at the post with Speers and Chief Petawabano, making their plans for their winter trapping. Both Glen and Chief Petawabano had a record of all the camps, where they would be, the names of all the members of their camps, and when they would be expected to move to a new camping area.

Glen enjoyed his annual "fling" attending the fur auctions at Montreal. Buyers from all over the world participated in the auctions. Mistassini furs were always among the finest offered. Russian buyers always bid on them. When Glen was away, the company employees welcomed the opportunity to relax a bit, but everything was shipshape again before he returned.

Glen also could see how using airplanes rather than the usual dog teams would enable him to complete his scheduled winter bush visits more efficiently. Bush pilots and their planes were hired from Seven Islands and other places from which summer fishermen were flown into the bush. Those pilots had little or no business in the winter and welcomed an opportunity for winter flying. The biggest problem was that the plane radios were set to contact their summer air bases; Mistassini was far beyond their range. When the planes were flying in Mistassini, the pilots were unable to use their radios. Glen studied all the safety requirements for winter bush flying. A pilot flew him into each camp twice during the winter months of January through March to collect furs and drop off food supplies, such as flour, sugar, tea, and lard. During a typical winter he flew nine to ten thousand miles. In 1980 he had fifteen years of flying that add up to many miles of winter flying in an area noted for its dreadful weather. He admitted that he had had some tight scrapes, but "one gets used to them!" He knew that he would be in for a rough time if a plane were forced down in winter.

Before my first flight, he warned me that if the plane is forced down, one has only twenty minutes to start a fire. If you do not have a fire within twenty minutes, there is no sense wasting your energy trying to start a fire. You will not survive. You need a good pair of snowshoes to travel in the chest-high soft snow, as well as an ax, food, warm sleeping bag, and a good supply of matches. Do not rely on those Boy Scout one-match fires here! Glen had survived two crashes when he gave me this advice.

About a year later, his plane was forced down again. About 1965 when they were leaving one of the camps, a cable attached to the right ski snapped and wound around the wing, locking the flaps in place, so that they would not operate. They were airborne. In order to use up fuel, the pilot decided to go on to Nichikun. The ski was flapping. Glen opened his window. The outside wind-chill temperature blowing into the cabin was at least −50°F. He tried to grab the ski and unwrap the cable from the wing, but he could not. He was probably fortunate that he was not able to catch hold of the ski. It could have pulled him right out of the plane.

As they approached Nichikun, they prepared for a crash landing in the snow. Glen grabbed some skins from the back of the plane and placed them in the front for padding for both the pilot and himself. The pilot had the stick to hold on to and brace himself. Glen braced himself against the skins. When the plane landed, the strut from the dislodged ski broke through the fuselage, preventing the plane from flipping over. The pilot checked to see that Glen was able to get out and then jumped out, expecting the trader to do likewise. The pilot took precautions, getting away from the plane in case it burst into flames. When he did not see Glen, he went back to find out why he had not jumped out. With no thought of danger, Glen was throwing out the pelts from the wrecked plane. Company first! Finally the pilot convinced Glen that he should leave the plane until they were assured that it would not burst into flames. When the plane did not return to Mistassini, everyone was greatly concerned. The following day a fellow bush pilot who knew Glen's flight schedule went to look for him with a spotter. They found him and his pilot, both safe at Nichikun. Glen and his pilot returned safely to Mistassini after their night out in the bush.

Several years later a very bad stretch of weather prohibited flying. Glen's bunkhouse was full. Two pilots were bunked at the Anglican rectory. Glen was behind on his visits and anxious to catch up with his schedule. The temperatures were borderline for flying. He wanted to get on with the trading in spite of the unpredictable weather. All the pilots were flying. Glen and Kershaw, his pilot, left early for a full day of bush camp visits. Kershaw hoped to return early, so he could go to Chibougamau to celebrate his fortieth birthday that evening. Glen had a reputation of taking all the proper safety steps and sometimes remained overnight at an Indian camp. No one was really alarmed when the plane did not return. He always left a record of the camps that he was going to visit. This time no one could find his schedule, nor had he told anyone which camps he was visiting. It was probably the first time that Glen broke his own rules. When they didn't return the second day, Kershaw's companion took a spotter to search for them on the third day. They returned without sighting the downed plane. No one wanted to call the RCAF spotting team unnecessarily, but the next day everyone agreed it was a legitimate request. The RCAF had faster planes with a much longer range and professional spotters, so that they had a much better chance of finding downed aircraft. It was located on a lake near a camp. Glen and Kershaw were lucky that the incident had occurred on a lake where Indians were camping. They were safe, enjoying life at a hunters' camp, although Glen was becoming upset that he was missing good flying weather and was unable to maintain his schedule. Due to the extreme temperatures, an engine oil seal had cracked, causing the oil to leak. The men were returned to Mistassini, but the plane had to remain on the frozen lake until mechanics could fly in and replace the faulty oil seal.

Glen built two small posts in the north, one at the old Nemiskau post and the other at the old Caniapiscau post, each about 250 miles away from Mistassini. He flew all the building materials and supplies in for both posts. The Indians of those areas could help themselves to what they needed and leave a record of what they took. They were on the honor system. This saved Glen much time and money. It was also a great convenience for the hunters in those areas. The Indians never cheated, but hungry bears broke into the stores for food several times. Once a bear broke in, ate about a hundred pounds of sugar, piled up the empty bags in a corner and went to sleep on them. Before ambling away, the bear finished eight pounds of lard and some flour. His tracks remained on the flour-coated floor.

As 1980 approached, Glen began to prepare for retirement. At first, this new phase of his life appeared to be a long way off, not an immediate reality. Then there were doubts about severing his relationship with the Hudson's Bay Company. HBC built a modern department store in the new Mistassini village area, away from the shore of the lake. The waterfront was no longer the central point of activity. Glen's office was above the main business floor, where he could oversee his kingdom. One day he proudly showed me his new telephone system. He could talk to any department without leaving his desk! The new system included his own line unhindered by those of the other departments. The electronic age had arrived at Mistassini, at least for government buildings, schools, and the Hudson's Bay Company! A young businessman who knew about business but little about furs was sent in as Glen's assistant. As one can imagine, friction grew between the veteran fur trader and the young merchant. Their special areas of knowledge were miles apart. Although Mistassini had not changed, the world had. Animal lovers all over the globe were declaring that wearing furs was no longer stylish. It was time to be kind to animals; trapping was a brutal act. The James Bay Hydro Project was already disrupting the Mistassini hunting territory system that Glen had helped shape. Seeing his world dissolve was difficult for Glen, a common feeling for people who are so involved in their small entities that they fail to take a realistic view of the situation around them.

Glen's fur-trading post was a well-organized and well-planned business enterprise. He cared for the Mistassini people but never showed favoritism to Indians or whites. His life was the fur trade. I asked Glen what he would do when he retired. His dream was to go to the Arctic to film birds, "That's where the birds are, you know!" He retired and returned to British Columbia. He found it difficult to adjust to life where he was now a stranger and no longer in charge. Life there must have left him bored and restless; he had always been an active, hard worker. Finding people who shared his interests would have been difficult for him. His retirement was short; he was soon working again for the Hudson's Bay Company, this time in the Arctic. News of Glen was very fragmentary. Little was known about his final days. Adjustment to HBC in the Arctic must also have been a challenge for him. We learned that he died, but nothing about the circumstances or even where he was when death overtook him. His death marked the end of a chapter of the great days of the Hudson's Bay Company in the fur trade at Mistassini. For me Glen Speers represented the finest of those who devoted their lives to the lonely Northland. The Mistassini Cree were lucky to have had him as their fourth Hudson's Bay trader.

# XVI

# THE SPRING GOOSE HUNT

Spring arrives late at Mistassini. My observations were made between 1970 and 1985. Global warming may have changed the timing of spring a bit now. Usually the snow began to melt, forming pools of water by mid May. The high sun and dry air melted snow quickly. River and lake ice took on a darker shade from the warmth of the sun and the lengthening days. Winter is considered the open season in the North, as one can go almost anywhere with snowshoes, dog team, or skidoo. As the days get longer, sunlight transforms the crust on the snow into a fragile shield that easily crumbles under the hunter's weight, dropping him through several feet of snow to the ground level. The Mistassini spread spruce boughs on the regular paths in the camps, a method like snowshoes that permits one to walk on the surface without sinking into the snow.

River and lake ice also become a thin, fragile sheet, wearing away from the warmth of the sun and friction of the flowing water. These conditions are extremely dangerous for travel. Hunters procure sufficient food to last several weeks before packing up and leaving the last of the winter camps for the spring goose camp. They travel on the snow while conditions are good and set up their goose camp before the spring melting begins. The hunters usually plan their trip to include a stop at one or more brooks where whitefish or other species will be running during their early spawning season. The spring fish will be a welcome addition to the menu. In former times, the threat of death from starvation was very real to the northern Indians. According to personal histories and parish records, starvation occurred most frequently in the early spring, when breakup restricted and immobilized hunting groups for three to four weeks.

The coming together of friends, combined with the coming of spring and summer seasons, offering new opportunities was a happy time. Spring Goose Hunt is still considered a national Cree holiday with a school vacation period allowing all the children to join their families in the goose camps. Every six-year-old can imitate the honking of a goose. During the several weeks of spring breakup when traveling was impossible, the Indians learned to depend on the miracle of the migratory waterfowl for food. Hunting usually took place early in the morning or shortly before dusk. A special thanksgiving ceremony honored the first geese killed. Everyone shared some of the fowl. Although the Waswanipi, Chibougamau, and Mistassini Cree are not on major migratory routes, usually enough birds are killed to meet the food requirements of these people.

Long ago Mistassini Cree devised a method for cooking geese, probably known to all northern Indians. A string is tied to the neck of a goose. When the goose is hung beside the stove to roast, the goose revolves clockwise and then counterclockwise as the string winds and then unwinds. The goose receives heat evenly and cooks uniformly. Dripping fat collects in a pan placed below the hanging goose. They store the feathers in bags and use them for stuffing pillows or lining winter clothing.

The people enjoyed removing layers of clothing in the spring warmth. Spring was also a time to carve new canoe paddles and check to see that canoes left on racks during the winter had not been damaged from winter storms. When the ice cleared from lakes and rivers, the Mistassini Cree prepared for open-water travel. The Mistassini village is deserted. HBC personnel take inventory, just as is done annually at stores everywhere.

Schools were operating in the village in 1970. The Cree decided to permit the teachers to learn first-hand about the hunt. It was a reverse type of educational program, given to thank the teachers. During the national Cree holiday vacation, a special camp was set up for the schoolteachers, but not one came. The Mistassini people were disappointed, not understanding why the teachers had not accepted their invitation to their special camp. Actually the teachers were just as enthusiastic to vacation for several weeks in their towns and with their own families as the Cree were to go to the spring goose hunt. When the Cree understood this, other means were found to thank the teachers.

Information concerning decoys and blinds is scarce and incomplete. Very few researchers have ever seen or experienced the Mistassini Cree spring goose hunt. Since few people other than the Indians have observed the hunt, very little has been published about it. In fact, some

Mistassini people said that I was the first person not officially connected with the village to visit a spring goose camp.

The camps are far enough from the actual shooting sites so that camp activity does not spook the birds. In the mid 1980s, some men built a large, sophisticated, wooden-roofed blind, fully protected from wind, snow, and rain, on the shore of the Mistassini village. Many rubber-plastic decoys were placed within easy shooting range of the blind to draw the geese within range. Before daylight, the men settled quietly in the blind, so they would not disturb the early bird activity. A young anthropologist Edward Rogers arranged, with the help of the Hudson's Bay Company manager Wilfrid Jefferys, for Ed and his new bride Jean to honeymoon during the winter of 1953–54. The honeymoon spot, Alfie Matush's winter camp, near the Temiscamie River that flows into Lake Albanel, was indeed an isolated family camp. Ed's tent was given a spot in Alfie's campsite. Ed was the first anthropologist to make a meticulous study of the Mistassini Cree. Apparently Rogers was the only person to publish descriptions of Mistassini duck blinds. His observations were limited to the Matush winter camp. Hunters constructed a framework that supported spruce boughs stuck and woven into it. They could hide and shoot from behind it. In the fall, they made a framework for woven spruce boughs placed in canoes, providing a camouflaged floating shooting platform for hunting waterfowl. I found camps in 1970 still using this style blind.

Hunters lured waterfowl by decoys. Then, when seeing geese, hunters would call the birds in by imitating their call. Rogers describes decoys made from bundles of small alder and willow twigs by forming them and tying them together,[1] similar to those that were popular on James Bay. In 1970 young people made decoys faster from spruce logs about a foot long and attached a head painted with the proper colors. An older hunter had a more elaborate, carved wooden duck partly painted, partly covered with a tattered remnant of cloth from worn-out clothing to decorate the decoy head. Now the rubberized, inflatable decoys of little weight and bulk purchased at the Hudson's Bay store were the preferred decoys. Waterfowl migration begins when greens appear through the diminishing snow cover, usually beside open fringes of lakes and rivers. The hunters are expert callers and can persuade a bird in flight to change course and return, coming within easy range of their guns.

International migratory duck laws permit native people to hunt waterfowl during the spring migration. The bird kills during the spring migration are low but very necessary for food for the Indians. Emmett

McLeod, the son of a fur trader, went to Moose Factory during the depression, and the HBC hired him. Soon after learning about the beaver conservation project on James Bay, the Hudson's Bay Company transferred him to the post at Mistassini. Later he married a Mistassini girl and became an independent trader. He instituted a similar conservation program at Mistassini in which the Indians kept records of all animals and birds that they killed. The statistics had been kept for twenty years. The annual total of ducks and geese killed by a hunting family ranged from twelve to forty, enough to supply the people's needs but not to noticeably reduce the flocks of migrating birds. For the two- to three-week period, the kill averages were less than two birds a day, certainly not enough to cause much excitement from an observer's point of view. The most common ducks killed are black, wood, American mergansers, and scoter. Glen Speers, the manager of the Hudson's Bay Company at Mistassini, added mallards to the list and said that black ducks and mallards had the same name in Cree. The Rev. John Gull confirmed that the Waswanipi also used the same word for black ducks and mallards. The common geese killed are the Canada and brant. Only an occasional snow goose was shot. The upper mandibles of all waterfowl killed are strung on the heavy brown twine or rabbit-snare wire available in every camp and hung on a branch in respect for the bird killed.

After the spring goose hunt, the Mistassini people had a thanksgiving ceremony in gratitude for the successful winter harvest of food and furs. They usually held this ceremony when most of the people returned to the village. It was a convivial and festive atmosphere for the reunited people. The fur traders must have enhanced the Native celebration.[2] "The best parts of the game animals, particularly the grease therefrom, were saved up during the winter for the spring feast."[3] It appears that the spring feast was sometimes combined with the Thanksgiving feast usually held in the spring after the goose hunt.[4] Now the village Anglican Church celebrates Thanksgiving at this time; a rogation service asking God for a generous harvest is held in the fall, before the hunters go into the bush.

The typical Mistassini hunter carries his gun in a leather case that his wife or mother made of moose hide and attractively decorated with colored material. He has a moose-hide or canvas backpack that is usually decorated with brightly colored threads sewn into floral patterns, or colored material similar to the decorations on the gun case. The birds will go into his pack. Slung over his shoulder is a small, oval, decorated moose-hide ammunition pouch. The patterns are spiritual representations shown to women in their dreams as good luck symbols. These patterns are applied as decorations on hunting equipment, such as backpacks, gun cases, and ammunition pouches. Hunters need all the good-luck help that is available.

James Bay Cree live in the heart of an area heavily populated by waterfowl. They once crafted their traditional decoys from bundles of willow twigs woven with two stubby legs inserted into the bundles. This craft has almost become a lost art known only by a few, to sell the decoys to summer tourists. Bay hunters had found that going into much detail for decoys is not necessary. They simply cut short pieces of a log about a foot long, attached a head, and placed the decoys in the snow along the shore. Today most of the younger men buy the rubber-plastic inflatable decoys. Their blinds are made by building up walls of snow, leaving an opening at one end. A thick layer of spruce boughs covers the floor for insulation. Willow and spruce boughs from the surrounding trees are stuck in the snow around the blind to help it blend with the environment and hide the occupant. The hunter sits and waits for birds to fly within sight, and then he calls them within shooting range.

May 7, 1973, was a nice spring day in Mistassini. The temperature rose to a high of 54°F. The scoter were beginning to return. Fish were beginning to enter the smaller streams. There were 46 goose camps that year. Twenty hunting families had not returned. I accompanied Father Blaber to five goose camps for a short service and to check on the people after their long winter in the bush. There was a great variety in the camp setups. The George Matush camp was probably the largest, composed of nearly sixty people. It was a tremendous family gathering, a time to catch up on family matters. George Matush had a very good camp. Plywood sheets were set up on the inside of the canvas, adding a bit of stability and insulation. There was a propane stove as well as a barrel stove inside the tent. George had a comfortable store chair from which he presided over his large extended family. There was a storm front farther south, so there was very little bird activity. Geese will not fly through a cold front.

The smallest camp was a double tent. Mrs. Edwards and a son resided in one section; Ronnie Loon and his family were in the other. One camp consisted of all young people, either school students or recent graduates. It was a well-organized camp. The young people were often teased by the elders that they no longer knew the rudiments of hunting. These high-spirited young people were out to prove otherwise. I expect that they did.

We stopped at Temiscamie River a hundred miles north of Chibougamau at the Tom Coon camp. Tom was a fishing guide at the government View du Poste Camp. There was a sick girl in the camp who was a big concern to them. They were glad to see their minister. While Father Blaber was evaluating her condition, young Tom, about twenty years old, told me that when he was small he missed his dad so much when he was away hunting and checking his traps nearly every day. He would ask his dad when he would return. His father drew a circle in the snow and stuck a small stick in the middle that cast its shadow on the circle. Then Tom's father marked another spot on the circle and said that when the shadow reached that point he would be home. The impatient boy made frequent trips looking at the shadow, so that he would know when to run down the trail a short distance to wait for him.

One of the tents had a large bathroom plunger tied to the crosstrees. I could hardly restrain myself from laughing because camps had no running water and the streams and rivers were just beginning to open. I was told that it was the school janitor's camp. The plunger was his most useful possession, here a humorous symbol.

The younger children in all the camps enjoyed using their slingshots to shoot at stones, knocking them off larger ones. They were all very good shots. The spring goose camps provided a happy interlude marking the change of seasons from winter to spring, and the time spent at the camps was enjoyed by everyone.

# XVII

# CHANGING PATTERNS OF LIFE
# 1970 TO 1985

During visits between 1970 and 1985, I could easily see the many changes that were taking place at Mistassini each year. At the time of my early visits (1970), most travelers came to the village by water. The settlement was a small gap in the virgin wilderness, bounded by water on two sides. The general landscape changed as the James Bay Hydroelectric Project developed. On my first visit, the prominent structures were the Hudson's Bay Company buildings by the lake (the store, warehouse, and manager's house), the Anglican church and rectory, about ten small log cabins, and the independent trader Emmett McLeod's buildings on McLeod Point. Soon there were annual improved housing projects. Streetlights would compete with the bright stars, moon, and northern lights. The program to electrify government buildings and the school included the impressive old log church, St. John the Evangelist. No plan provided for electricity to Indian housing. There were several tribal office buildings in the designated village area that were still to be developed. In 1970 old tent rings could be easily identified near the Hudson's Bay Company and the church buildings. In the new village plan, both Hudson's Bay Company buildings and the church had to move to land stipulated for them to be far away from the projected flooding level that the James Bay Hydroelectric Project would create.

Dogs roamed freely during the summer, but in the middle of August hunters began catching and chaining their winter work animals. Thus their owners were assured of their presence when the families were ready to move to winter quarters. While chained, the dogs howled at all hours, often keeping us awake. A party preparing to leave for their winter hunting camp had five canoes tied one behind the other. Some were for people, some for a mix of baggage, dogs, and people, and others just for baggage and dogs. Winter hunting camps had an average of three families. Hunting families arose very early. Most were on their way by 4 a.m. In the summer, the sun was well above the horizon by 4 a.m. Indians usually arose before the sun; the old-time fur brigade paddlers were canoeing by 4 a.m. before the wind rose. They stopped about 9 a.m. for a hearty breakfast and then continued on their way.

Mistassini was the end of the road, the jumping-off place to wilderness adventure. McGill University sponsored a Mistassini Anthropological Project. It was a busy place. The traders were busy, the McGill anthropology students were busy, prospectors and miners were sometimes present. The people were hunting and fishing for their daily food. Visiting students were showing much interest in the Cree. McGill professors assigned students to make various specific studies of Native people. The Mistassini Cree proudly cooperated with them. Generally the people felt that they were now important in the eyes of the strangers. It was a great opportunity for young anthropologists to study this group who had retained their lifestyle with so little change and remained almost unknown to the outside world. These studies provided a chance for lasting friendships to form between anthropologists and Indians. Unfortunately most students saw their Mistassini projects as only a necessary step toward their diploma and their informants as the source of required information, not as potential lasting friends.

The informants' position was that the student received a diploma, what the Indians called a "union card," ensuring the student of a good-paying job, while the Indians received nothing. The students sometimes doubted the accuracy of the informants' material, but they were always reassured that the information was valid, whether in reality it was or not. Parts of the sessions were frequently followed by lots of laughter, sounding as if each informant were trying to top his predecessor's story.

The older children home from school did not always look forward to spending their vacation in the bush with their families. One had to give up so many niceties to return to the basics with their families. It was a far different life from what they had become accustomed to at school in La Tuque. Some teenagers opted to remain in the Mistassini village with relatives. Others lost their bonding to their parents, feeling that they had been betrayed by them when they were sent to school. In the evenings, Adrian Tanner, a University of Toronto graduate student in anthropology, usually had a following of teenage boys at his cabin, enjoying Adrian's musical tapes, conversation, and food.

In the casual Mistassini way of life, it was not unusual for the vacationing children to feel bored with the limitations of the Mistassini village. One summer day, three twelve-year-old girls decided to visit school friends in Senneterre, about 250 miles to the south, where there were activities like those at school. They hitchhiked but never arrived at their destination. For several days the authorities concentrated on the Indians for information regarding the missing schoolgirls. Someone overheard a young, drunk miner in a bar telling a gory story about raping and killing the girls. Police followed through, finding the mutilated bodies in an off-road gravel pit. The Quebec court did not want to convict a white man for such a heinous crime. The case became extremely lengthy and was not solved during my time in the area. The lengthy procedure and denial by the Quebec people did not improve Mistassini-Quebec relations and was not a credit to the province.

Soon after the road came to Mistassini, Sam Gunner became the first Mistassini Cree to buy a vehicle and obtain his driver's license. He received the contract for the daily mail run and the hospital run to Chibougamau. One spring day Sam was driving along the well-known gravel road on a hospital call. Suddenly something stretched out all across the road in front of him. It was not a branch or sapling, because it was moving. He had never seen anything like it. Mystified, he slowed but still ran over it. He looked back in the rearview mirror and watched it writhe away into the bush. There are no snakes native to Mistassini. He wished he could have stopped and raced back to investigate the squirming monster, but he had to get to the hospital. He noted the place along the way, so familiar to him, figuring that anything run over by the four wheels of the heavy van could not be far off the road. He would stop and investigate on his way home. Word soon circulated through the hospital and then all over Chibougamau about the monster snake. Sam stopped on his way home and searched the surrounding area, finding no trace of the creature. The Saint-Félicien Zoo was notified, but no such creature had escaped. No evidence was found that the snake ever really existed. Chibougamau residents could not accept the tale and passed it off as a drunken Indian's imagination. However, most northeastern Indian tribes living on large bodies of water or on the coast have traditional sea-serpent stories that play important roles in their heritage. Could Lake Mistassini have its sea serpent too that might follow schools of migrating fish up small creeks to other lakes?

Annual government housing contracts were another result of the road. Now large construction equipment could easily drive to the village site. Streets were cut through the village as directed by a Quebec City plan. The government habitually approved Indian housing in the federal budget in late summer, but did not take into account the subarctic weather conditions. Jobs were put out to bid in August. The winning contractors were expected to complete their work by the end of the year. Any unused funds at the end of the year were to be returned to the federal government's treasury. Funds were not available to complete an unfinished project in the following spring.

There was no housing for workmen at Mistassini. The closest housing was at Chibougamau sixty miles away. Freezing temperatures and snow begin in September. The workers demanded that their workday include the sixty-mile portal-to-portal trip. Construction did not begin until September or October, when snow had already begun to accumulate. The Indians felt that due to the late start, the men were rushing the jobs. Shoddy work resulted. The Indians doubted that the properties were being properly inspected in the rush to meet the end-of-year deadline. The Indians assumed that since the housing was for them, Indians would produce much superior construction to that of the present builders. I had heard the same complaint made by Maliseet Indians twenty years earlier on New Brunswick's St. John River. The Mistassini decided to establish their own housing company.

The young school group, unprepared for the bush, learned to drive and operate big equipment. They were sure that they could win the bids, because they could eliminate the sixty-mile portal-to-portal daily fee and put the two hours daily travel time of each worker into actual construction time. Much to the consternation of the big-city contractors who were accustomed to being awarded large government contracts, the Indians' low bid won! The Mistassini Cree were building for themselves and did excellent work. This solved the work problem for many young, school graduates looking for employment in Mistassini. They have continued to win housing contracts.

Vehicles were taking their place beside newly built homes. The extended-cab pickup trucks with a full-size box were popular. Then came the all-terrain vehicles, not as toys but as an easier means of penetrating the wilderness.

The James Bay Hydroelectric Project marked the end of the long span of the fur trade as Mistassini's primary economic enterprise. The landscape was changing. Some large areas were to be inundated. Some lake and river areas were to be drained. Hydro-Québec hired Indians to cut lines through the wilderness without telling them why they were cutting the lines. Then Hydro-Québec told them that due to dam construction reservoirs would be on one side of the line. Hunting was banned on the reservoir side of the line. Some hunters who flew long distances to their hunting camps noted that every hunting territory that they flew over appeared to have a line through it, reducing its size and capability to support subsistence hunting for the bush families.

Meanwhile, the Mistassini were impressed by the way Glen Speers used planes for bush camp travel, even when weather was not very good. Paul Petawabano learned to fly and obtained a job with a local bush-flying service for the Mistassini flying venture. He saved his money and soon purchased his own plane and established his own flying service. Mistassini people preferred to fly with one of their own. Air service became more popular for transportation to and from the bush camps. Many tribal members felt that the Mistassini should establish their own flying service rather than pay non-Indians to fly them to their camps. The tribe agreed to send five young men out to take flying lessons. Mistassini Flying Service increased the size of its fleet. When the James Bay power project began, the Indians observed the greater flexibility of helicopters. They sent another five young men out to learn to fly these craft and added helicopters to their fleet. Their flying service was growing. More employees were needed; more young men who lacked bush education but wished to remain at Mistassini could do so.

During the 1970s many people who had never had much actual money found employment that paid for their services with cash or checks. No one had established a bank in Mistassini yet, but Chibougamau had several banks. In 1972 Charlie Brien went to Rev. Ken Blaber and showed him his new checkbook from a Chibougamau bank. He was the first Mistassini resident Indian to open a checking account and deposit his money in a bank. Charlie had opened a restaurant, attracting the ever-increasing number of strangers visiting the village: government employees, teachers, anthropologists, building contractors, drivers for delivery services, sportsmen, and the occasional tourist.

In former times the Indian could rely on fur prices as being fairly stable when he went into the bush, although he was operating on prices that were set for the previous year. In 1974 the fur business passed through some unfortunate changes. New communication systems enabled those at the post to contact other posts regarding fur prices on an almost daily basis. Fur prices fluctuated every day, just as the stock market, the price of the dollar, and the value of gold do. The polar bear population was decreasing. Polar bear skins from the coast brought the best prices and were considered excellent investments.

The fur business was going down. The James Bay Project was breaking up the trapping grounds. The animal-rights groups were convincing people all over the world that trapping was cruel to animals and animal furs should not be worn. Their answer was to replace the natural furs with synthetic fibers. Synthetic fibers fabricated from oil were an environmentally unfriendly alternative. In one day the price per beaver skin dropped from $125 to $100. How does one explain that to the trappers who have no contacts with the outside world? In 1972 the small village of Mistassini lost $50,000, a big loss to their economy. It was very difficult for the Indians to understand that the problem was the world economy, not just the Hudson's Bay Company. Resentment against the furriers ran high at Mistassini, but there was little that they could do. The Mistassini killed their animals quickly and painlessly, nothing like what their opponents described them as doing. It was the beginning of the death of what was once a flourishing market and the Mistassini people's principal source of income.

Glen Speers retired from the Hudson's Bay Company. Furs were no longer the primary business of the company. A new manager was hired to emphasize the services of a store, but he lacked experience with furs. Apparently the new manager studied Glen Speers' system and began making many changes to policies, which upset the Indians. The Cree felt that many new policies favored the Hudson's Bay Company at the expense of the Indian.

An independent fur buyer found his way to Mistassini at the time when many trappers were becoming angry at the Hudson's Bay Company's change in direction. The new dealer paid less for mid-grade furs but more for poor furs than HBC did. The major difference was that Glen credited trappers' accounts and did not charge freight to take goods to the camps when the primary purpose of the flight was to collect furs. However, the competitor paid cash for the furs, shifting the transportation cost of store goods to the trappers. Some Indians thought that they were getting a better deal from the new man. In reality, I thought that the bottom lines from the two competing fur buyers were about equal. Some trappers changed their allegiance to show disapproval of changing policies. Two Mistassini Indian employees of the Hudson's Bay Company decided to start a store in competition with their employer, thinking that many Mistassini residents would prefer to do their business with them. Three or four years later, when government grants to promote new businesses were no longer available for the two Indians who had started the other store, they decided that they lacked proper business experience and were ready to sell the store. The Indians had not stopped buying from the Hudson's Bay Company. Two of the white Hudson's Bay Company clerks decided to buy the Indians' business. The clerks had acquired more business acumen and were able to compete successfully with the Hudson's Bay Company.

One summer an Anglican Church youth group arrived to work on several projects for the village. In prior days, Mistassini trash and garbage were not seen as a problem. Indians wrapped fish, meat, and other items in biodegradable birch bark or similar wrapping. Now almost everything arrived in plastic, tin, or glass containers. No proper disposal site for the waste existed. Members of the youth group created a dump site; barrels were placed at certain areas of the village, where the villagers could drop waste items. A schedule for pickup to the disposal area was devised. This greatly improved the village image. I wondered if waste concentrated in the disposal area would attract bears to the village, but this problem did not materialize as it did in some James Bay work camps. Hunters were glad to be asked to kill the work-camp garbage bears, until they soon discovered that garbage-bear meat tasted quite different from the wild bear meat. Interest in the garbage bears quickly waned.

Traditionally, it appears that the women's routine was regulated by a special chore designated to a specific day. I never learned the full routine. Monday was washday. The fetching of water from the frozen lake, heating it, and washing with a washboard is hard work. However, the village plan developed at Quebec City included a water system pumped from Lake Mistassini to all parts of the village and principal buildings. The pipes were to be set at nine feet below the surface to prevent freezing. A young Indian high school graduate working on the project told the engineer that the pipes should be eleven feet below the surface to be safe from frost. The engineer did not appreciate being corrected by a young Indian and retorted that he had an engineering degree. The pipes were set at the nine-foot level. On a very cold, −70°F, windy, January day, a very distraught nurse suddenly exclaimed that there was no water at the nursing station. The Quebec City engineer's office was contacted. The engineer was sorry, but his busy schedule would not permit him to leave his warm office. He was sure that the Indians could take care of the problem. They did. They dug the pipes up from the frozen ground and re-laid them at a depth of eleven feet. Running water returned to the nursing station. Water stations were established at convenient points in the village for people to obtain their water. The people no longer needed to haul a toboggan with containers to the lake and break through three or four feet of ice for their water. The Mistassini were quick to label these water stations "nipi tipi," or "water building." Friday or Saturday was the day to harvest diaper moss. As young people with small children began to be assigned to Mistassini, Glen Speers added the new disposable diaper styles like Huggies or Pampers. The Indian mothers tried them and most found them much to their liking, quickly adding them to their shopping lists. Store diapers reduced the workload of going into the bush and harvesting the moss diapers. The old moss Indian diaper picked in the woods and then hung on a line to dry began to lose its appeal. It was said that the moss diaper was superior, since the children never suffered from diaper rash when wearing them, as they did occasionally with the store product.

Hunters have noticed changes among the animals as well. When the snowmobiles were first used, the hunters said that caribou would not cross a snowmobile track. But since then, caribou have ranged farther south and have crossed roads. They may have been forced to seek food farther south, as their primary feeding grounds became flooded by the James Bay project. While caribou have moved south, moose have moved north. Older hunters said there were no moose in their area until after the time a series of forest fires had destroyed large tracts and encouraged new growth to the liking of the moose.

Isaac Shecapio was chief, a fine man who looked after his people well and was loved by them. His father and grandfather had held the position of chief. It seemed to this elderly man that his world had suddenly turned upside down. There had been many good years, but now confusion seemed to reign. The only escape was to go into the bush. He, like Waswanipi's Diom Blacksmith, felt that the time had come to turn over the chieftainship to a young person with more understanding of the invading white man's world. For the first time, a generation gap was known at Mistassini. The school children were on an entirely different wavelength from the bush people. Many children had difficulty recalling their language. Due to the lack of trapping experience, many children did not know some of the terms in the hunter's vocabulary.

Some children returned home from school with a drug problem. At first the Indians didn't know how to handle it. Then one of the families encountering the drug problem decided to spend the summer in the bush instead of the village, thus cutting off the drug supply. Others did likewise.

Apparently, the children who had been to school were influenced by consumerism. For any of the schoolchildren and youths who desired to spend a winter in the bush with their family, it meant additional bulk and weight in their winter outfit. The trapper was not one to make an immediate purchase of a new item; he had to convince himself that the new object would be advantageous to him. Elders chided young people about how much easier life now was than it had been. They were a people who were accustomed to following parents' instructions. Progress and change were slower to develop for the inlanders than those in closer touch with white communities. They had to be assured that they would benefit from progress and change.

In the last half of the twentieth century, there was a move to interest more Cree in becoming priests. Too many churches were always without priests. Mistassini leaders interpreted the term "missionary parish" as a demeaning expression. The bishop or one of his committees appointed the missionary without Indian involvement, just as nurses and teachers were selected. The community, at least ninety-five percent Indian, could easily support an Indian clergyman accustomed to their way of life. Convincing young school graduates to become priests was not easy. They felt that they were turning their backs on their Indian heritage by becoming priests of the Anglican Church. Many white clergy of the diocese disagreed among themselves regarding the policy of ordaining Indian priests. Some had the attitude that a priest should have the full training required for priesthood and be willing to serve any church anywhere. I never knew an Indian who wanted to serve in any place except his own village.

The opposition always declared, "But there might be!" The long educational period away from home in a culture foreign to them did not appeal to the Mistassini. There had to be an understanding between both cultures to develop a realistic program in the eyes of the Indians for the ordination of Indian priests. And the program would have to be acceptable to both the candidate and his spouse. I heard many discussions regarding this problem. The need for priests forced the program to be developed.

The Indian is a very spiritual person. His life was controlled by various spirits such as water spirits at falls and rapids, spirits of the forest, spirits to guide the hunter, and spirits of the air. Although they are seldom, if ever, seen, traditional tales describe them. They are not just cardboard images. Spirits often make themselves known to hunters by certain actions, or one might see the results of their work. The spirits are watching, although they remain unseen.

Children, when very young, learn how to deal with the spirits to prevent some of them from harming family members. There is a fear element to most spirits, for they are easily angered if ignored or forgotten. Some are of a demanding nature, requiring tobacco or food. Examples are the water spirits, who demand a gift of tobacco for a safe trip through rapids or for successful fishing. Other spirits are benevolent, guiding a hunter to food, or foretelling of the future.

The hunter must be brave enough to go into a small tent and call upon these spirits who test his courage by shaking the tent up and down and speaking in weird voices. The spirits of the dead are in the magnificent aurora borealis that frequently lights up the winter night sky, and in the Milky Way, and watch over their loved ones below to protect them. A bit of food is cast into the fire. The smoke that rises to the heavens from the food offering provides sustenance for family spirits. I recognized that

CANON REDFERN LOUTTIT AND REV. JOHN GULL AT THE CHURCH
OF ST. MICHAEL AND ALL ANGELS, MIQUELON

this practice was surreptitiously performed before the evening meal but said nothing to indicate my recognition. Pre-Christian traditions are still deeply embedded in the Mistassini philosophy of life, especially when it concerns living or dead family members. I was once invited to attend an Iroquois ceremony to honor their spirits, represented by carved masks. The family carvings were fed in special ceremonies in which they were given corn to satisfy their hunger. A guest should not be critical of such meaningful ceremonies but respect his host's beliefs.

I once showed a film depicting New York City life, in which some footage was shot from high above, looking down from the top of a skyscraper. The heavy traffic, both pedestrian and vehicular, hustled this way and that. It made it seem that pedestrians took their life in their hands every time they crossed the street. Traffic in the city was just as fearsome an image to the forest dwellers as the wild forest animals would be to many a city dweller.

# XVIII

# THE MISTASSINI INDIAN GOVERNMENT

During childhood Smalley Petawabano[1] lived with the Kurtness family at Lake St. John until he moved to Mistassini, where there were several other Petawabano families. He had an excellent school record and felt that the Mistassini Cree needed school education. He was always interested in the reserve education programs for both the youth and the adults. Smalley was a very capable young man. Elders assumed that since he was a good student, he had gained knowledge and experience of the workings of the white world. Mistassini needed a person who could bargain successfully with white leaders. Smalley was in his early twenties when he was elected chief to oversee the growing Indian village that was to have many features of a modern Canadian town.

As the village developed, a bureaucracy evolved that followed in the officialism of a typical Canadian town. Each bureaucratic representative wanted a building or at least sufficient office space for his work and an adequate staff. The chief was also to oversee and work with several Quebec Government agencies new to Mistassini. Each representative of the government agencies was pushing for space for his specific project as well. The head of each office thought that his work was more important than the others and wanted the chief's backing. It was an entirely new situation for the chief, who did not possess the bureaucratic powers that most of the Quebec civil servants supposed that he had. The bureaucratic system was also the way to obtain grants to develop the village. The chief was the spokesman for the tribe. He met with Quebec Government representatives and took the proposals to his Council members. Usually this meant flying to the bush camps and making presentations to each Council member individually to obtain opinions. The Council made the ultimate decisions. Chief Petawabano wisely did not attempt to preempt the Council's power.

Although there was a huge load of tribal business, the chief received no pay. Smalley was seldom able to take time to hunt, as a family provider should. Many successful hunters gladly shared a portion of their meat, fish, or poultry with their leader. It was nearly time to elect a new chief. The tribe also needed a band manager, a salaried position. Smalley felt that was the niche for him. He applied for the position and received the appointment. He then directed tribal affairs as band master. In Canada the term "band" refers to a particular group, such as the Mistassini who

CHIEF PETAWABANO

are members of the much larger Cree tribe. The Mistassini were lucky to have a man of Smalley's caliber and abilities during these trying times; Petawabano stood up very strongly for the welfare of the entire tribe as various branches of Quebec's bureaucracy became established at Mistassini. The Cree will always remember his strong leadership.

In spite of being confined to desk work most of the time, Smalley retained a strong physique. One of the feature events of the annual tribal

CHIEF PETAWABANO IN WEIGHT CARRYING CONTEST

powwow was the weight-carrying contest. The weights were 250 pound bags of sand. Each round was increased by an increment of 250 pounds up to a total of 750, then by 100 pounds, and finally by 50 pounds. In 1970 Smalley won by carrying 1,000 pounds; the following year he carried 1,100 pounds. The contestants did not have to pick up the bags. They were placed on the contestant's back, so that the weights balanced, not overly weighted on either side, which might throw the carrier off balance. Each competitor had to walk a prescribed course. The load was increased for each new round, but the length of the course was decreased. There were always at least six contestants, bona fide bush people, trappers. Several men would almost achieve carrying the same

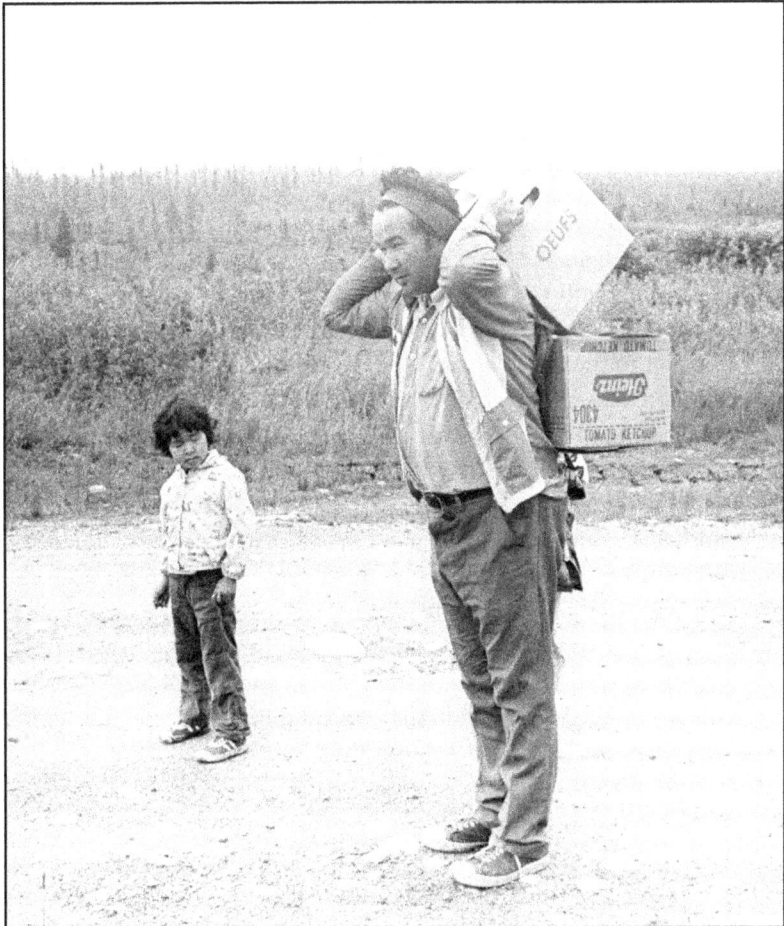

PHILIP VOYAGEUR USES A TUMPLINE TO CARRY HOME HIS PROVISIONS.

weight as the chief, but no one ever equaled or outdid him. I was sure that some hunters could have carried a greater load than the chief, but outdoing the chief would have been unethical and disrespectful. A young man added that it was their way, really not much different from some of our contests, where prizes were created so that almost all the contestants receive an award.

The James Bay chiefs also held their annual weight-carrying contest. Smalley was usually the winner. One year he carried 1,200 pounds. Such contests require good balance and footwork. A slip and the weight being thrown off balance would create a dangerous fall, probably causing damage to internal organs. There are people who when portaging carried greater weights, but there was never a person present to record the event. People of the wilderness could not rely on machines; they had to learn to handle great weights as a requirement of bush life. Chief Petawabano was a rugged individual with tremendous energy and was capable of analyzing problems, determining the best course for his people, and approaching the various government bureaus to obtain the results that he wanted. Smalley knew the importance of education for the years to come. He wanted his son to be a band master, prepared to face the unknown challenges the Mistassini Cree would encounter in the future. After arranging with the Anglican priest in Chibougamau to accept his son as a boarder, he took his son out of the local Mistassini school and enrolled him in the Chibougamau high school, enabling him to acquire an education equal to that of the white students. Smalley wanted to prepare his son to be able to understand and compete favorably with the white competitors and someday follow him as band master.

As Quebec imposed its ways on the Mistassini, there was often much to disturb the conservative Indians. I recall that once there was a big quandary among the village people, but I can't recall exactly what the problem was. I made my way to the rectory, expecting to find Father Blaber trying to straighten out the fracas. He was home. I asked him why he wasn't with the Indian leaders trying to sort the problem out. He replied that the Indians didn't need him; they would find a solution. They have had problems before, and they have worked them out. It is much better that way than to provide a paternal answer. Indian Affairs was much too paternalistic. If the Indians are left alone, they will find a solution that suits them better than any that is tainted with paternalism. And so it was that in a day or so, all was quiet again.

It is to Smalley's credit that he survived the many changes that took place while he was chief and band master. He can take much credit for the development of the present village, many businesses like the home construction, the flying service, the Mistassini schools, and the two-way radio system. He also led the fight to protect the Mistassini homeland from the James Bay Hydro Corporation's plans. He was effective in the process of bringing widely distributed people together in a relatively small area. In addition he was instrumental in creating jobs for the trappers who could no longer make a living trapping. All these problems would tax the best of our politicians.

Along with the other James Bay Cree, the Mistassini Cree decided to fight the James Bay Corporation without the help of other Indian or advocacy organizations. It was their first experience of a court case in a system quite foreign to them. Although they lost the case, they came closer to winning than any other Indian tribe had in pursuing their fight through the Canadian courts. The Mistassini were very able in governing their own affairs.

The leaders wanted more control of their schools. Their aim was to have the authority to select all school board members and empower the school board to select dormitory monitors, teachers, and all other staff. The Mistassini wanted to develop a program so that the students could visit parents' or grandparents' camps for a week to experience the traditional life. They believed that the school should plan a meaningful educational program that provided practical instruction to the students to help them become useful citizens in Mistassini. It often seemed that the present system encouraged the young people to leave for the cities. Leaders needed good students to fill village administrative positions.

# XIX

# James Bay Hydroelectric Project

## Here's Why

by D. C. Butterfield[1]

Here's to the deer and the caribou
To the moose and the mighty bear
I hate to think we'd be on the brink
If the critters and creatures weren't there,
And here's to the stars and the Milky Way
To the sun and the "man in the moon"
I can only hope that we learn to cope
While the time is so opportune,

And here's to the forest and fountains
To the rills and the rivers and lakes
To the whales in the waters, and all the otters
And the beauty a sunset makes,
Here's to the fir and maple and the mighty oak
And to the mountains that touch the sky
I can only plead that we must succeed
And avoid the obvious . . . why!

Here's *not* to the places of people and power
Of consumers and credit and cash
As they glom and gore for always "More!"
While turning our planet to ash!

The James Bay Hydroelectric Project was the Quebec provincial government's best-kept secret. The local people involved in the project knew little about the preliminary activity, such as cutting lines and surveying for the huge project. The Indians hired for the actual line cutting, for the most part, did not know the purpose of their work. I could not help but see the preliminary work of mapping and surveying the territory. Although I did not know the full scope of the project, I was aware that it was another subarctic hydroelectric project. It seemed to me that all the nations having some subarctic land were destroying this narrow ecological band with their destructive hydro. I noted that environmentalists hearing word of the immense hydroelectric plan shrugged it off as a tall tale. The James Bay Hydroelectric Project is much too big and detailed to go into in depth here. It greatly affected the Mistassini Cree and ended the fur trade as it had operated in their lives for more than three centuries.

In 1970 most of the area was officially labeled as "unmapped." In far-off Quebec City and Montreal the politicians' images of wilderness resembled wasteland having little value waiting for development. Hydro-Québec (a government-owned corporation) drew up a large plan to generate electricity from the power of the impressive waterfalls on the five large rivers flowing into James Bay. This energy resource made it possible to export electricity to New York City and other places. Hydro-Québec hired all kinds of scientists to prove that the plan would not be harmful to the fauna nor upset the environment. The reports claimed to prove that hydroelectric power is the cleanest energy source on earth.

The project leaders were so confident that their scientists, most of whom had never been in the territory before, would give the project a five-star approval. Construction even began several years before all the scientific reports were completed. The project costs were almost double the estimates. Hydro-Québec began the project with no fanfare or announcements to the media about it. It was kept very secret until the generators were ready to be turned on.

Indian concepts of land are quite different from those of the white man. The land supports all life. If one harms the land, all life on that land will be harmed. The hunters know that they are just a small part of the total life that relies on their existence from the land. If a hunter desecrates or mistreats the land or the life on the land he, too, will be affected. The towns of Chapais and Chibougamau were to the Indians' examples of the truth of that hypothesis.

Indians pointed out to me their sacred family burial places. I realized that these sacred places would soon be covered by water. It seemed to me that the fact that water would cover the land containing their family graves was not a reality to them. It was customary for families to visit these sites to show respect for their forebears by leaving tobacco. There was no plan or thought to save these remains from the flooding. There would be no place for the Indians to go to visit and venerate those who had gone to the other side. Hydro-Québec distributed a brief summary of the project and plans written in Cree to the Indians throughout the James Bay area. This included maps of the anticipated flooding at the Mistassini village. As an unintended consequence, the James Bay Project brought the bands together, strengthening their ties. All the chiefs met at a James Bay site to discuss the project. They were unified against the project. They reacted by meeting on a beach, building a big fire, and burning all the documents, thinking that was a significant way to show their disapproval and terminate the project. Although the burning of the documents signaled the James Bay Indians' unified disapproval of the project, their opinion did not affect the politicians who saw the project as their economic destiny.

Although the Indians disliked the James Bay Project, their innate humor comes through in the example of this gibe, following the Quebec bulldozers invading the Mistassini lands and destroying their hunting territories, although no agreements had been made about the land. Indian Commissioner: "You know, Chief, the Great White Father has sent me down to speak to you. You know the white man loves his red brother."

"Ugh!" replied the chief, "white man love very ground Injun walk on."

The James Bay Project stimulated both younger and older men, who had tried other means of making a living, to return to the Mistassini hunting lifestyle. There was a steady increase in the number of winter hunting camps. Glen Speers (the HBC manager), band elders, and Anglican missionaries provided the following statistics.

| Winter | No. of Camps |
|---|---|
| 1969–70 | 42 |
| 1970–71 | 45 |
| 1971–72 | 51 |
| 1972–73 | 57 |
| 1973–74 | 62 |
| 1974–75 | 70 |
| 1975–76 | 77 |
| 1976–77 | 84 |

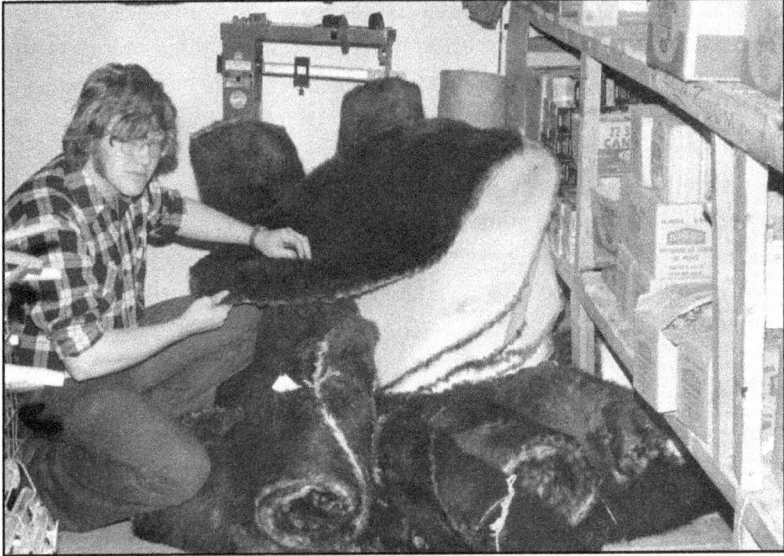

BEAVER SKINS TO BE SENT TO THE FUR AUCTIONS

The people were going back to the land, their heritage. Their image and definition of a Mistassini man was that of an extraordinary, strong, rugged hunter who could defy the worst elements that nature could throw at him. The population was also increasing. It must be remembered that the tabulation included what were formerly the separate posts of Nemaska, Nemiskau, Neoskweskau, Nichikun, Kaniapiskau, and Chibougamau. In 1952 the population of these groups together totaled 646.² By 1970, eighteen years later, the figure had more than doubled to 1,329, according to the band census. These counts were probably low because they lacked a good communication system, and no one actually traveled from camp to camp for specific census figures.

In 1971 Glen Speers made up an impressive 5,600 bundles of Mistassini beaver skins to send to the fur auctions. The Mistassini were on a tightrope balancing act, trying to maintain sufficient food animals in their territory for their future, yet harvesting an adequate number for a healthy lifestyle. Every year more sportsmen were flying into the camps, where they were practically guaranteed a caribou or moose.

In 1972 the Mistassini in the fifty-seven hunting camps depending on wild food killed an average of only two and seven-eighths moose per camp and three and a half caribou per camp.

Unfortunately, I could not obtain the number of game animals killed by sportsmen in the area. The same year, sixty-eight Waswanipi families harvested one hundred and five moose, providing an average of less than two moose per family. Sportsmen killed thirty-three moose in the Waswanipi territory, approximately a third of what the inhabitants of the area killed in a year. Such statistics alarm the Indian who relies on these animals for food. Small animals and fish make up much more of the Indians' food than the large animals do. The quota system for beaver has provided an ample number of pelts harvested each year to meet the hunters' store needs. Many men feel that a similar quota system should be imposed on the large game animals to maintain the balance of food animals.

The Mistassini are very much aware that as white men move into an area, the animals disappear rapidly. There was a saying among the Cree that, "You can tell an American because he will kill all he can and take as much with him as he can; you can tell a Canadian because he will kill all he can and eat it there." The Indians showed much concern toward the changes that were soon to occur in their land. It was discovered that mercury levels peak in newly created water systems about ten years after they are created. The inhabitants can no longer rely on the new waterways as a safe food source for at least ten years or perhaps longer. These new threats have forced the change to a money economy from the beaver economy.

The white freshwater landlocked seals of Ungava were one of the area's greatest secrets and mysteries. Indians and Eskimos have long known about them. A. P. Low's report states that he saw three white seals and that Indians told him that thirty were harvested a year. Ornithologist Clyde Todd heard stories about them while studying Ungava birds in 1935. On his advice in 1938 ornithologists Arthur C. Twomey and Kenneth Doutt[3] of Pittsburgh's Carnegie Museum included in their Canadian Government grant application funding to search for and procure a freshwater white seal specimen in Ungava. With the help of James Bay Eskimo and Cree Indian guides, the rare freshwater white seals were observed and a specimen taken to the Pittsburgh Pennsylvania Museum of Natural History for further museum study. After lengthy research, this rare mammal was finally, officially recognized as a distinct species in 2008.

The Mistassini bush people whom I knew in the 1970s and 1980s had little changed from the guides that Dr. Arthur Twomey and Dr. J. K. Doutt employed in 1938 on their expedition to the Seal Lakes, more than three hundred miles north of Mistassini. I have tried to portray these Indians who, although they killed animals for food, were not butchers of animals or of people. Their killing practices were a solemn rite for the sustaining of life, and not to be abused. The images of these people are not to be confused with the "Hollywood" interpretation.

There were times when the ornithologists Doutt and Twomey could not continue their trek to the white seal lakes. They usually simply rested and talked. One gray, lonely day, with the world silent and barren all about, Doutt and Twomey crouched near the blaze, waiting for the tea water to boil, and discussed the Japanese invasion of China. Their earnest tones and intent faces brought the curious Indians about them in a few moments. Such earnest discussions invoked the following conversation.

"What are they saying?" the men asked George (the head guide).

"We are speaking of war," we told George to answer. But George thought for a while and then finally admitted that he knew no word for war in the Indian language.

"Describe it then," we said. "Didn't these Indians ever fight one another?"

"No," said George, "I don't think so.

"Men divide into groups," George told them, translating for us as he went along. "They are enemies. They have guns more terrible than any you can imagine. They shoot off hilltops like this one (pointing) without any trouble. They kill hundreds of men with only one loud shot!" By this time the astonishment and shock of the natives was plain to be seen.

"Do white men shoot each other as we shoot the seal?" asked one of the Ruperts finally, as though he couldn't believe it. When George answered yes, they all looked at each other obviously excited.

Through the afternoon that followed, George told us, the Indians went on discussing this strange thing . . . And this was not the only illustration we had of the high regard which the Ungava Indians have for human life . . . they certainly are unwilling to kill.[4]

Slowly it became apparent that there were too many outside forces pressuring their world. The Mistassini had lived a life adapting to the fur traders' rules; now they realized that if they were to continue living on their land, they must adapt to a new order of things. Now some of these stalwart people regulate the water of the newly created dam world and others operate huge machines. They have found a new niche in life, just as the Iroquois steel bridge builders did. They will continue to live on their land, their heritage. Let us hope that the Quebec Government will not only listen to these people of peace but work to give them sovereignty within their province and a life of respect and dignity.

Before 1970, targets were set on the ground to photograph the unmapped Mistassini territory from the air, a modern mapmaking procedure. The Indians who were hired to cut lines were not told the purpose of their work, but they found that it was an attractive source of income. It soon became apparent to the tribal leaders that the Indian workers, now looked upon as being rich, were aiding a project that would break up the Indian territory and disrupt the Indian way of life. Tribal leaders dissuaded their people from working on the project. They often referred to those who continued to work for the project as traitors.

Well-paid Quebec workmen came unannounced, without asking permission, to arrogate the land, under the assumption that they were the true owners. The Mistassini viewed them as the destroyers of the territory, the inhabitants' source of food and the basis for their way of life. It was a dispossession of land similar to the sending of the Acadians to Louisiana. The Indians decided that they would fight for their lands in the white man's way, in the courts. A people who had no legal training and limited knowledge of the system took a stand in the Quebec provincial court, which follows the French legal system.

The tone of the provincial justices was that electric power was more important to the province than the hunting rights providing subsistence food for Indians. For the people who had never been in the area or had no intention of going to the area, the argument seemed to make sense. Unfortunately there were very few people who understood the economics or the Indians' coexistent system with the land. The strangers invading the territory were the descendants of those who had come to the New World three centuries ago, having continuously redeveloped their land but still in need of a proper economic base. They were now prepared to eradicate an ongoing economy that had proved itself for well more than three hundred years. Quebec political leaders saw the development of the primeval Mistassini territory as an answer for an economic base for the future of the province.

The Mistassini and Waswanipi communities hired a lawyer in an attempt to gain an injunction against the James Bay Project. The hearings began in the fall of 1972 and continued into the spring of 1973, the longest injunction hearings in the history of Canada. Hydro-Québec continued work throughout the hearings. Months went by while the

Indians waited for a verdict. Work continued on the James Bay Project while the Indians were waiting for a decision. No attempt was made to stop the work, as if the administrators knew that they would win the case. Finally in November the judge decided in favor of the Indians. All across Canada, Indians celebrated an Indian victory. But it was short-lived.

Again, Indians had evidence that work had never completely terminated. In less than a week, three higher judges overruled the decision and decided in favor of the James Bay Hydro Project. The Indians decided to appeal. It was no surprise that work continued. The Indians said that if the work continued at its present rate, some major dams would be so far along that the damage to the land would be irreversible. The courts quickly turned down the Indians' appeal. The Indians spent much tribal money in their effort to fight fairly in the court system. The Indians could feel proud that they had planned their case and presented it very well. But the fact that they came closer to winning against the Quebec Government than any Indians had in a Canadian Government case before them was of little consolation. The Indians received little economic benefit from the project. The workers left a shattered land with their high earnings to spend elsewhere.

No alternative plan for the loss of land or way of life was offered the Indians. The Indians were positive that the court was not fair to them. The Indians' attitude toward all white men changed, and they became more unified against the white man than ever before. Finally the province offered payments to the hunters, to be given between Christmas and New Year's each year. The Indians had to be present in the village to receive their stipend. This was another example of how little the government knew about the Mistassini territory.

The managers of the trading posts on the St. Lawrence River had always offered their trappers a big party between Christmas and New Year's Day. Their Indians came in with furs, traded, and enjoyed partying and dancing before returning to their trap lines. The Mistassini Christmas-New Year's period produced the finest furs, while the St. Lawrence River trappers took the finest furs after New Year's. (Since the Mistassini area is colder earlier, the animals' winter coat comes in earlier than in the St. Lawrence River area.) Therefore, the Mistassini trappers preferred to remain at their camps, but they were forced to return at holiday time to receive the provincial payments due them. Those who did not appear at the village received no provincial payments. Although it was their prime trapping season, Mistassini trappers were forced to return from the trap lines during the Christmas-through-New Year's period to receive their government money. The condition of furs declined as winter progressed. As the season passed, many animals engaged in fights resulting in wounds that damaged their pelts. The trappers were in the habit of remaining at the trap lines during that period.

Caribou were gathering to make their traditional crossing of the La Grande River when the floodgates were opened for the first time. The leading caribou started to cross the river and were swept away by the increased force of the swift current. The caribou had not the slightest hint of the vastly increased intensity of the flowage. The lead caribou jumped into the river and was quickly swept away as were his trusting followers. The exact magnitude of the slaughter was unknown. It was obvious that the incident could not be ignored. An early media report stated that 650 caribou were drowned. Later estimates were more than double that figure. The Indians were notified of the incident and were invited to salvage what they could from the carcasses. Unknown numbers of hibernating bears in their dens and beaver in their houses drowned and could not be salvaged as the water rose in the reservoir. There were no limits on the number of animals the project could kill, but game wardens had been ready to arrest Indians on the slightest suspicion of breaking the white man's law. I wondered how many New Yorkers were enjoying reading their Audubon or Sierra Club publications by a lamp lit by electricity made available from a Quebec grid due to the increased electricity produced for Quebec from hydro dams at LG2 on the La Grande River in the heart of the Mistassini territory. A volunteer at the Bowdoin College Arctic Museum commented that we can't change our ways. She was glad that the needed electricity was produced "up there, not on Maine's wild rivers."

The independent fur trader who resided at Mistassini, Emmet McLeod, had as much experience and knowledge of Mistassini beaver as Glen Speers did. The trappers had been keeping records of not only the animals that they killed in their territories, but the number that they saw. Emmet kept a tabulation of the numbers and sent a copy to the Department of Conservation in Quebec City each year. In January 1974, Emmet estimated that there were 13,000 beaver lodges containing 60,000 to 65,000 beaver within the 60,000 square mile Mistassini territory. There were an average of 6,500 beaver harvested each year. The largest annual harvest of beaver in his records was 9,500.

A trapping control system was developed. Each beaver skin must have a tag. Only a tagged skin could legally be sold. An untagged beaver skin had no market value. Each headman of a territory received a certain number of tags based on a percentage of the number of beaver that he estimated were in his territory the previous year.

Both Emmet McLeod and Glen Speers claimed that the tags worked well and were reliable; otherwise there would not be a fairly consistent harvest of mature beaver each year. If the skins of young beaver outnumbered the mature, it would be a sign that the beaver were beginning to disappear. All the signs showed that the beaver populations were healthy, in spite of more than three hundred years of harvesting them for the fur trade.

Hydro-Québec hired Garrett C. Clough, biology professor at the University of Rhode Island, to make a survey of beaver in the La Grande River watershed. His survey found 0.75 beaver per square mile, concluding that it was a rather small population of little concern to the project. Although the Indian's twenty years of statistics were available in the Quebec Department of Conservation, they were considered too unreliable to have any significance. A scientist's opinion was considered of much higher value than that of the fur traders or trappers who had been in the area for more than thirty years and whose livelihoods depended on furs.

After the first huge reservoir was filled, the southern migration route of waterfowl changed. The rich feeding ground at the mouth of the river had been completely washed out with all its food resources on which much wildlife depended, from very minute lower forms to whales. The food supply for migrating snow geese disappeared; they somehow discovered the rich farmland near Montreal, where they had been considered rare, as a substitute source of food. It seemed that the snow geese now came to haunt the Montreal farmers in revenge against those who had obliterated their northern food resources! Retribution, I'm sure!

Rich food resources at river mouths, the base of food chains, had been washed away, eventually damaging the North Atlantic fishing banks. It was known that these river mouths always attracted many species of fish to spawn and then return to the Atlantic. After the opening of the La Grande River Dam, the loss of a nourishing fish resource in James Bay, with food-chain links to the fish in the Atlantic, may be little known but could be a factor to the dwindling Atlantic fish supply now blamed on over-fishing. It is possible that the hydro project in western Quebec that was to stimulate the province's economy could be an impediment to the important fishing economy of people of eastern Quebec, Nova Scotia, Prince Edward Island, and the New England coast.

On one visit to Mistassini, I was surprised to see a TV antenna on

almost every house. I marveled that the village now had electricity.
Then I learned that the hydroelectric project administrators had still not
planned to supply the Mistassini people with electricity! Their stated plan
was to ship the electricity produced on the Mistassini territory to New
York City, Mistassini government buildings, to the school, Hudson's Bay
Company, and the church buildings. Electricity for Indian housing at
Mistassini was not included in the plan. As a protest, almost everyone
attached a TV antenna to his roof. It was a silent but very visual protest
that brought exclamations of, "Oh, you have TV up here!" The visual
protest brought the desired result: electricity to the Indian homes.

There was no way to harvest the drowned black spruce of the virgin
forests in the roadless areas of the projected reservoir. The plan was to
leave the drowned trees untouched to rot in the water. A year or two later
the scientists discovered that the rotting spruce left in the reservoir areas
would cause the water to become toxic and would kill or poison all wildlife
that lived in the water or came to drink it. The toxic condition would last
at least eighty years before the water would again be potable. Something
had to be done! Two large dredge-style barges were constructed. Huge
boilers were on the decks. Crews worked day and night hauling the trees
aboard and burning them. Acrid smoke filled the air for many days The
smoke covered many miles and heavily veiled the sun, creating similar
conditions to a long drawn-out period of overcast days.

I had seen the destruction caused by the New Brunswick Power
Company's dam project on the St. John River, once a magnificent
waterway and home to many species of fish and other life. Turning a
meandering river into a reservoir destroyed the Atlantic salmon and
sturgeon spawning beds. The greatly magnified current from the dam
quickly swept the fish-nesting areas away, as well as the minute life that are
the rich food resources for the food chains upon which so much wildlife
depends. The dams created electric power but did not provide a cheap
source of energy to attract big business to the area. Labrador's Churchill
Falls, with a drop of 245 feet, was seen as a productive hydro project.
The province ignored the rights of the Native people and has never
negotiated with them for the use of the land. The Churchill Falls Dam
that was to bring renewed life to Newfoundland has not yet transformed
that province to one of great prosperity. Quebec is Newfoundland's
biggest customer. The project is a notable engineering event. However, it
was extremely destructive to large areas of natural settings that attracted
a wide variety of wildlife, food that was a wonderful resource to feed the
native people.

In 1967 Arthur Sorensen contacted me regarding a trip to Labrador's Churchill Falls. I wanted to photograph this unique, magnificent natural feature and readily agreed to take him there. At the end of May, with our canoe tied to the roof, we drove to Seven Islands on the north shore of the St. Lawrence River. There was still snow on the ground and more coming down. We were told of a road from Esker to Churchill Falls. We left the car and canoe at the railroad station and boarded the train for Esker. The Quebec North Shore and Labrador Railway connected Seven Islands with Schefferville. The train was composed primarily of empty ore cars with two passenger cars attached to the rear and followed a river with mountains on either side. Many spectacular, icy waterfalls descended from great heights. Several men were getting off at Esker. A man checked off their names as they jumped off into the snow. He did not have our names and told us to return to the train and get off at Schefferville. I told the checker that we wished to see and photograph Churchill Falls, one of the highest waterfalls in the world. He replied that we would have to obtain permission from Joe Smallwood, the prime minister of Newfoundland. He continued, "How do we know that you are not Arab spies coming to blow up the falls, so that Egypt will retain the honor of having the largest dam in the world?" I didn't see any telephones attached to any trees from which to call the prime minister. We made a hurried decision to disembark, go around the rear of the train and on into the bush. When we found a place that was easy to hide our camp, we stopped and spent two weeks roaming around central Labrador. Ironically, several years later I was invited to a New Year's party in Gananoque, Ontario, where I was introduced to the recently retired energy minister of Newfoundland. He was interested in hearing my story and said that he would gladly have given us the needed permission, since the government had only one photograph of Churchill Falls before the water was diverted to the Newfoundland and Labrador Hydro project.

The great dam projects spread across the subarctic. Scientists must examine these areas to determine if the destruction has been worth the gain. It appears that some third-world hydro projects are created to prove that their engineers also can construct gigantic projects. Will we ever know the true destruction of water life, plants and trees? The transforming of large areas of dry land into huge reservoirs, and the draining of rivers and lakes, are major factors of our global warming. Scientists must become concerned about the changes in landscapes, to guarantee that such projects do not result in unexpected detrimental changes that could be devastating to us, outweighing the benefits of the dams. Today's major agrarian concern is that the world is not producing sufficient food to feed everyone. The scientists must find new, harmless sources of energy. It is not a case of "we are not going to change, but I am glad they are doing it up there." There must be more concern about the adverse effects of projects to people beyond the limits of the project. Wind and water currents carry pollutants across international boundaries.

The populations living in the subarctic around the world are usually small, often so low in number as to be considered insignificant; the inhabitants do not have to be informed about the plans that will change their land, environment, and way of life. In spite of the government's shameful treatment of them, the Mistassini people have shown great versatility in reacting to the situation. The Mistassini saw the Earth as the precious Mother, providing sustenance for all life. Matthew Iserhoff stated to me that: "God gave the Indians the land to protect, the white people did not know the value of the land and were ravaging it, and the land would no longer be fit for animals. The Indians had to protect the land, since the white people did not know enough to do so. White people will thank the Indians in years to come."

Indian oral history emphasizes that Indians are the caretakers of land conceived by their creator for a hunting territory. Animals were created for their use, as long as there was no abuse. Nature and the great outdoors always provided new experiences. The responsibility that had been their predecessors' was always passed on to an ever-present younger generation. In return almost all their necessities would be provided. It was a life that had not changed. Over the years Hudson's Bay Company managers introduced improved, new gear that made the hunter's life easier, contributing to hunting and trapping success. The usual result was additional furs for the HBC traders.

# XX

# Winter Bush Life: Philip's Camp

The flight from Mistassini to Philip Voyageur's camp, about one hundred miles north, took about an hour. From the air, the land had an uninviting, rugged wilderness appearance of snow-covered rivers, lakes, and rolling hills. Several years earlier a James Bay Hydroelectric Project helicopter was flying some men to a work site, probably on about the same flight path my pilot was following. A typical subarctic, whiteout blizzard suddenly blew up without warning. The helicopter slammed into an unseen hill. Philip's camp was just over the next hill. Philip's family was doing chores inside the protected wall of their tent and heard the crash above the shrieking storm. In spite of the strong gusts blending the new snow with the old, causing whiteout conditions, Philip knew that he had to go out to investigate and see what he could do for the unlucky travelers who had tried to defy the storm by flying into it. He and his son quickly put on their heavy jackets and grabbed a large coil of rope, tying themselves together so that they would not become separated. The visibility was so poor and the wind so strong that the men, bent over for protection from the biting storm, could not see more than two feet ahead. It was hard going and difficult to hear one another. They could see almost nothing. They made little headway. They fought their way forward foot by foot. Fighting the storm was extremely tiring. Swirling snow erased their trail in no time. They decided that the conditions were so hazardous that for their own safety they should return to their tent and wait until the storm abated.

The weather cleared during the night. The men rose early to set out on their rescue mission. It did not take long to find the downed craft less than a half mile from their camp. The search team looked inside the helicopter but found no one. Then they searched around the craft but still found no trace of anyone. The wind would have obliterated any tracks

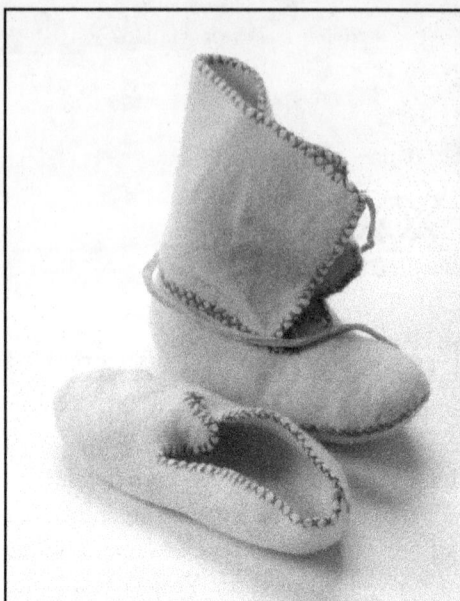

LOW INSERT, HIGH LINER

within minutes. They found a note inside the helicopter stating that the men had started back to James Bay, a distance of more than one hundred miles. Later, an organized professional search team failed to find any trace of them. To this day their remains have not been found. Their disappearance is another of the many mysteries of the North. If they had remained in the shelter of the craft, the only sane thing to do under the circumstances, they would soon have been rescued and would have received excellent treatment from the Voyageurs. It was most likely that if the crash victims had attempted to follow a compass course, they would not have known enough to compensate for the variance between true north and magnetic north at the crash site and were quite far off their intended course. The pilots were trained to figure the variance from magnetic north, but it is doubtful whether the Quebec workers flown in would know the variance, even if they had a compass.

Before I went into the winter bush, I made what I

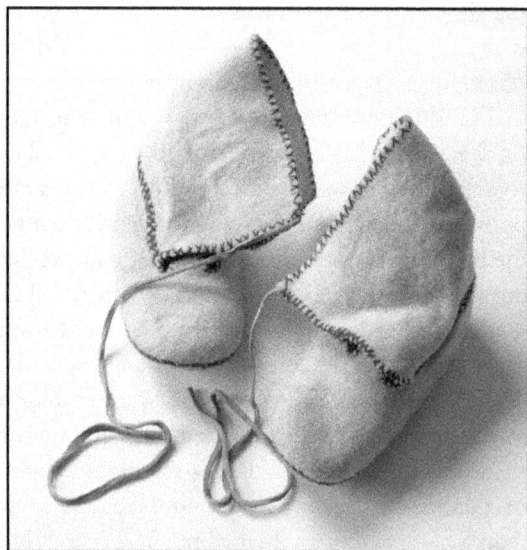

THE COMBINED INSERTS READY FOR THE LEATHER OUTER COVERING

thought was a careful purchase of a fine, insulated L.L.Bean boot for the conditions I was to find. When I arrived at Mistassini, a friend saw me wearing the boots and asked me what boots I was going to wear in the bush. I pointed proudly to my new insulated boots. "No," he said, "you will freeze your feet in them." I looked astonished. I replied, "What should I wear?" My friend stated, "Get a pair of moose shanks. The well-cured skin breathes. If you do a lot of walking, your feet won't sweat. Since the hide breathes, moisture does not build up and accumulate to freeze once you stop and rest a bit." Were these archaic technologies that we have not yet equaled?

I figured that I was out of my element at Mistassini and should take the advice of a well-meaning hunter familiar with subarctic winters. I was directed to a cabin where a woman would make me a pair of boots. She instructed me to take off my boots and put my feet on a piece of cardboard that was on the floor. She traced around my foot, creating her pattern for my boots. That was all there was to it. I was to return in the morning for the boots, which I did.

There were my new boots called "moose shanks": a packet that consisted of a low, heavy duffle moccasin insert, a high inner heavy

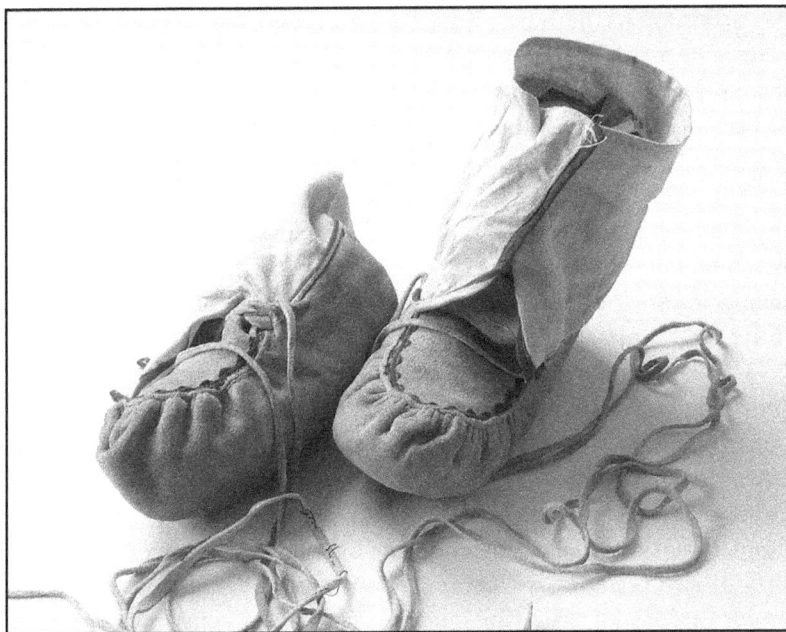

MOOSE SHANK BOOT WITH ITS DUFFLE LINER AND DUFFLE INSERT, THE TYPICAL WINTER FOOTWEAR FOR THE MISTASSINI INDIANS.

duffle boot lining, and the outer soft moose-skin shell with canvas top. Formerly these boots, about a foot high, were entirely of moose skin, peeled from the lower leg. The restrictions on hunting in the early 1970s reduced the number of available moose skins. So when I got my boots, the moose shank did not reach the top. The HBC stocked much canvas, a good replacement for the top of the boot; the canvas was used to extend to the top of the boot. I happily paid the $20 price. These boots have been traditional, winter footwear for all the Mistassini bush people and were also standard for the northeastern Maine and Canadian Indians. I felt much better prepared for the worst that the weather king might throw at a greenhorn in the bush.

The standard children's sock, sometimes used by adults as well, is a rope of twisted rabbit skin wound around the foot and lower leg. When it is very cold, one, two, or several pairs of socks are worn with the boot. I once saw an old pair of moose shanks pulled over a new pair. The boots took the name of "moose shanks" because they were made from eight or ten inches of the hide above the moose's ankle, peeled down to the ankle. I was happy that I took the advice to buy the boots.

From the air the ground looked extremely inhospitable. Soon the lake appeared. I saw the tent near a barrier of black spruce that offered protection against the north wind. Then the plane's skis touched the snowy surface of the lake, and we taxied towards the tent. A dozen quizzical faces peered in wonder at this white guy who had accepted an invitation to become a temporary member of an Indian winter camp, when winter was at its coldest and stormiest. I had arrived at Philip's camp.

The pilot wisely left promptly, since the temperatures were already beginning to drop, and he had another camp to visit. It was a lonely moment as I wondered if I was really up to this rugged life and cold temperatures. I couldn't hesitate. I must act enthusiastically. I would never forgive myself if I turned this invitation down.

I looked out over the lake, a part of an extensive hunting ground providing food for many generations of Voyageurs. I had visited Philip's father, Willie, now in his 90s, here several times. His trapping days were over. His children had heard about the new home for senior citizens established in Chibougamau. They felt that their parents, Willie and Clara, deserved to enjoy the comforts of a home for senior citizens in their golden years. They were the first Mistassini people to move into a senior care facility. The Chibougamau facility was sixty miles south of the Mistassini village. Their children, evidently, were not aware that the home assigned males and females to separate sections of the building, even if they were a married couple. The two Voyageur helpmates who had lived for many years together, providing support to one another in the harsh northern bush life, were now in comfortable living quarters, quite civilized, but each separated from the other. Neither parent was fluent in French. Each of them felt very much alone, seldom having a visitor with whom they could converse in their native tongue. This was one of many unanticipated conflicts between the Indian and Canadian cultures when certain customs clashed head on.

Willie was the son of Solomon Voyageur, who was regarded as the greatest Mistassini leader. Solomon Voyageur was the chief for many years. He was born about 1860. He said that the family who adopted him underfed and overworked him. He felt that enduring these hardships produced the man that he became. His grandfather and great-grandfather were Hudson's Bay factors. His grandfather was in charge of a company post, and his great-grandfather was in charge of the Rupert House Post. It was not a surprise that Solomon was appointed to head the fur brigades from Mistassini to Rupert House. Nanuwan of the Chibougamau Hudson's Bay Company also had great respect for him and wrote:

> There are many stories about his strength when he was guide of the Mistassinny brigade on their three hundred and sixty mile trip with thirty-foot canoes to Rupert House; how he carried seven hundred pounds over a half mile portage; how when they met the Woswonaby [Waswanipi] brigade on the middle of a portage and there was a dispute as to who would carry over their load first, Solomon himself wrestled with and overcame all the men of the Woswonaby canoes. By these stories you might think him a giant of a man, but he is even under the medium height and probably never weighed more than one hundred and fifty pounds. Even now, in his age, he has a frame of steel, and I myself have seen him carry three hundred pounds over a portage and in the winter haul a like amount on his toboggan from Chibougamau to Mistassinny . . . For more than thirty years he has been the guide of our brigade and in that time never lost nor damaged fur nor supplies.[1]

Solomon has many descendants at Mistassini. The stories about him are still popular. He is the Paul Bunyan folk hero of the tribe. These stories, emphasizing strength as a major factor in the selection of a chief, support what the Waswanipi people said regarding Diom Blacksmith.

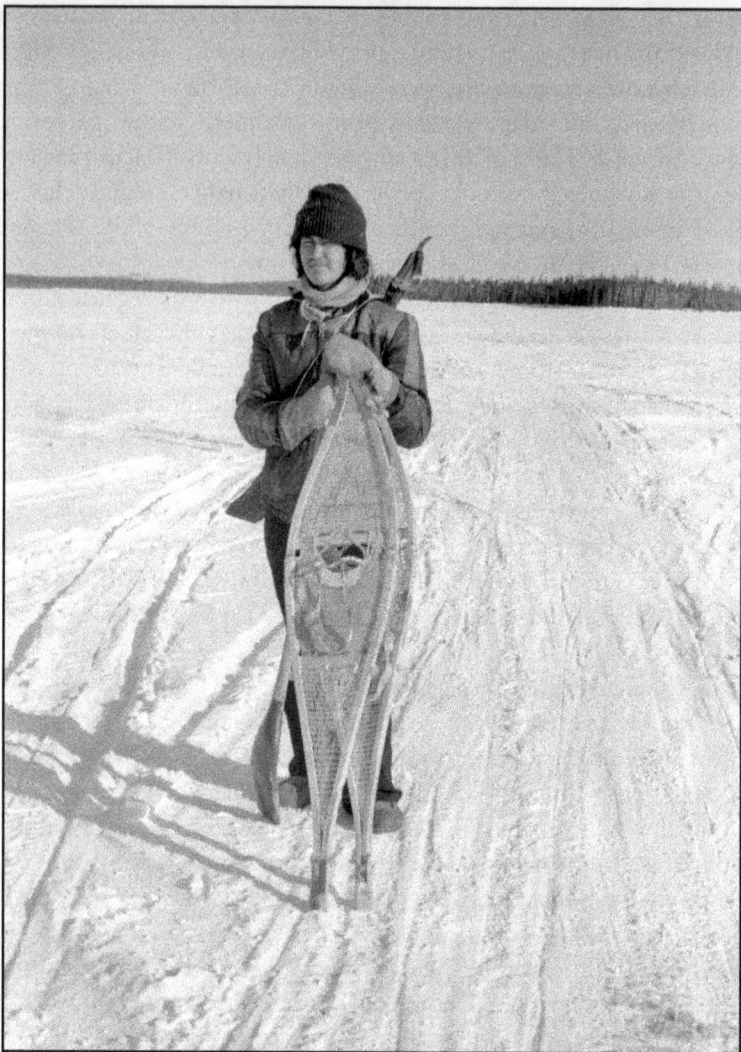

MICHAEL'S COUSIN DEPARTS FOR HOME, A TEN-MILE WILDERNESS
TREK THAT INCLUDES CHECKING TRAPS AND HUNTING. NOTE
ENCASED GUN, TRAPPER'S SNOW SHOVEL, AND TRAIL SNOWSHOES.

In 1950, the Mistassini and Waswanipi elders began discussing the concept of school education for the children. After several years they concluded that one child from each family that approved of school education would be sent to school first. Solomon's son Willie decided to send Philip with the first group to go to school. He was sent to Sault Ste. Marie, one thousand miles from home. When he returned to Mistassini after nine years at school with no opportunities for vacations or visits home, Philip was more than ready to learn his bush heritage from his father, a very able hunter. When the government built the school in Mistassini, it needed a name. The government got it right by asking the people to name it. The almost unanimous opinion was to recognize their greatest Chief; the school is the Solomon Voyageur School. Philip Voyageur, an influential elder of the band, was one of Solomon's descendants still living at Mistassini.

An older brother, Reuben, lacked a school education. He remained with the family and excelled in learning the bush life. Reuben had two sons in their late teens. Philip's teenager, Michael, had learned many hunting skills while accompanying his two cousins and uncle. The three teenagers were well versed in the skills of traditional Mistassini men.

Ten miles of wilderness and snow separated the two families. Reuben and Philip inherited Willie's hunting territory that before him belonged to Solomon. It had received proper care and still produced adequate food for each family. The two brothers, one with school learning, the other with bush expertise, were very close and each supported the other in his own way. Reuben's and Philip's children were learning how to care for the land, so that they and their families could continue to enjoy living from its bounty.

Both families included young children below school age. Babies

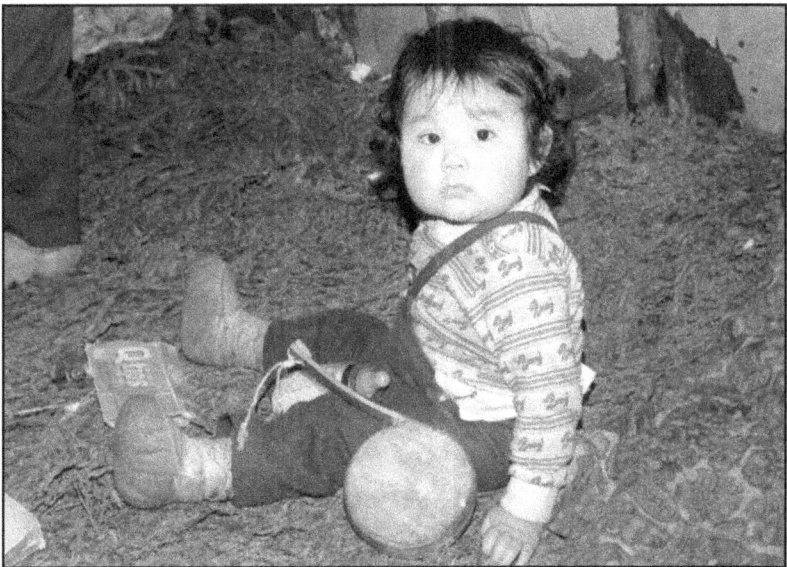

Everyone likes a baby.

were an important part of every camp. All the others in the camp could display their emotions freely when with the youngsters, since everyone likes a baby. The adults worked at their tasks intently, but relaxed when they gave a few minutes of attention to the young ones. The moments devoted to children provided laughter and voiced approval of the baby's development. A baby adds much to the life of a camp that would otherwise be dreadfully dull. The Voyageur camp was unusual in that there were no grandparents in it. Customarily, grandmothers have the knack of giving a little help or encouragement when it is needed, even slipping a treat to a young hunter before he starts off in the morning. Sometimes grandmothers have the role of midwife for the birth of a new grandchild. Winter camps enjoyed the participation of three generations, thus completing the family unit. Many older men, not feeling at ease in adapting to village life, gave their pension funds to a younger hunter who accepted the elders as a part of their extended winter family. These elders helped as much as they could and were not just a drain on the food supply. These Indians lived honestly, ate well without overindulging, and used their money wisely. Their success depended on a mutual husband-and-wife endeavor.

The Mistassini economy was quite different from the white man's economy. The Indian economy could stand still and be a success, since there was no point in making great sums of profit. Wandering tribesmen were limited to what they could carry from place to place. Many Hudson's Bay managers never understood why trappers did not have more furs to sell them. As long as the trappers could pay for their winter hunting and trapping outfits, that was all that was necessary, whereas the outside world must continually increase profits by at least ten percent to be thought successful. Stockholders, managers, and company owners all demand higher profits. As the companies make money, the world's natural resources are reduced. As the supplies are consumed, explorers search for new resources, causing the world to react in ways that are out of our control. The Indians were happy to have their economic level stand still at a point where they had sufficient food year after year. A successful business that thrives through three or more generations usually receives honors and awards in the white man's world. At Mistassini there are no special accolades or honors given the hunter families who live successfully on their territories for several generations. They do this by respecting their land so that it maintains the proper balance of wildlife that is necessary to continue to support human life within it. Their only reward is knowing that they and their family have survived another year.

Nature restocks the land quickly when the one entrusted as its keeper uses it properly.

I had felt it necessary to go north to comprehend the actual harsh winter life of the northeastern Canadian Indians, who cherished the stimulating subarctic cold. Here I was gazing at white everywhere. Banked with snow, Philip's tent stood in a small clearing. This would be my home for several weeks. I turned and followed Philip and his family to the tent. Philip escorted me into the tent and to the back left-hand corner, saying, "This is your room." He continued with simple instructions: "Put everything that you do not need now in the supply tent. When you get up in the morning, take your sleeping bag and hang it outside. If it is snowing, put the sleeping bag in the supply tent until you need it in the evening."

The introduction was brief. From my corner "room," I surveyed the tent and found it neat and tidy, uncluttered by unnecessary belongings. The "kitchen area" was at the front of the tent. The small stove near the middle radiated heat in all directions, but little penetrated to the far corners. The sleeping space for the two teenage girls was at the far right. The baby's cradle, suspended from ropes, was also in their corner "room." The two preschool children, about five and six years old, had the space between Philip and his wife Mary, who were in the center. Michael, their 16-year-old son was on the left side of his parents, and I was beyond in the left-hand corner. In my mind I noted that Indians from Maine and the Maritime Provinces had similar sleeping arrangements when their housing was in the tent or single-room-cabin stage.[2]

I went outside the tent. In front of it were several high racks containing preserved meat and fish, frozen solid in the −30F° to −50F° temperatures dominating the winter season. A storage tent was to the left. Beaver skins hung curing on long rope lines tied between trees. Laundry dried on other lines. The freeze-drying process must have been an efficient ancient practice discovered thousands of years ago by dwellers of the colder regions. Philip stored snowmobiles and his fuel supplies in shelters near the shore of his lake.

The Voyageur hunting territory had passed down from one generation to the next for an unknown length of time. Each successive group of children had learned where each species of animal, fish, or waterfowl could be found in their 90 x 25 mile hunting territory. The children would learn the terrain and geographic conditions creating the typical environments for all species of wildlife necessary for sustaining their life. Hunting territory, a segment of a vast virgin forest, was their "supermarket" and "building supply store," providing everything from food to wigwam frames. There was no need to trespass on another's hunting territory.

Here I was the guest of Philip Voyageur, a Mistassini Indian hunter and trapper in his winter quarters. This Voyageur bush family consisted of a cradle baby, two other children not of school age, and three teenagers, plus the two adults. Reuben, Philip's brother and nearest neighbor, lived ten miles away with his wife and two teenage boys, both proficient hunters.

That night the mercury plummeted. The stars of the Milky Way shone extremely bright in the crisp air. The northern lights flashed, danced and sparkled brilliantly, presenting a gala performance. Northern heavens show off a marvelous display of outstanding beauty for those who can withstand the cold hardships and enjoy it.

The week before I arrived the temperature hovered between −50°F and −70°F. No one goes far from the warmth of a fire under those conditions. Temperatures can rise or fall rapidly. One night the temperature dropped sixty degrees; one day the temperature rose sixty degrees but was still below freezing. Indians know the weather well and adjust to the changes. One secret of their success is that they learn the signs that foretell the changes and prepare for them. Commercial forecasts are not dependable for those who are able to receive them in the bush.

Work was delegated to all the members of Philip's camp except the youngest. Philip and Michael were the hunter-providers. They left punctually between 8:00 and 8:30 every morning to check trap lines and hunt when weather permitted. There was no hunting on Sunday unless food was scarce. The family enjoyed being together. The day's feature was the headman leading hymn-singing and reading Bible selections from their Cree hymnal and Bible.

There was always work to do for everyone. Edna, Philip's wife, was "boss," overseeing the camp duties, both inside and outside the tent. Primarily the oldest daughter's duties were outside the tent, such as cutting, splitting, and carrying firewood; filling the water pails from a hole cut in the four-foot-thick lake ice; gathering spruce boughs; stretching, scraping, and preparing larger hides such as moose and caribou. Her younger sister did the inside tasks, such as laundry, food preparation, cooking, tending the stoves, tending the babies, "knitting" a new spruce-bough floor, and fleshing furs. These were the household chores that women were expected to perform when they married.

Upon the hunters' return, the younger children of about six years old went to meet them at the edge of the lake. Their contribution to camp life was to carry quarry up to the tent and give it to their mother. In former days, when hunters killed animals they returned to camp and told the women and children where to find the food so they could retrieve it. The animal became the mother's property when it was brought into the tent. The women had the skills to create elegant articles from the hides.

Edna was a person of great energy. She arose early each morning, supervised breakfast and the children. She prepared lunches for the two hunters. Each morning one of the girls took a basin of hot water, soap, washcloth and towel to the patiently waiting headman for his daily ablution. No Arab sheik could have enjoyed this ritual any more than this northern hunter did in his snow-banked canvas tent. When he had finished, she would bring a basin of hot water, soap, washcloth, and towel to me in my "room."

Breakfast was then served to each in his own area. A colorful oilcloth was spread on the spruce bough floor for each person's breakfast. This, like other meals, was a silent time; each person was absorbed in their own thoughts. Like all other meals, breakfast consisted of meat, fat, bread, and tea. The fat was served in a separate dish to be spread on the meat, as we spread butter on potatoes or bread. The hunters, especially,

Voyageur family sitting comfortably on
newly knitted spruce bough floor

burn many calories out in the cold temperatures all day, therefore food containing a high fat content is important for them. I did not need all that fat. It would take a bit of time for my body to become accustomed to it. Moose and caribou steaks have little fat, so they were fried in a skillet with melted lard within a half inch of the rim. The fat completely covered the meat and was absorbed by it. In spite of scraping off as much as I could, there was still more than I needed.

I mentioned to Philip how impressed I was with the variety of meat and the diversity of food preparation. Philip replied that when he was a boy, food consisted primarily of fish and rabbits. Now the diet is more varied during the winter trapping season, when large and small game animals are killed. Both moose and caribou have changed their migration patterns. In the 1970s technology gave the hunters snowmobiles, so that they could cover at least twice the territory they used to cover on snowshoes. By 1990 the James Bay Hydro Project had destroyed so much of the ecology that the land could support fewer animals. The summer diet is primarily fish. In the fall and spring, waterfowl are added to the menu. Although meat was basic to every meal, menus were delightfully varied. There was a large variety of meat stored on outside racks, where it remained frozen solid. One never knew when a period of bad weather would prevent hunting for a week or more. Having the larder full was best. There was moose, caribou, rabbit, beaver, and occasionally other small game such as otter, muskrat, ptarmigan, spruce partridge, and fish such as northern pike, lake trout, walleye, or whitefish. The North supports a wide variety of food resources. There were varied ways of cooking meat: frying, baking, boiling, or stewing it. Vegetables were almost entirely lacking. Once a week Edna served commercially packaged instant potatoes. Onion was from time to time added for flavor, as was salt and ketchup.

Some anthropologists pondered over the lack of some vitamin sources in the Indians' diet, such as vitamin C. There is no known rich natural food source that provides vitamin C for the subarctic people. In 1970 anthropologists assumed that subarctic Indians had a source for this important vitamin. To my knowledge the source is still unknown. At least one anthropologist suggested that subarctic people might have the capacity to manufacture their own vitamin C, just as dogs do. Probably Indians traditionally used a local source such as Vitamin C-rich spruce needles for teas as they did in Maine and the Maritimes. In World War II the Germans turned to the spruce for tea. Formerly the Mistassini may have enjoyed a spruce-needle beverage, but I am not aware of documentation for this hypothesis. If they prepared spruce or birch tea, the introduction of store tea ended the use of spruce tea long ago. School children were introduced to oranges, orange juice, and many vegetables. They generally accepted oranges, but the Mistassini had a reputation as meat eaters, declining most vegetables and fruit. Gardening as most southern tribes did was impossible in the bush. Since vegetables were practically unknown, they were considered a foreign or exotic food, which the Mistassini were not eager to try.

Late in the afternoon my host asked me when I liked to eat, six o'clock? It seemed like a question that was really a statement. I answered affirmatively, thinking that their suggested time would fit their schedules. Then I discovered that the hunters had their dinner-hour first, after which the women ate. After everyone was finished, they spread a brightly colored oilcloth on the bough floor; my meal was placed on top of it. My dinner was usually different from what the others were eating. They assumed that I preferred store bread, so ordered some to come on the plane with me.

When I finished, Philip said that bedtime was eight o'clock. That meant being in bed, so the babies would get their sleep. This appeared to be the only rule to which they strictly adhered. It was perhaps overemphasized in my memory, because it did not fit my body clock. Adjusting to the early bedtime hour was the most difficult thing for me. When I had finished dinner, the family was ready for an evening snack before retiring. Michael had acquired a taste for French toast while at school, and that was now his preferred snack. The early bedtime saved on candles and Coleman lamp fuel. With emphasis that gave it the sound of a command, Philip strongly suggested that I wear a wool hat to bed. As I pulled my wool hat down over my ears, I noticed that all were wearing their wool hats. I found it excellent advice. The two woodstoves glowed with a slight cherry tint and purred pleasantly. It must have been about 90°F near the stove but at least twenty degrees cooler at the outer limits where I was. The high temperature helped people fall asleep quickly. Slowly, quietly, the cold came in and took over.

About 3 a.m. one of the girls restarted the stove. When I awoke, I was aware that I could see my breath. I felt the effects of the fat beginning to work, reached for my Pepto-Bismol and discovered that it was frozen! The wake-up temperature in the tent was −64°F.[3] I was surprised that my small thermometer was able to record such lows. The rush of cold air racing up the frozen stovepipe sounded like locomotives speeding through the tent. Soon the pipe warmed, and the stove returned to its reassuring purr. The tent warmed up surprisingly quickly. Then it rained on me! As we exhaled during the night, the warm emission rose and condensed and froze upon contact with the frigid canvas ceiling. During a cold night such as this, an inch or more of ice adhered to the ceiling. I learned to estimate the outside temperature by seeing how thick the ice was above my head. A half inch was equal to –40°F, three quarters of an inch equaled –50°F, and an inch equaled –60°F. Warm air from the stove rose, quickly melting the ice that had formed. Thus rain descended on me. What a great introduction to life in the winter bush camps!

Then I realized that I did not escape a case of diarrhea. This is an unpleasant malady under the best of circumstances, but here in a tent where the outside temperature was –60°F, the trips to the outhouse were quite an experience. I was quickly making many adjustments: climate, food, sleeping schedule, language, and entire lifestyle. It was like suffering from jet lag. I realized that my school, college, and graduate studies had not prepared me for living in the subarctic bush. I was also at least six years older than Philip, who sympathized with me by saying that when he went to Mistassini, the store food affected him in the same manner. He preferred to remain in the bush.

There are many uses for spruce boughs. The principal use is for tent floors. Every week or ten days they "knitted" a new springy, aromatic, bough floor, covering the dried-out former floor that became a good base for the new floor. The floor required a large quantity of boughs, which became a soft mattress on which to sit or sleep. It also filled the tent with a pleasant fragrance. There was no way or need to sweep, mop, or vacuum the floor. Most of the dirt sifted down through the boughs; hot, melted, spilled fat dripped down and through the boughs. During winter when several feet of snow are on the ground, sand and mud were insignificant. Family members and visitors were expected to brush off snow and dirt from their clothing and boots before entering a tent. For this purpose, a small pile of boughs was conveniently left at the entrance to the tent. Snowy clothes were not appreciated in the tent. A fresh floor did much to create a pleasant atmosphere in the camp. The fragrant boughs were pleasant to sit and sleep on and generally raised the people's spirits.

After the hunters left on their skidoos in the morning, the women began their duties. I found that Edna was as handy outside with a chainsaw as she was inside with a needle and thread. If there were skins to be prepared, she could make wooden stretchers for them. Almost every kind of animal skin required a specific type of stretcher. Large animal skins required a good-sized frame set sturdily in the ground.

Edna could carve new fishnet floats. Wet floats continually needed replacement, since they quickly lost their buoyancy. Edna's skills also included: fashioning moccasins or mittens from moose or caribou hides; setting and checking rabbit snares; skinning rabbits into long thin ropes for weaving into blankets, jackets, or socks; harvesting spruce boughs; and doing many other things that a good camp required.

In Maine and the Maritimes, the Indians had found they could weave baskets from black-ash wood splints to form containers for many purposes. Mistassini is beyond the range of the trees suitable for splint production. Mistassini people used moose and caribou hides as material for containers and usually decorated them beautifully with beads, bright-colored threads, or moose hair colored with plant dyes.

Philip, like most of the hunters, was now using skidoos in the bush. It was necessary to fly skidoos in, as well as barrels of fuel and oil for the long winter months. Most of the young men had taken courses in skidoo maintenance and took care of their machines very well. These were working machines for the Indians, not recreational vehicles. They added to the overhead of trapping, but offered the advantage of covering more ground in a shorter day. In the worst cold, the skidoos were limited to a top speed of 25 mph. The increase in wind chill produced white spots of frostbite on most of the hunters' faces, even when protected by a wool cap, hood, and scarf. The hunters usually returned between 3 and 4 p.m., ready for a hot meal of pan bread, meat, and tea. At school Michael had become fond of ketchup, which was added to his plate here. The women and children ate later.

Indians are very much aware of the beauty of their primeval surroundings. This extended visit to one camp provided the opportunity for me to see some of nature's winter wonders. Often magnificence appears unexpectedly. One night a light snow covered the tent roof. I rolled up my sleeping bag to carry it to the storage tent. The newly fallen snow covered everything, and the tent's new bright white coat shimmered in the sunshine. I deposited the sleeping bag in the shining white storage tent and marveled at the surroundings. By the time I returned, the stoves had consumed their fuel; the tent had cooled. The white cape had transformed into a sparkling luminous icy coat, a fanciful ice castle. That too disappeared quickly as they fired the stoves up again.

The snowshoe was an innovation from ancient times by those who lived in northern New England, the Maritimes, and farther north, where the winter snow depth reaches several feet. Moving any distance would be impossible without snowshoes, if one had to break a trail in soft, dry snow of any depth. The Mistassini Cree, like other northern tribes, developed several different snowshoe styles for specific conditions and purposes. The beaver-tail style, a rounded form, was for breaking trails. The person breaking the trail was soon relieved by another, since it was very hard work. Those who followed wore a long, narrower trail snowshoe. The length of the man's trail snowshoe equaled the height of one's eyes from the ground, the woman's from the chest to the ground. One could travel much faster with snowshoes when the trail was broken.

A person on snowshoes can quickly tell the temperature with considerable accuracy. The wooden frames make a crunching sound on the frozen surface. The tone is distinctly different for every ten-degree change in temperature. The characteristic sound for a specific temperature was quickly learned. It is surprising how sound travels in the subarctic silence! An alert listener, as well as animals, can hear the high-pitched swishing snowshoes quite a distance from the source. Hunters needing a quieter approach to their game found that by binding cloth around the snowshoe frames they deadened the telltale sound of their presence. A hunter can send a greeting a good half mile in the crisp subarctic silence.

A HOMEMADE CROCHET-TYPE NEEDLE IS INSERTED AT ONE END OF A RABBIT-SKIN ROPE THAT IS STRETCHED OUT. THE HANDS ARE RUBBED BACK AND FORTH RAPIDLY, WHILE HOLDING THE HOOK BETWEEN. THE FUR RUFFLES OUT COMPLETELY ALL AROUND.

TWISTING A RABBIT-SKIN ROPE

Philip's father had hunted and trapped on snowshoes. When Philip was old enough to accompany his father, they considered that ten miles a day on snowshoes was their limit. That meant ten miles out and then

THE RABBIT-SKIN ROPES HAVE MANY USES: THEY ARE WOVEN IN BLANKETS, CHILDREN'S JACKETS, AND WRAPPED AROUND FEET AND ANKLES AS SOCKS.

PHILIP AND MICHAEL START OUT ON A HUNT.

ten miles back to the tent. Father and son plodded home as the darkness grew deeper.

During the shortest days of the year it was dark by 3 p.m. About midafternoon they stopped, built a fire, and had a tea break with a bit of meat and Indian pan bread that had extra fat in the center. When the bread was warmed, the hot fat melted into it, heating and softening the crusty, frozen bread. By the time they finished eating, the moon was rising, reflecting its light on the white carpet, turning the night almost into day. They donned their snowshoes again and continued home, often under the multicolored, flashing northern lights. The cold nights had their own special beauty, showing off a multitude of shiny stars in the Milky Way and the glamorous northern lights. They usually arrived home about 8 p.m., where the younger children were eagerly and impatiently waiting for them. They showed as much elation as could be shown any father returning home from a factory or office.

Now Philip could cover twenty to twenty-five miles out with his skidoo and return in daylight. However, the cost of snowmobiles and gas cut into his profit. What difference would profit make in his world? Money should be spent to improve one's life and make the work easier. Often Philip would give Michael a separate section of the trap line to check. I was impressed how diligently sixteen-year-old Michael inspected his skidoo every night, making sure that it was in fine shape for the next morning's journey. He took every precaution to prevent a breakdown on the trail.

The intruders from the south introduced skis to the area. The young Mistassini Indians found skiing an interesting pastime, but to my knowledge they never included the ski in the bush camp paraphernalia.

The Indian sled dogs were large animals, a mongrel mix that grew large and very strong by their third year. They could be ugly and could not be trusted. If not watched carefully, they might kill a small child. However, they were good sled dogs, as long as they knew who was their master. They were by no means a house pet but were chained in individual spruce-bough shelters at the edge of the clearing. Caribou hair is hollow, a fine insulator. The hunters spread caribou hair for bedding on the dog shelters' snowy floors. The dogs were left to run and forage for themselves all summer. In late summer or fall, the men caught the dogs to ready them for their winter work. Some had to be retrained. When they were three years old and their master no longer felt safe with them, he had to kill them. They were of uneven temperament and could turn mean and ugly without much notice. It was easy to understand why the snowmobile replaced them so quickly as standard equipment.

Some families replaced the annual contingent of new puppies by

MICHAEL KILLED A CARIBOU.

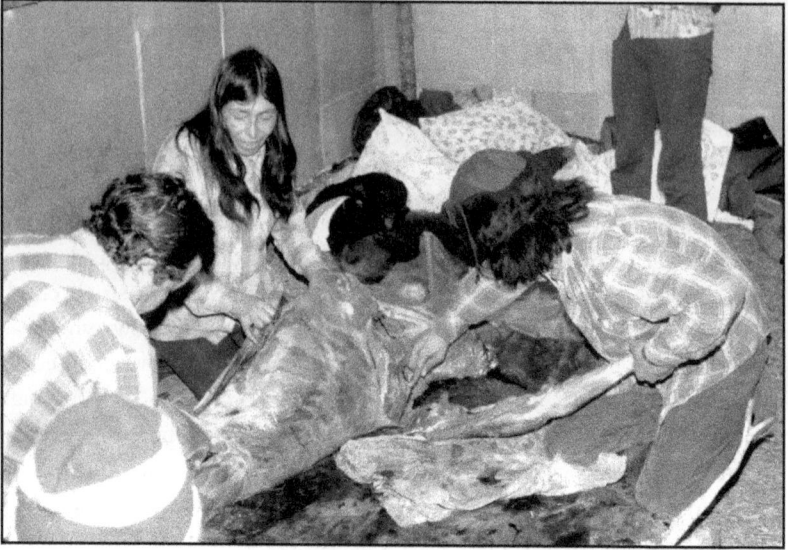

THE CARIBOU WAS IMMEDIATELY SKINNED AND BUTCHERED.

purchasing small lapdogs from the Chibougamau pet shop for children's tent pets. House cats were recent acquisitions admitted to the tent and were valued much more than dogs. Both were tied with stout cords, so that they could not bite through the cords and escape outdoors, where

SPLITTING CARIBOU LEG BONE FOR MARROW

they might freeze to death, become a choice morsel for a predator, or become confused and lost in the great wilderness.

The small children, not yet walking, remained in cradles or baby bags most of the time. They were not given the opportunity to crawl and

PHILIP CARVES CARIBOU HEAD FOR TONGUE AND CHEEKS.
VERY LITTLE IS WASTED.

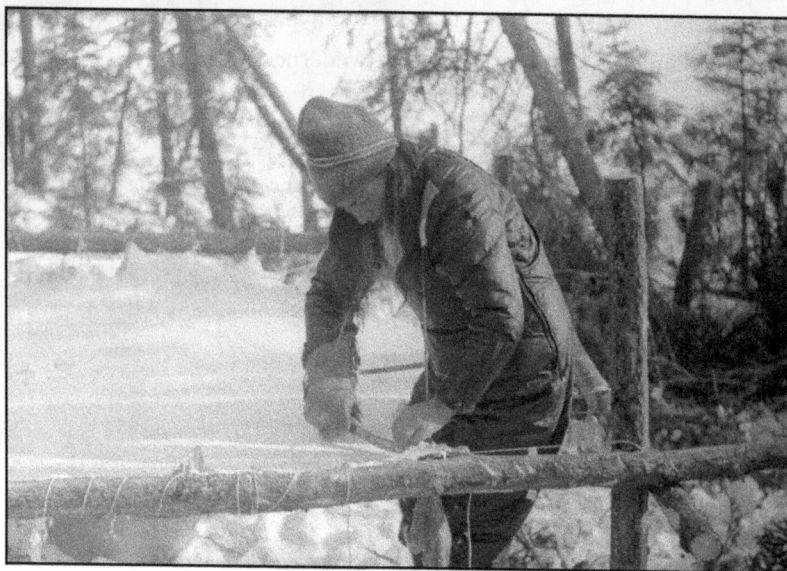

EDNA SCRAPING A CARIBOU SKIN

explore the tent freely. If they crawled out of the tent on their own unnoticed, there was always the chance that they would freeze to death. The beginning walkers were tethered, to keep them away from the stoves. In the summer the cook stoves were placed outdoors, so they do not overheat the tents. Parents had much work to do, so they turned over the responsibility of babysitting to children of a rather young age.

Michael and Reuben's two teenaged boys went on an overnight trip. They were to return the following morning. In my thinking that would be nearly noon, but since Indians rise at an early hour, it meant before 10 a.m. When the boys did not arrive, I could see the tension rising on their parents' faces. The boys became the center of what little conversation there was. I tried to calm fears by saying that the boys probably enjoyed sleeping late. Reuben replied in a contemptuous growl, "Our boys don't sleep late like yours do!" The tension continued to rise. I did not know what to say. The silence said more than the small talk. Suddenly I saw a crack in the stoic, granite faces. My eyes and ears detected no change out on the lake. The faces became smiles, yet I could not hear or see the boys. In a few minutes, tiny figures appeared on the far side of the lake. I marveled at Reuben's hearing. I guessed that he was five years older than I was, yet his ears were so much more acute than mine. For most of his life he had had no motors, chainsaws, factory hubbub, radios, or TVs blaring, or all the daily noise levels of our cities. This was an important example of why it is necessary to shield our precious ears from so much of our unnecessarily created clamor. It appears that many of our TV popularity scores are based on their sound levels. In our world, our senior citizens now take hearing aids for granted as a necessity.

When Philip was a boy, caribou were seldom killed; moose were unknown in his hunting territory. I became aware of some changes in animal ranges in the few years that I was in the territory. Some of these changes were the result of man's changing the land.

Moose skins were valued as the material for boots, snowshoe webbing, bags, drums, ammunition pouches, gun cases, mittens, and moccasins. Caribou skins had a finer appearance and were used when possible for the same accessories. Michael killed a caribou with his .22 rifle. The animal was frozen solid when he arrived at the tent with it. Upon arrival, he took the caribou into the tent to thaw. Then it was immediately skinned and butchered.

Unfortunately the caribou skins have a problem. I noticed a number of holes in the skin that were not bullet holes. When the caribou is feeding on the mosses, it picks up parasite eggs that it swallows. The eggs hatch, and the worms work their way into the caribou's bloodstream. Eventually the young worms eat their way out through the skin, leaving their distinctive escape hatches as evidence. The worms fall to the ground where they lay their eggs and begin a new cycle. The skins of the caribou

STRETCHING A CARIBOU SKIN

THE POST HOLE THROUGH FOUR FEET OF ICE;
THE START OF SETTING A NET UNDER THE ICE.

killed early in the winter are in the best condition. By late winter some skins are so full of holes that they are virtually worthless for anything but long strands of snowshoe webbing.

CLEARING ICE FROM THE HOLE TO PASS THE NET THROUGH ON -40°F DAY

SETTING A NIGHT LINE

Fish and rabbits were the most reliable sources of food for the Mistassini. A night line was set for fish in the late afternoon.

I suggested setting it in the waterhole. They thought that fishing in the waterhole was ridiculous; a fish would not come to a waterhole. A new hole was chipped through the four-foot-thick ice. A line with a weight on the end of it was dropped to measure the depth. Then one end of a line was tied to a crotch stick; the other end was baited and lowered so that it was close to the bottom where the fish were. The crotch stick was placed upright by the hole. A small spruce bough with all the short needle branches cut off, except a tuft on the top, acted as a flag. The bough was set in the snow at an angle and through the crotch of the stick. When a fish took the bait and ran off with it, the "flag stick" on the fork was pulled down, notifying the fisherman of his catch. Other northern bands also employed the method that the Mistassini had for setting a net through four feet of ice, a well-established procedure. The day that Philip was to show me how they fished with nets in the winter, the temperature was −40°F. with strong winds. It was going to be a cold job.

Edna helped with the preparation of the gill nets, a time-consuming occupation. The 125-foot net had to be repaired. New net floats were cut from dry wood. Once wet, they usually never dry out, so no longer retain good floating qualities.

Some net weights also had to be replaced. A large, white hump sat by the lake. Philip brushed snow off, exposing a big pile of fist-sized water-worn, rounded stones. Philip said that his father had told him that if he always replaced net sinker stones to the pile, he would never have to go searching for them. I wondered how many generations had used this pile of net sinkers.

When all the net preparations were completed, we went to a time-tested spot, where Philip's father had set his nets and probably many generations before him. Philip cut a series of seven holes in the ice in a straight line about fifteen feet apart. Each hole was about three feet long. A rope more than a hundred feet long was tied to one end of a twenty-foot sapling that was lowered into the first hole and pushed with a shorter pole toward the second hole, where Edna held it with a spud. (A spud has many purposes. It can have a long or short handle. Woodsmen fashioned it easily for the purpose at hand by simply cutting a stick of the required length and angling one end. It is sharp and similar to a spade.) Then Philip pushed it to the next hole. They repeated this procedure until they reached the last hole. Philip untied the rope from the pole, and Edna held it while Philip attached the net to the other end back at the first hole. He lowered the net into the hole. Then Edna hauled her rope, pulling the net under the ice until she returned to the first hole. The net was stretched underwater from the first hole to the last hole. Philip cut two spruce saplings, and all but several branches at the top were trimmed from them. Each tufted post was set at an end, marking the position of the net, and the net was tied to both posts.

The net was hauled several days later with a harvest of three lake whitefish, an eight-pound and a ten-pound northern pike, two walleye, and a ten-pound lake trout, providing about seventy pounds of fresh fish for the larder. Lake trout and whitefish have a caloric value similar to that of moose or caribou. Fish is an important and dependable food source in the subarctic. Generally, little was known in 1970 about subarctic Indian nutrition, other than what Gonzalez wrote in *Changing Dietary Patterns of North American Indian Children*.

> An extremely high caloric intake, consisting largely of protein and fat, is characteristic of the Arctic and Subarctic cultures. The body probably requires more calories simply to maintain warmth in the severe winter months. The high protein diet is associated with a metabolic rate, which also raises the amount of calories needed.[4]

Fresh milk was not readily available at Mistassini until after the roads were built, and then it was frequently sour. HBC ordered it more for the growing white community than as a replacement for a broth made by boiling fish and fish bones, a beverage that provided much needed calcium, essential for a strong bone structure and teeth, especially for

PHILIP'S AGE-OLD BONE FLESHER IN USE

the young children. There was no practical way to ship fresh milk to
the camps. The canned, condensed milk replaced the boiled fish bone
broth that is almost a thing of the past. In the 1970s the nurse noted
that the Mistassini had a high rate of broken bones. She believed that the
problem was due to a lack of calcium.

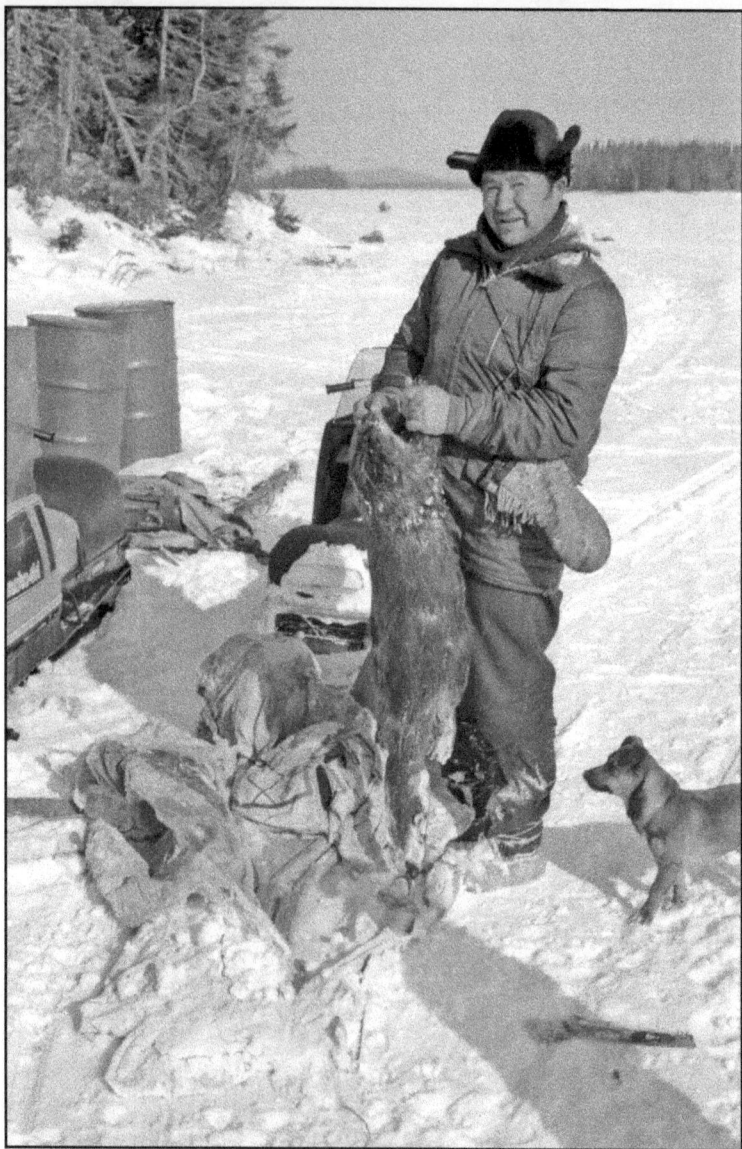

PHILIP RETURNS WITH A FINE BEAVER.

Women had a responsibility in the preparation of skins while the men were hunting. After the trappers had returned with a beaver, the "inside girl" had the task of removing the skin. I was surprised to see a scraper fashioned from a moose leg bone as a tool to remove the skin from the beaver. These are tools that are frequently found in archaeological sites,

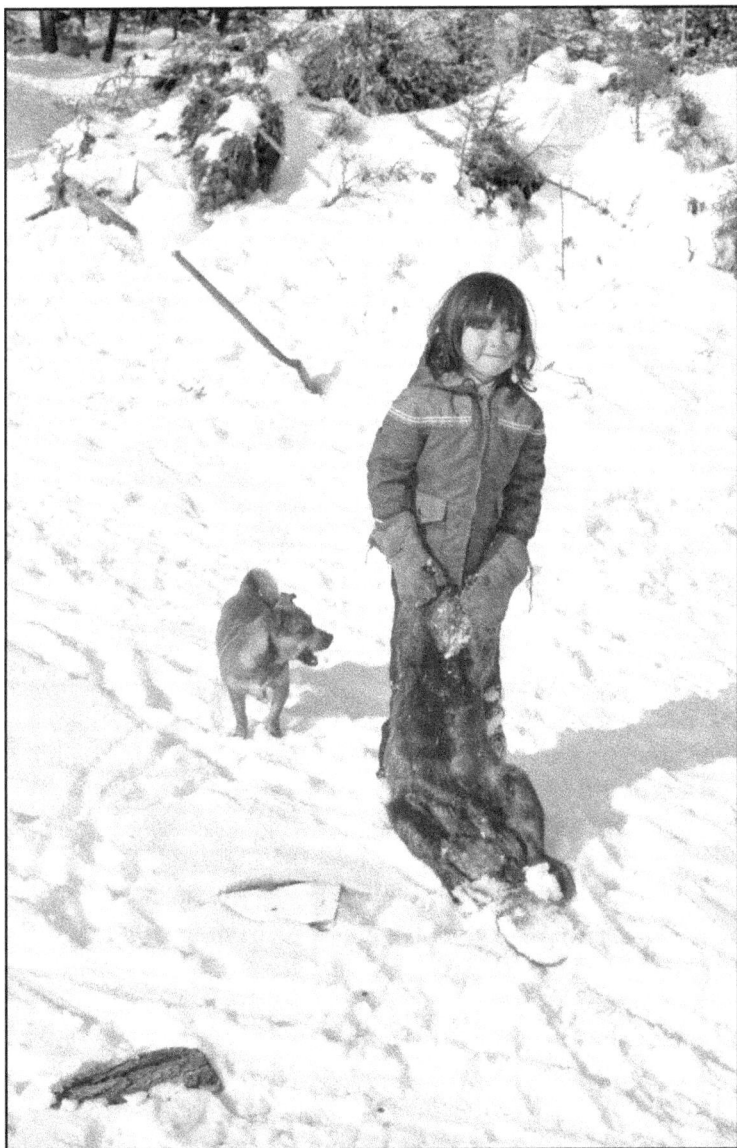

PHILIP'S DAUGHTER TAKES THE BEAVER TO HER MOTHER IN THE TENT.

yet here it was in use before my eyes! Better archaeological reports of the area are needed to establish dates. The beaver is a difficult animal to skin. The pelt doesn't want to part from the body. Philip remarked that they had not found a steel tool that was as good as the age-old bone flesher for skinning a beaver.

A large plastic sheet was placed over the spruce bough floor as a working place. A stout post about eight feet long was pushed at an angle into the dirt below the spruce boughs at the edge of the plastic. The beaver was hung on the post and skinned. The beaver meat was removed to the larder, and the skin was stretched over the post and the fat scraped from it. Very little of the animal was wasted. The government had warned against eating organ meat, since mercury and other toxins accumulate there. Animal hearts and livers were always eaten until mercury infiltrated the water and food supply. Wild animal predators instinctively know that animal organs provide necessary nutrients and vitamins, and they devour them first. White men's carelessness in the handling of dangerous chemicals has put the northern hunters' health at risk. No type of compensation was ever considered for these innocent people. The Indians watched the wealthy sports fishermen come to the government fish camps, catch and eat the toxic products of the lakes and rivers that government representatives warned the Indians not to eat The Indians were confused. Why did rich sportsmen spend so much money to catch and eat the same fish that Indians were forbidden to eat?

Moose and caribou hides are stretched outside the tent. A large square framework was set up outside near the lake, where the skin would receive drying sun and wind. Slits were cut at short intervals in the large skins for ties to the framework. These fastenings were tied as tight as possible while stretching the skin. The skins were scraped on both sides; the outer coat to remove the hair, the inner side to remove the fat. Again, specialized bone scrapers were made for scraping the large skins. After the scraping was finished, the skins were left on the stretchers to dry.

The skins of marten, mink, muskrat, otter, and other small animals, peel off quite easily, like a glove. The animals vary in size, so each requires a special stretcher. The characteristic small-animal skin stretcher consists of two long side pieces shaped ovally to the contour of the animal. The two side pieces are inserted first, and then a wedge-shaped spacer is driven between them, forcing the skin to stretch. Beaver skins require a round frame. Slits are cut all around the edge of the beaver skin. A springy sapling is cut and tied in a rough circle, to which the skin is tied. The sapling fights to gain its release by straightening out to its normal

PREPARING OTTER SKIN STRETCHER

shape, thus keeping a constant, even pressure on all sides of the pelt. Wolf and lynx skins do not require a stretcher; they are just hung up to dry. Wolf skins have the warmest furs.

The Mistassini Cree have great respect for the white man's technology, but are not ready to accept all their marvels into their daily life until it passes a well thought-out approach for improving their accustomed ways. Elders had studied two-way radio systems. The Council decided to apply for a grant to authorize a two-way radio station providing communication services between the tribe office and bush camps. The government officials were very skeptical of the plan, not having the slightest notion how the band would benefit from it. This was another example of government ignorance about Mistassini and its bush population. The project was not approved. Why would Indians want a two-way radio system? The grant application for the project was sent again the following year. In the mid 1970s the grant was approved. The two-way radio system became an umbilical cord from the camps to the village. This two-way communication system has proved to be one of the most practical innovations for these people. In the winter all camps are contacted with a wake-up call at 7 a.m. and given a weather report, other important information, and the opportunity to report any sickness or problem. Emergency information can be sent any time. The system had a range of ninety miles. Since the farthest camps were three hundred miles from the band office station, substations were established at ninety-mile intervals. Large batteries similar to those used in vehicles powered the substations. The batteries were returned to the village routinely to be recharged, while newly charged batteries replaced them.

Philip's camp was a substation. He forwarded the 7 a.m. reports to

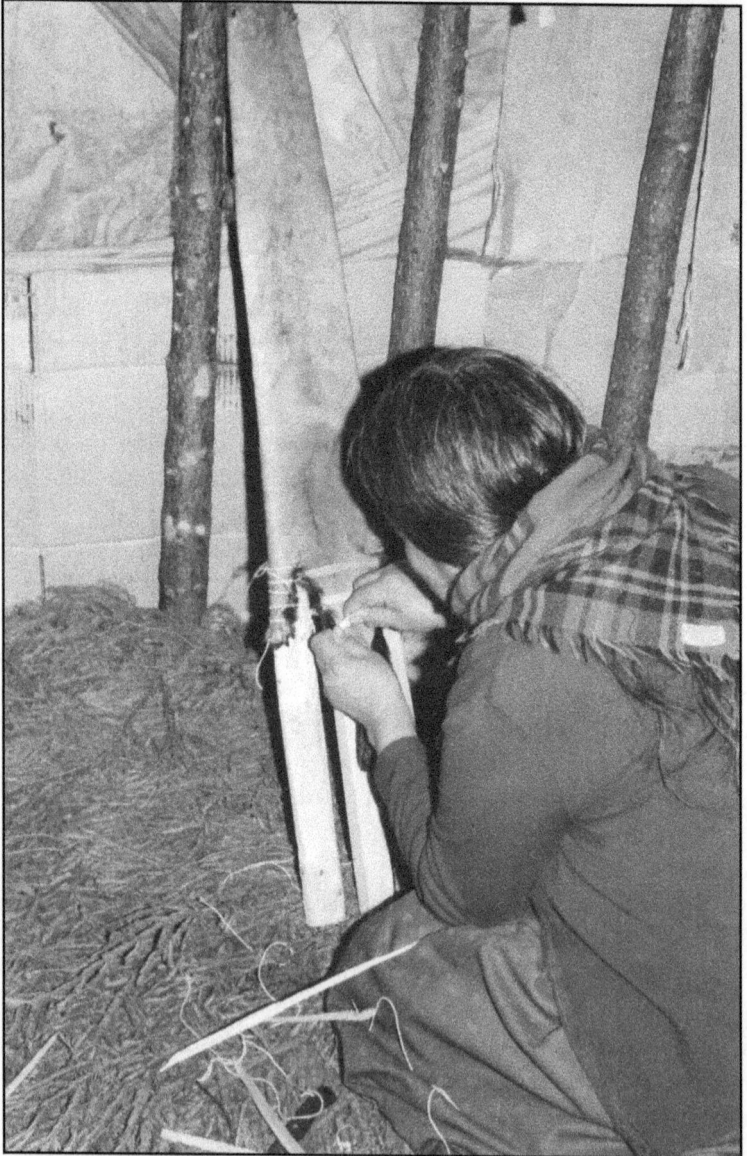

FITTING AN OTTER SKIN TO A STRETCHER

the camps within the next ninety-mile range. If there were messages regarding needed medical attention, Philip forwarded them back to the band office. Philip received several messages regarding medical problems that he forwarded to the band office while I was there. A woman cut her leg badly with an ax, another woman's nose had been bleeding for three

OTTER ON STRETCHER

days, and a third woman had birthing problems. The former generation could have healed many medical problems without outside help. Now the people had learned to rely on the white man's doctors and nurses. It would not take long for a doctor to be flown up, if weather permitted.

The bush people have felt that the white man's custom of brushing one's teeth was unimportant for Indians and referred to the beaver whose yellow teeth were strong and sharp as a knife. One night I woke up to a little girl's shrill crying in the stillness of the cold subarctic night. Everyone in the tent was awake. The hunters found the disturbance particularly upsetting. They needed their sleep to recharge them for the rigors that they would confront on the morning's trail. It was with difficulty that the parents learned that the cause of the child's pain was a toothache. Edna instructed the older sister and Michael to take care of the youngster's problem. Michael found a piece of strong thread, tied a noose in it, put it around the painful tooth, and handed the thread to his sister. The crying continued. With a hearty jerk the tooth came out; the youngster stopped crying immediately in the middle of a loud blat. The tent was quiet; the child did not emit another whimper. In no time everyone was back to sleep.

In the morning Philip explained to me that they order candy for the kids, but there is no place to hide it in the tent where the kids cannot find it. The girl had lost a baby tooth, but in a few months the permanent tooth would come through. He concluded that they would not order any more candy. An advantage of the road was that fresh milk, eggs, ice cream and other perishable foods were delivered on a regular basis. The disadvantage was that junk food (including favorites of the school students) also was delivered regularly. These foods were almost unknown at Mistassini before the road extended into their community. The dentist who came in the summer before the road was built had little to do. The weekly deliveries of junk food increased the dentist's business. The children discovered junk food when they went away to school. When children came to the bush camps, parents wanted them to have foods they liked, not realizing the damage that some do. Consequently, the junk foods went to the camps.

Candy was often used by teachers as a reward for good grades or good behavior. A teacher found that her first graders generally had very poor teeth, some rotten to the gums. Some teachers stopped giving their students candy except on Halloween and Christmas. On one of my early visits to Mistassini, I talked to the summer dentist. He said that most of the bush people had excellent teeth until they decided to live in the village where junk food was readily obtainable. The meat diet was good for teeth and gums; chewing on fat and gristle naturally cleaned the teeth. Since a tooth cleaner or paste was not used, the teeth took on a dark shade similar to the teeth of the bush animals.

Generations of living in an invigorating climate have taught the James Bay Cree the best method of dressing for protection from the cold. Some early anthropologists made the assumption that Indians did not perspire. In reality perspiration is the worst enemy of the northern people; the people learned how to control it. The rugged outdoor activities can easily generate sweat in the pleasant minus-thirty- to minus-forty-degree temperatures. When such activity terminates and one becomes inactive, the cold can slowly penetrate and freeze escaped body moisture. Northern methods of dressing inhibit perspiration from forming on the body. Normal garb for the winter hunter consists of one or two pairs of winter underwear, two or three wool shirts and wool pants and one or two winter jackets or a snowmobile suit over them. Feet are dressed with up to six pairs of socks protected by porous handmade, moosehide boots that "breathe." Heavy moosehide mittens, handmade and lined, cover the hands. They are tied together with a cord that passes through the sleeves and over the shoulders. When it is necessary to use the fingers, the hunter quickly and easily withdraws a hand from the mitt and reinserts it in the hanging mitt after the task is completed. Ears are radiators, depleting body heat if left unprotected. A vital part of the hunter's wardrobe are a wool hat, a hood, and one or two scarves, protecting the face and leaving openings for the eyes. It is difficult to replace lost body heat, and hypothermia will quickly develop. Many years of dealing with the cold have taught them that layers of clothing are the proper winter dress. During the warm midday, a layer can be removed and later replaced as needed. A hunter might take off a jacket and hang it on a branch to pick up on his return trip later that day, when the temperature declines.

Pastors Swindlehurst and Cartlidge strongly opposed conjuring and sorcery. There are two types of conjuring; one done for retribution or punishment against a fellow trapper, the other as a means to find game. The first kept people on edge. One never knew when one might be the subject of a conjuror's ill will. The second type was a power gained by hunters to provide them with information on where game could be found. Similar practices are generally known among third-world nations.

A common form of the second type is the Shaking Tent. Maine and maritime Indians used it as well until they lost their hunting territory lifestyle. For years the enlightened Europeans would not accept the shaking tent as anything more than a ruse. It was not until about 1950 that anthropologists began to take this practice seriously, when a nurse assigned to northern Canadian Indians described the phenomenon from an academic point of view. The tent is a special, quickly constructed, small, round tent. The shaman enters and contacts a spirit helper, Mistaapew. The tent jumps up and down; strange voices and noises are heard. A person must be powerfully brave to contact Mistaapew, the Mistassini's only spirit who speaks to them in their own language. Most headmen could perform the shaking tent. It was part of the bush education to be a headman. Older teenagers were usually taught by grandfathers, who take the boys into the forest for their lessons. It appeared to me to be a mental attitude of highly concentrating one's mind until one felt that one was entering the spirit world. These periods of high mental positions were painful but necessary as equipment for hunting. For years the shaking tent was not done publicly in a village site, because the missionaries forbade it. The priest could claim that there was no conjuring, but once in the bush, hunters acted in the traditional ways of the bush. The shaking tent was done in Philip's camp, as it was a characteristic of the hunting camp life. They felt that it was a security key to obtaining food. Providing food was the chief goal in order to sustain life.

The Mistassini have been called a spiritual people. They shared a world also inhabited by several spirits, very real to them. Some spirits were clearly identified, such as Mistaapew, whose work can often be distinctly identified in the bush surroundings. They also had very clear images in their minds of the various cultural spirits. When missionaries spoke of spirits in the Christian context, it was easy for these spiritual people to comprehend their realism and the importance of their powers.

Under ordinary conditions, the men did not hunt or trap on Sunday. One should not shoot a gun on Sunday but could use a slingshot to bring down small birds for food. Philip was a lay reader at the church and led a service of Bible reading, prayer and hymns on Sunday to his family. Hymns were played on a small, battery tape player, the members of the family joining the singers.

The early missionaries had done their job well, but apparently there was no conflict between benevolent conjuring and Christianity in the Indian mind. It was not something that they would readily admit participating in to their white neighbors; both the conjurer and the missionary offered benevolent spirits to help the Indian. Some circumstances required help from every source available.

In the confusing days when the people were losing their hunting territories, and money was becoming more important in their lives, some hunters decided to use their shaking tent powers to demonstrate the phenomenon to white men by selling tickets to the event. One hunter decided how much money he needed, then how many tickets he needed to sell at a specified price to meet his goal. He found that the required number of tickets sold very easily. The ancient Indian laws declared that if they abused the powers, the hunter would lose his power of obtaining Mistaapew's guidance and aid. I did not learn if Mistaapew considered that finding a source of money was as important as finding the source of food animals. The performing for money was a new application of the shaking tent's power. No one seemed to know if it would be interpreted as an abuse of the power.

Indians consider tea an important beverage. Many have never had coffee. There are many ways of preparing tea. In the Maritimes, I have had Indian tea so strong that it would melt the quills off a porcupine. Mistassini tea was at the opposite end of the spectrum. Each morning in Philip's camp, a pail of tea was made to last the day. It was on the weak side and sweetened with cans of condensed milk. In the morning it was hot but quickly cooled. It was left where anyone wanting to quench his thirst could fill his mug during the day. They gave me a separate pail of tea.

Philip, like other fathers, carved wooden toys such as canoes, cars, airplanes, and even helicopters for their young sons. Some craftsmen were very creative with their carvings. A string was attached to the toy, and a stick was tied to the other end for the boys to hold and pull the toys over the snow, ice, or sand. Children also had sleds, and parents made some runs for sliding. One summer I watched out of the corner of my eye several boys and girls about nine or ten years old playing "house." They played outside near the edge of their camp and constructed their "house" of forest-edge stuff—a fine home. They even had a play fire. Finally they became aware of my interest. In a split second they trashed it, and they were gone, almost like birds. They knew the important things of a camp. Beginning at the age of six, girls are given the responsibility of taking care of their younger siblings. The girls gradually take on women's work, such as preparing the skins and cooking. Although I have seen Indian dolls in museums and Indian craft stores, I have never seen an Indian doll in a camp.

A routine schedule of washing clothes was kept in the bush. The washing process consumed many pails of water, carried from the four-foot-thick icy waterhole to the tent, heated on the stove, and poured into a tub, where the clothes were scrubbed on an old-fashioned washboard. The wet, clean clothing was hung on an outside line to freeze-dry. Every camp had a wash line of colorful clothing breaking up the monotonous white that surrounded the small camp clearing.

The time was coming for me to leave Philip's camp. The days had been full. There was so much that Philip and his family had taught me in a short time about Mistassini culture and life. For me, it was a marvelous and unique experience to observe the typical Indian life the way it was intended to be. It was a rich, genuine, although simple life, in which all of nature received respect. There was nothing synthetic about it. They were hardened all-season people, enjoying the outdoor life throughout the year. Everyone was too busy to become burdened with cabin fever. I was never aware of a controversy between individuals. Each went about his or her duties smiling as if it was a privilege. It was his or her share as a member of the family community. Whereas the other world emphasized specialization, Philip and Reuben were jacks-of-all-trades and were very good at all of them. They knew so much more about real life than those who make scheduled visits to a store, take a finely wrapped package off a shelf, pay for it, and take it to a heated home, where one pushes a switch for light or heat or goes to the kitchen sink and in moments has heated water. As the head of my house, I am nothing more than a master of switches; with a click of a switch, I get light, heat, or hot water. I know very little about the source of my electricity, my water, or my heating fuel. The Mistassini world did not displace people, destroy wildlife and ecological systems, release toxins into the air and water systems that would harm people near and far. They did not break down processes or cause global warming. The life that lacked the luxury of a master of switches required activity, creativity, versatility, vivacity, and independence. Such a life created its own destiny. Their lifestyle might be described as one of scientific simplicity. Many youngsters who were sent to school lost the training and desire for such a life, settling as masters of switches; this is where they saw their future.

The weather forecast predicted a storm coming before noon. The morning communication from the two-way radio system announced that my plane would land about 7:30 a.m. I was given a choice for breakfast and selected boiled beaver. After breakfast I quickly packed. The plane arrived. The pilot was anxious to return before the storm began. There was a quick handshake and "goodbye" and "thank you" to each member of the camp. These were real people. Some choice food parcels were sent to village relatives who were no longer able to enjoy a hunting camp life.

From the air it was a privilege to admire the pristine snowscape below, intersected by rivers with notorious falls and rapids so roily that they seldom froze and continued to create steam-like mists that rose high above in the coldest weather. Near one such site a small herd of caribou rambled. How much longer would these conditions exist? One might think that as wilderness becomes scarce, it would become more valuable. Once it is gone, it can never be replaced exactly as it was. My camera caught images to record a lifestyle the way it was before mammoth machines encroached on a fast-disappearing, virgin wilderness.

This image of life in a Mistassini subarctic wilderness hunting camp in the winter of 1979 portrays a full, industrious life that recognized that its completeness was dependent on the ecology around it. It was a life that understood and taught the necessity to respect all life. The Mistassini code of ethics, based on at least several thousand years of experience, understood that any disturbance of that balance upsets a part of their own fullness of life. The Mistassini ethic established strict regulations to maintain the precise balance necessary to uphold and increase the richness of their way of life. Certain events that occurred hundreds and even thousands of miles away have had deadly effects on the happy inhabitants who have tried to maintain their good life in the fragile, subarctic zone. Governments and private corporations must proceed with broad-based ecological studies before advancing projects that could change the land affecting those living hundreds or even thousands of miles beyond their boundaries. The Quebec Government had made extensive studies concentrating on the wildlife of the Mistassini territory. The government was convinced that it could proceed without endangering the species living in the area. It appears that studies regarding the native people were not considered as important as those for the fauna. The inhabitants were pawns for the government's chessboard, to displace at will.

Philip's camp was one of many camps. There is just as much individualism in the camps as there is in households beyond the Mistassini territory. Every camp was interesting to visit, for no two were exactly alike. When the white strangers moved into Indian settlements, they made little effort to fit in with the Mistassini way of life. They expected that if anyone were to change, it would be the original inhabitants. Little actual cross-cultural exchange took place by either group until the road created an easy link to Chibougamau. Some Mistassini Cree were experimenting by purchasing large, plush chairs and putting them in their tents, where they took up much space. Others took portable generators into their bush camps and enjoyed electric lights and some appliances such as washing machines. Early bedtime saved much on artificial light, whether produced by the generator, propane lanterns, or candles.

Before returning to the outside world, I spent several days at the rectory with Father James Collins. It was good to have several days of transition before having to return to the other world. Jim and his wife Marilyn enjoyed the challenges of serving these northern Indians. They made a good team. Jim fitted into the situation well, and the Mistassini liked him. He enjoyed visiting the bush camps and seeing the people in their non-village setting. Usually it was like seeing two different people. The bush was their genuine lifestyle; the village was like a new set of clothes that did not fit quite right.

Often the priest was the only easily approachable white person for the Indians to visit. He also represented the white men who cheated the Indians and was one of the few they could easily find. He represented all white men and became the whipping boy for their many misdeeds towards the Mistassini. Soon after Rev. Jim Collins' arrival, a young man knocked on the door. The visitor was obviously quite drunk. He had a rifle and said that he had come to kill Jim. The visitor could hardly stand and was visibly wobbly. Jim told him that he was so drunk that he couldn't hit him. "Go home, put your gun away, and go to bed. Come back tomorrow." The story made its way around the village. Generally the people were angry at the young man and disciplined him in their way. Then they went to Jim and apologized for the incident and wondered why he hadn't reported it to them. Jim was new in the village. He was sure that he wouldn't see the young man again and didn't want to cause unnecessary trouble for him.

The incident was an example of the change in many Mistassini people's attitude towards white people since the McGill anthropology program began in 1966. When the program commenced, the people were elated that the white strangers were for the first time taking an interest in the Mistassini.

We talked about some Indian customs. One of the biggest mysteries to Jim was how the Indians know that a family member has died many miles away when there is no telephone or other means of communication. I had been asked this by others before him. I told Jim the story of a previous Mistassini missionary. A village death was reported to a new missionary a few days after had arrived at the mission. All the close relatives were in the bush. The missionary felt that he was responsible for notifying the family in the bush. He packed up and started to the deceased one's camp. Before long the missionary came face to face with the family who were returning to the village. Yes, they knew about the death. He too, wondered how. The owl was the usual harbinger of bad news for many northern groups. Other omens represented woeful tidings. The normal white man's reaction to the Indian's story is that it is unbelievable and just a superstition. It may be, but I know from experience that such signs are well known to all northeastern Indians and are very reliable. A communication warning system quickly and accurately notified the next of kin long before they had the sophisticated electronic systems of today's world. However, the ancient systems seem to fade away quickly when they are no longer necessary.

On the morning of my departure, Marilyn Collins took me to the bus station in Chibougamau, where she had errands to do. All my gear had been subjected to the odors of wild meat blended with those of cooking fat, smoke, and animal hides that had permeated all my clothing and porous belongings. I had become so accustomed to these camp smells that I was completely unaware that my gear harbored them. I took a seat near the front of the bus. I saw people in neighboring seats sniffing in various directions; then they moved farther back in the bus. It never dawned on me that I was the object of their displeasure. There were many empty seats and few stops. Finally we arrived at the stop where

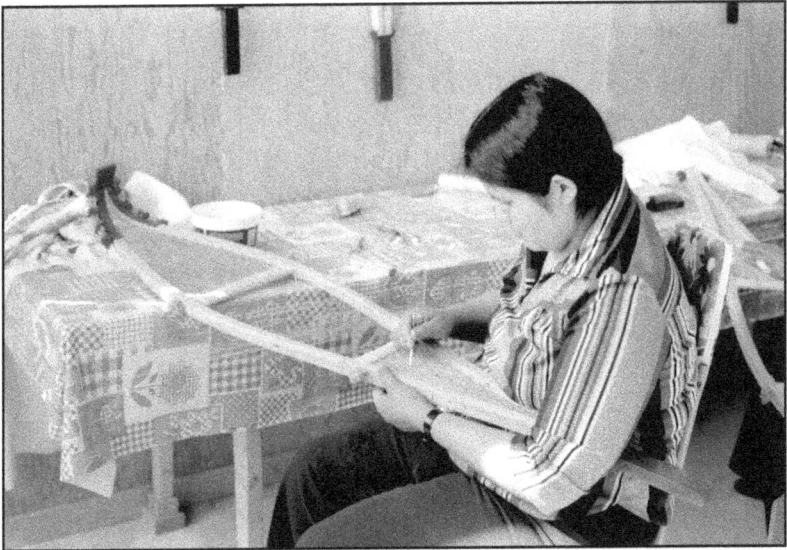

MAKING SNOWSHOES

I had to change buses. I had about an hour to wait, so I selected lunch from the simple menu the bus station offered, a meal that reflected a different way of living. The vegetable salad was a delectable change, but it did not really fuel an active person in a cold climate. The bus arrived. I was glad to be on my way again. Stops became more frequent as we neared Ottawa. Passengers had to fill the seats close to me, sniffing and looking toward me. Finally we were there. Edyth was waiting for me. I recounted some of my experiences on the way home. It was not until I reached home that I realized that my clothing and gear reeked with the smell of animal fats, wood smoke, and hides. It was my souvenir from the great lone land of Mistassini! My clothes required several cycles in the washer and then drying outside in the suburban city air to become acceptable to city people again.

# EPILOGUE
# THREE HUNDRED YEARS IN THIRTY

The thirty years between 1960 and 1990 were difficult for the Mistassini. During this period they moved from primarily a beaver economy to a high-tech people. They should be congratulated for making such a fast transition, one that took us three hundred years to accomplish. However, the trapper community looked with sadness as their land was torn up unmercifully. The flow of some mighty rivers was reversed, a diversion that would send warmer water north, instead of colder water south. How that will affect the ecology is still unknown.

The Mistassini philosophy still recognized life's circles. People danced in circles. The circle was a complete object. Individual dancers connected with one another, completing a circle. All of nature's creations had a place in circles. The sun and moon moved in circles, creating day and night. The seasons were circles, completing a year, and so it was with life. The Mistassini Cree had never been at war nor made a treaty with the European strangers. Then the mammoth machines came, attacking their land, destroying nature's circles. It began a period of questions. Are the Mistassini to be or not to be trappers? Are they to be or not to be a nation of modern construction engineers? These questions were argued back and forth between the trappers, whose reputation was worldwide, and the young Cree, who, having been "away" to school, saw bigger dividends in the destructive development of their land, now no longer in their control. Adept young people developed businesses ranging from home construction to road building and dam building. Some in the industrial world have begun programs to demolish dams that block the freedom of wildlife up and down rivers. Quebec is convinced that dam building is where its future economy lies.

The population of Mistassini has exploded to more than 15,000, mostly young people who no longer remember or experience the necessary training for trapping. While population was on the increase, the changes in the land drastically reduced the wildlife. Mistassini leaders sadly concluded that the dwindling wild food supply, such as caribou, fish, and beaver, was no longer a viable economy. The changes to the land became irreversible. The land will never be the same again. The hydroelectric project has replaced the Hudson's Bay Company as the principal source of income. The young people born into the confusing years of fast changes have shown the ability to adapt positively. The young Mistassini people were like the hard ore ripped up from their land and shipped out to become useful metal. Now they will fill the high-level tech positions, not the pick-and-shovel or ax-and-chainsaw jobs of their fathers and grandfathers. They will man the massive machines and equipment regulating the flow of water, while the tribal leaders investigate other sources of development and income. They have found a new niche in life, just as the Iroquois steel-bridge builders did. They will continue to live on their land, their heritage. They are the generation who have the responsibility to find ways for the future generations to succeed in the territory. Let us hope that the Quebec Government will not only listen to these people of peace but work to give them sovereignty within their province and a life of respect and dignity.

# Glossary

**Atikamekw (formerly known as the Tête-de-Boule).** The accepted name for the tribe south of the Waswanipi.

**band (as in Mistassini Band).** It appears to be a Canadian term for Indian groups having a local, residential area and belonging to a large tribe.

**Basques.** A people living between Spain and France, who in the sixteenth century were noted to have the best seamen in the world. They came to North America, established fisheries, whaling stations, and traded with the Indians, from Labrador to Newfoundland and northern Maine.

**birch bark biting.** The craft of biting designs into thin, small sheets of birch bark.

**BP.** Before present. Used by archaeologists in place of AD or BC.

**bush.** A common term for the woods and forests, used among woodsmen from northern Maine to northern Canada. The northern forests are commonly called the "northern bush" by northern people.

**bush pilots and planes.** The term for the pilots who fly their bush planes with skis/pontoons into the northern, uninhabited forest areas to transport missionaries, traders, sports hunters and fisherman.

**bush, virgin.** Forests that have never been cut over.

**capote.** A cape with a hood on it.

**chert.** A type of stone having flint-like characteristics that make it a fine stone for creating arrowheads or any sharp tool.

**chert, Ramah.** A specific type of chert found in Labrador, having extremely fine quality for arrowheads, scrapers, and knives.

**country food.** The term for the wild food of trappers and others living in the wild.

**dogsled.** A sled carrying hunters' and trappers' supplies, pulled by dogs over the snow and ice.

**dog team.** A team of trained dogs for pulling a sled in the winter over the snow and ice.

**factor.** A Hudson's Bay Company head trader, manager or agent, established for trade with trappers.

**fallow.** Condition of a field let to rest for a period of time to regain nutrients in the soil.

**flesher.** An implement to scrape hair and fat from a skin.

**First Nation.** A name devised by Indians to replace the term Indian, emphasizing that they were here before the Europeans.

**French North West Company.** French fur trading company.

**fur brigade.** Formerly the year's furs from the fur trade were sent to the coast by a group of canoes that were called a "fur brigade." The canoes returned with supplies.

**jerkin.** Close-fitting jacket or short coat, also of leather.

**Labrador Trough.** A specific area in Labrador where highly valued chert is found.

**larch.** A tree that is a deciduous conifer found in northern Canadian forests.

**moose scapula.** The shoulder blade from a moose. When burned, the cracks create a map which is interpreted by the burner as to where game can be found.

**muskeg.** Unstable swampy ground that is frozen most of the year.

**Pine Tree Line.** An early-warning system, alerting the military that enemy planes were coming over northern Canada.

**portage, on portage.** When traveling by canoe, a carry around a falls or rough whitewater.

**sheath knife.** A knife worn on a belt in a special device called a "sheath," usually worn by woodsmen, hunters, and trappers.

**shaman/shamanism.** Sometimes referred to as a "conjurer" or "conjuring." The practice or method of contacting the spiritual world to learn where to find game.

**snare.** A snare is a device with a noose to catch small animals or birds.

**spirit animal helpers.** Hunters are helped by spirit animal helpers. Usually the spirit helper is identified during a youth's training years.

**spud, long spud.** Pole for poling a canoe. The pole also keeps the person from slipping when the canoe hits a rock.

**tumpline.** A carrying aid which has a strap that goes around the head to support a heavy pack on the back.

**tundra.** Flat, level land, frozen most of the time.

**Ungava.** Large peninsula in northwest Quebec. Some people or maps sometimes include Mistassini and Labrador.

**Waswanipi band master.** The person responsible for taking care of the daily Waswanipi tribal business. He received a salary, whereas the chief only received a token payment.

**Woods Cree Indians.** Northern Indians living in woods, in contrast to Plains Cree Indians out West.

# Notes

## Preface

1. The late Andrew Dana, a Penobscot, was recognized by academic linguists as the leading Penobscot linguist. Dr. Frank T. Siebert, an authority on the Penobscot language, referred to Dana as his chief source of information. I also found Andrew Dana valuable as a Penobscot resource. He corrected me, saying that in Penobscot the word is both singular and plural. It is incorrect to attach an *s* to make it plural. Since then I have followed Andrew Dana's advice about the Penobscot language.
2. Few people realized the significance of this forgotten trail. John Gould satirized the experience with the title *The Old Trail to Houlton* in his *Dispatch From the Farm* series in the *Christian Science Monitor,* Thursday, Sept. 24, 1964, as it was by coincidence the year that I-95 was being extended from Old Town to Houlton.

## Chapter 1: A Dream Comes True

1. Frederick Remington, *Man with the Bark On*, (Harper & Brothers, 1900).

## Chapter 2: Mistassini Territory

1. Hare, "The Present Day Snowfall of Labrador-Ungava," 658–659.
2. McCaffrey, "Archaic Period Occupation in Subarctic Quebec," 165.

## Chapter 3: Tadoussac

1. Whitehead, *The Old Man Told Us*, 7; Barkham, "The Basque Whaling Establishments," 515–519; Calloway, *Dawnland Encounters Indians and Europeans*, 9.
2. Whitehead, *The Old Man Told Us*, 7.
3. Martijn, "Commentaires sur la "Frise des Sauvages" à l'église Saint-Jacques de Dieppe, France," 319–324.
4. Alston & Danielsson, "The Earliest Dictionary of the Known Languages of the World," N.p.
5. Jones, *Gentlemen and Jesuits Glory*, 24. Two Catholic priests and a Huguenot clergyman joined the Sieur de Monts expedition of which Champlain was a part.
6. Coverdale, *Tadoussac Then and Now*, 13.
7. Ibid., 14.
8. Ibid., 15.
9. Shea, *The History of the Catholic Church*, 303–328.
10. Oldmixon, "The History of Hudson's Bay," 385; Cooper, "The Culture of the Northeastern Indian Hunters," 275; Skinner, "Notes on Eastern Cree and Northern Saulteaux," 79; Nicholas N. Smith, *Field Notes*.

These reports of Iroquois war parties collected at different Cree villages and in different time periods illustrate how much the Cree feared the Iroquois.

11. Larouche, *Le Second Registre de Tadoussac*, 4.
12. Loc. cit.
13. Ibid., 154.
14. Crépieul, *Jesuit Relations*, 249–267.
15. The earliest French missionaries used the numeral 8 for the French "u" sound consistently from the seventeenth century into the nineteenth century.
16. Crépieul, *Jesuit Relations*, 255.
17. Speck, "Family Hunting Territories," 399, 400, 403.
18. *Dictionary of Canadian Biography* Vol. 2, s.v. "Albanel, Charles."

## Chapter 4: The Hudson's Bay Company Becomes Established.
1. P. C. Newman, 1985. *Company of Adventurers*. For those wishing to know more about the Hudson's Bay Company, Newman's well written account presents a realistic and readable view of the times and people.
2. Francis and Morantz, *Partners in Furs*, 95–96.

## Chapter 5: Missionaries
1. *Dictionary of Canadian Biography* Vol. 4, s.v. "Evans, James."
2. *Dictionary of Canadian Biography* Vol. 12, s.v. "Horden, John."
3. *Dictionary of Canadian Biography* Vol. 12, s.v. "Horden, John."

## Chapter 6: The Great Lone Land of Moosonee
1. Scanlon, *The Preacher's Book*, author's note.
2. Swindlehurst, *The Great Lone Land of Moosonee*, unpublished manuscript, 1–14.
3. Scanlon, *The Preacher's Book*, 20.
4. F. Swindlehurst, *The Great Lone Land of Moosonee*, unpublished manuscript, 21.
5. Scanlon, *The Preacher's Book*, 11.

## Chapter 7: The Government Takes an Interest
1. Hurlbut, "Mistassini," 471–474; Low, "The Mistassini Region,"11. The Laure map is a fine example of early mapmaking. There are many references to it.
2. Low, "The Mistassini Region," 11–28.
3. Wilson, *Chibougamau Venture*, 88–89.
4. Speck, "Indian Notes," 453.

## Chapter 8: Waswanipi
1. Skinner, "Notes on Eastern Cree and Northern Saulteaux," 57.
2. Cooper, "Some Notes on the Waswanipi," 460.
3. Petersen, *The Land of Moosoneek*, 218.

4. The Penobscot followed the new regulations; the Passamaquoddy persuaded the Maine Legislature to permit their new chief, elected in their traditional manner for a life, to continue to be chief until his death. Chief John Francis retained his office until his death in 1875.
5. Skinner, "Notes on Eastern Cree and Northern Saulteaux," 25.
6. Rogers, "The Hunting Group," 80–81.
7. Skinner, "Notes on Eastern Cree and Northern Saulteaux," 80.

## Chapter 9: Mistassini, A Hunting Community
1. Rousseau, "Mistassini Calendar," 34.
2. Pattison, "Pastor and Parish," 8.
3. Ibid., 17.
4. Drake, *Indian Captivities*, 82.

## Chapter 10: School Not A Complete Mistassini Education
1. Flannery, "An Analysis of Coastal Algonquian Culture," 269.

## Chapter 11: Paving the Way
1. Baker, "St. Alban the Maytr," 14; Scanlon, *The Inlanders*, 84.
2. Wilson, *Chibougamau Venture*, 4.
3. Scanlon, *The Inlanders*, 94.

## Chapter 12: Mistassini: The Beginning of a New Village
1. We became very good friends with the Blabers. A number of people came to see the Mistassini missionary hoping for help with a project. Ken warmly received these visitors and usually succeeded in obtaining something that would improve his work with the Indians in return. Ken kindly gave me a copy of his diary kept during the years he was at Mistassini.
2. Scanlon, *The Inlanders*, 7.
3. In Wabanaki cultural history, Kuluskap was once portrayed as a religious figure parallel to the Christian's Christ. He has since been reduced in power and stature but is still an important figure as the being who made the land safe for Indians. There are many geologic features in Nova Scotia, New Brunswick, and Maine that Indians say were the result of a Kuluskap event. Each feature has an interesting story of its origin.

## Chapter 13: Our Introduction to Mistassini
1. Sweat baths are a traditional healing method for many Indians. They also have religious significance. The sweat bath is performed in a small tent with a stone fireplace in the center. Stones are also in the center where the fire is. When the stones are hot, water is poured on them creating much steam. The door of the tent is closed. It is customary to include certain known healing plants that give off a fragrance. While one sits in the steam, certain

prayers are recited. One takes as much heat and steam as possible before leaving the tent. The steam bath can be for a single person or a group event.

## Chapter 14: The Change From Independence to Community Values
1. Jilek, *Salish Indian Mental Health*, 17.

## Chapter 15: The Role of the Hudson's Bay Company
1. Anderson, "Eastern Cree Indians," 31.

## Chapter 16: The Spring Goose Hunt
1. Rogers, *The Material Culture of the Mistassini*, 4.
2. Low, "The Mistassini Region," 23.
3. Flannery, "An Analysis of Coastal Algonquian Culture," 267.
4. S. Rogers, "The Hunting Group," 52.

## Chapter 18: The Mistassini Indian Government
1. Smalley Petawabano. There was no set way to spell Indian names. Most people spelled them the way the word sounded to them. I use the spelling that Smalley did. The name often appears with the *e* omitted, because the writer thought it was the proper spelling.

## Chapter 19: The James Bay Hydroelectric Project
1. D. C. Butterfield, (March 2007) by permission of Patrick Paul, editor, *Wulustuk Times*.
2. Rogers, *The Material Culture of the Mistassini*, 2.
3. Dr. J. Kenneth Doutt was an ornithologist for Pittsburgh's Carnegie Museum who enjoyed bird research in Labrador and the Ungava Peninsula. While in the Ungava area, his Indian and Eskimo guides mentioned white seals that inhabited two freshwater lakes. At first he concluded that the stories were myths. Seals living in fresh water not connected with the sea? Finally he decided that the stories from two of his most trusted guides would be worth checking. He convinced the museum to include search time to find and authenticate the white seals of Quebec's Upper and Lower Seal Lakes. In 1938 he brought back specimens that have been studied, and in 2008 the white seal was officially designated to be a new subspecies, *Phoca vitulina mellonae*. The Eskimo and Indians knew that these landlocked seals were different; their hides were the best for making special containers or clothing. It is thought that these harbor seals were cut off from the sea 4000 years ago by the rising land. They learned to adapt to the winter conditions of a freshwater lake, which are quite different from the ocean. At least for now, these rare white, landlocked seals have been protected from environmental changes that could result from the James Bay Power

Project. See J. Kenneth Doutt, "A Review of the Genus Phoca," pp 61–125, in Annals of the Carnegie Museum XXIX, 1942; "Subspecific status of the Freshwater Harbor Seal (*Phoca Vitulina Mellonae*): A Re-Assessment," *Marine Mammal Science* 10(1):105-110, 1994.

4. Twomey and Herrick, *Needle to the North*,109–110.

## Chapter 20: Winter Bush Life: Philip's Camp

1. Nanuwan, "Solomon Voyageur," 162–163.

2. Speck, *Penobscot Man*, 28.

3. I took a small thermometer to record the temperatures.

4. Gonzalez, "Changing Dietary Patterns," 25.

# Bibliography

Alston, R.C. and B. Danielsson. "The Earliest Dictionary of the Known Languages of the World." *In English Studies Presented to R. W. Zandvoort on the Occasion of his Seventieth Birthday.* 45. Amsterdam: Swets & Zeitlinger, (1964).

Anderson, J. W. "Eastern Cree Indians." *History and Scientific Society of Manitoba Papers* Series 3, No. 11, (1956).

Baker, Cyril A. "St Alban the Martyr, Chapais." *The Northland* (2) 29 (1972–3): 14–15.

Barkham, Selma Huxley. "The Basque Whaling Establishments in Labrador 1536–1632, a Summary." *Arctic* 37 (1964): 519.

Blaber, Rev. Kenneth. Unpublished Diary. Nicholas Smith Collection, 1966–1974.

Calloway, Colin G., ed. *Dawnland Encounters Indians and Europeans in Northern New England.* Hanover, NH: University of New England Press, 1991.

Church Records. St. Barnabas, Waswanipi Lake, Quebec.

Cooper, John M. "Some Notes on the Waswanipi." *Proceedings of the Twenty-Third International Congress Americanists* 20, Vol. 2, (1928): 459–61.

———. "The Culture of the Northeastern Indian Hunters: A Reconstructive Interpretation." *Man in Northeastern North America,* edited by Frederick Johnson. Andover, MA: Phillips Academy, (1946): 272–306.

Coverdale, William Hugh. *Tadoussac Then and Now: A History and Narrative of the Kingdom of the Saguenay.* N.p.: n.p., 1942.

Crépieul. *Jesuit Relations and Allied Documents,* Vol. 63, Edited by Thwaites, R. G. Cleveland: Burrows Brothers, 1896–1891.

Denton, David. "From the Source to the Margins and Back. Notes on Mistassini Quartzite and Archaeology in the Area of the Colline Blanche." L'émbassadeur essais archéologiques et ethnohistoriques en hommage à Charles A. Martijn. *Paléo-Québec* 27. Recherches amérindiennes au Québec. (1998): 17–32.

Doutt, J. Kenneth. "A Review of the Genus Phoca." *Annals of the Carnegie Museum* 29 (1942): 61–1125.

———. "Subspecific Status of the Freshwater Harbor Seal (Ponca Vitulina Mellonae): A Re-Assessment." *Marine Mammal Science* 10(1) (1994):105–110.

Drake, Samuel Gardner. *Indian Captivities, or Life in the Wigwam; Being the True Narratives of Captives Who Have Been Carried Away by the Indians, From the Frontier Settlement of the U.S. From the Earliest Period to the Present Time.* Auburn, NY: Derby & Miller, 1851.

Flannery, Regina. "An Analysis of Coastal Algonquian Culture." *The Catholic University of America Anthropological Series* No. 7. Washington, D.C.: The Catholic University of America Press, 1939.

Francis, David and Toby Morantz. *Partners in Furs A History of the Fur Trade in*

*Eastern James Bay 1600–1870.* Montreal: McGill-Queen's, 1983.

Gonzalez, Nancie L. "Changing Dietary Patterns of North American Indian Children." *Nutrition, Growth and Development of North American Indian Children. DHEW Publication No. (NIH)* 72–26. Washington, D.C.: U.S. Government Printing Office, (1972): 15–33.

Hare, F. Kenneth. "The Present Day Snowfall of Labrador-Ungava." *American Journal of Science* 249, No. 9 (1951): 654–670.

Hurlbut, G. C. "Mistassini." *Journal of the American Geographical Society* 39, (1888): 471–474.

Jilek, Wolfgang. *Salish Indian Mental Health and Culture Change: Psychohygienic and Therapeutic Aspects of the Guardian Spirit Ceremonial.* Toronto: Holt, Rhinheart and Winston of Canada, 1974.

Jones, Elizabeth. *Gentlemen and Jesuits: Glory and Adventure in the Early Days of Acadia.* Halifax: Nimbus Publishing, 2002.

Larouche, Léonidas. *Le Second Registre de Tadoussac 1668–1700 Transciptions.* Montreal: Les Presses de l'Université du Québec, 1972.

Low, A. P. "The Mistassini Region." *Ottawa Naturalist* Vol. 4, 1890.

Martijn, Charles. "Commentaires sur la "Frise des Sauvages" à l'église Saint-Jacques de Dieppe, France." *Recherches Amérindiennes au Québec* 11(4) (1981): 319–324.

McCaffrey, Moira, T. "Archaic Period Occupation in Subarctic Quebec: A Review of the Evidence." *The Archaic of the Far Northeast,* edited by David Sanger and M. A. P. Renouf. Orono, ME: University of Maine Press, (2006): 161–190.

Morantz, Toby. "An Ethnohistoric Study of Eastern James Bay Cree Social Organization, 1700–1850." *National Museum of Man Mercury Series, Canadian Ethnology Service Paper* No. 88. Ottawa: National Museums of Canada, 1983.

Nanuwan. "Solomon Voyageur." *The Beaver* March 1929, 162–163.

Neilson, James M. "The Mistassini Territory of Northern Quebec." *Canadian Geographical Journal* 37 (1948): 144–57.

Newman, Peter C. *Company of Adventurers.* Canada: Penguin Books, 1986.

Oldmixon, John. "The History of Hudson's Bay." *Documents Relating to the Early History of Hudson's Bay.* Edited by J. B. Tyrrell. Toronto: Champlain Society, (1931): 371–410.

Pattison, E. Mansell. *Pastor and Parish—A Systems Approach.* Philadelphia: Fortress Press, 1977.

Petersen, Olive Mackay. *The land of Moosoneek.* Toronto: Bryant Press Ltd., 1974.

Rogers, Edward S. "The Hunting Group—Hunting Territory Complex Among the Mistassini Indians." *National Museum of Canada Bulletin* No. 195. Ottawa: Department of Northern Affairs and Natural Resources Canada, 1963.

———. *The Material Culture of the Mistassini. National Museums of Canada Bulletin* No. 218. *Anthropological Series* No. 80. Ottawa: National Museum of Canada, 1967.

Rousseau, Jacques. "Mistassini Calendar." *Beaver 29,* No. 2, September 1949, 33–37.

Scanlon, James. *The Inlanders: Some Anglicans and Indians in Nouveau-Quebec.* Cobalt, Ontario: Highway Book Shop, 1975.

———. *The Preacher's Book at Rupert House 1902–1911.* Cobalt, Ontario: Highway Book Shop, 2008.

Shea, John Gilmary. *The History of the Catholic Church in the United States.* Rahway, NJ: The Meshon Company Press, 1886.

Shulgan, Christopher. "The Price of Peace." *Canadian Geographic* Vol. 125 (2005): 67–86.

Skinner, Alanson. "Notes on Eastern Cree and Northern Saulteaux." *Anthropological Papers of the American Museum of Natural History* 9(1) (1911).

Smith, Nicholas. Field Notes 1969–90.

Smith, Nicholas. "Food Versus Nutrition: The Changing Diet of the Mistassini Cree." *Papers of the Eleventh Algonquian Conference.* Edited by William Cowan. Ottawa: Carleton University, (1980): 128–134.

———. "The Spring Goose Hunt." *Papers of the Fifteenth Algonquian Conference.* Edited by William Cowan. Ottawa: Carleton University, (1984): 81–90.

———. "Three Centuries of Progress in Three Decades: Mistassini 1960–1990." *Actes du Trent-Deuxième Congrès* des Algonquinistes. Edited by John D. Nichols. Winnipeg: Université du Manitoba, (2001): 516–526.

Speck, Frank G. "Family Hunting Territories of the Lake St. John Montagnais and Neighboring Bands." *Anthropos* 22 (1927): 389–403.

———. "Indian Notes." *Museum of the American Indian, Heye Foundation* 7 (1930): 410–457.

———. *Penobscot Man.* Philadelphia: University of Pennsylvania Press, 1940.

Swindlehurst, Fred. *The Great Lone Land of Moosonee* (Unpublished Manuscript).

Tanner, Adrian. *Bringing Home Animals: Religious Ideology and Mode of Production of the Mistassini Cree Hunters.* New York: St. Martin's Press, 1979.

Twomey, Arthur C., and Nigel Herrick. *Needle to the North.* Boston: Houghton Mifflin Co., 1942.

Voorhis, Ernest. *Historic Forts and Trading Posts of the French Regime and of the English Trading Companies.* Manuscript. Ottawa: Department of the Interior, Natural Resources Intelligence Service, 1930.

Whitehead, Ruth Holmes. *The Old Man Told Us: Excerpts from Micmac History 1500–1950.* Halifax, N.S.: Nimbus Press, 1991.

Wilson, Larry. *Chibougamau Venture.* Montreal: Chibougamau Publishing Co., 1952.

# Index

New Brunswick Power Company
180

Newfoundland 12, 91, 180, 181

Newfoundland and Labrador
Hydro 181

New France 16, 18

New York 1, 27, 115, 163, 171, 180

Nichikun 27, 74, 104, 127, 143,
144, 173

Nitchequon 7

Nodway 17

Nonsuch 20, 21

Norridgewolk Indians 16

Northeast 10, 14

Norway House 36

Norwegian 38

Nottaway River 17

Nova Scotia 13, 14, 35, 180

O

Obalski, Joseph 48

Odanak 51

Ogdensburg, NY 119

Ojibwa 35, 38, 62, 95, 100

Oke, Elizabeth 37

Ontario 9, 34, 35, 37, 43, 82, 91,
92, 95, 96, 119, 181

Opemiska Experiment 89, 90

Opemiska Mine 89, 91

Orkney 26

ornithologists 174, 175

O'Sullivan River 17, 53, 59, 69

Ottawa 224

P

Pan-American Indian heritage 107

papoose 76

parents 36, 77, 78, 81–84, 87, 88,
110, 114, 116, 129, 138, 154,

161, 169, 186, 191, 204, 216,
219

Paris 47

Passamaquoddy 2, 64, 123

Patino Mine 103

Paul, Minnie 62

Peace Corps 31

Penobscot 1, 2, 231, 233, 235, 239

Petawabano, Smalley and Paul 100,
142, 157, 164–166, 168

Pickle Crow 95, 96

Pilgrims 18

Pilgrim's Progress 38

Pine Tree Line 111

Pittsburgh Pennsylvania Museum
of Natural History 174

Point Blue 50

polar bear 105, 158

Polar Bear Express 43, 45

Port Royal 14

Portuguese 12

powwow 80, 167

Prairie Provinces 37

*Prince Albert*, ship 37

Prince Edward Island 180

Protestant 14

Pustamaskow 17

Pusticamica Lake 62

Q

quartz 13, 64

quartzite 10

Quebec 1–4, 6, 9, 12, 13, 15, 16,
20, 23, 37, 47–49, 53, 60, 61,
71, 73, 74, 80, 82, 85, 86, 95,
99–104, 113, 118, 121, 122,
127, 130, 155, 156, 159, 164,
166, 168, 171, 172, 176–181,
184, 221, 225, 226

Quebec City 12, 13, 15, 16, 20,

**Nicholas N. Smith** was born in Malden, MA in 1926. After serving in the 9th Air Force in Europe during WWII, he received his B.A. in history from the University of Maine and a Library of Science degree from Columbia University. His advisor at UM suggested that he study Maine Indian history. His research in this fascinating subject has taken him to many university and special libraries in the U.S., Canada, England, and Germany. He is the author of many papers concerning the Wabanaki and the Cree of Lake Mistassini in Northern Quebec and received an honorary doctorate from the University of Maine in 2007. The author and his wife, Edyth, live in Brunswick, Maine.